npr

NPR

The Trials and Triumphs of National Public Radio

Michael P. McCauley

 COLUMBIA UNIVERSITY PRESS   NEW YORK

COLUMBIA UNIVERSITY PRESS
Publishers Since 1893
NEW YORK   CHICHESTER, WEST SUSSEX

Library of Congress Cataloging-in-Publication Data
McCauley, Michael P., 1958–
     NPR : the trials and triumphs of National Public Radio / Michael P. McCauley.
     p.   cm.
     Includes bibliographical references and index.
     ISBN 0–231–12160–1 (cloth : alk. paper)
     1. National Public Radio (U.S.)   2. Public radio—United States.   3. Radio broadcasters—
     United States.   I. Title: Trials and triumphs of National Public Radio.   II. Title.
     HE8697.95.U6M33 2005
     384.54'0973—dc22

                                                            2004061133

Columbia University Press books are printed on permanent and durable acid-free paper.
Printed in the United States of America

c 10 9 8 7 6 5 4 3 2 1

For Judy—who supported this book in every way,
and whose love has always sustained me

CONTENTS

ACKNOWLEDGMENTS

Though the phrase is now cliche, it took a village to make this book. First of all, I must say that it would never have been published without the loving support of my wife, Judy Groth. It cannot have been easy for Judy to give me all the time, space, and encouragement I needed to complete the project, not to mention the financial support she provided in covering the cost of several research trips, mountains of photocopies, and various other expenditures. She never quit believing in this book or its author. For these reasons, I can truly call myself a lucky man.

The research project that led to this publication began in 1994 at the University of Wisconsin–Madison. Robert McChesney, my graduate adviser, and William Hoynes from Vassar College read, and commented on, everything I wrote at that time. Others who offered early help include Michael Apple, James Baughman, James Danky, Joseph Elder, Roberto Franzosi, Edward Frederick, John Hochheimer, Stanley Kutler, Kurt Neuwirth, Robert Ogles, Kent Sidel, and Stephen Vaughn. Jack McLeod deserves special mention as a friend, mentor, and fellow scholar who provided excellent advice—both in his office and on the softball field. Jack Mitchell also holds a special place in my heart because of the countless hours he has spent honing my perceptions, keeping me honest, opening doors, and offering the sort of friendship and support one does not encounter all that often.

The Joan Shorenstein Center on the Press, Politics and Public Policy at Harvard University supported this project financially with a Goldsmith Research Award. Many thanks go to James Ledbetter and Henry Morgenthau III for introducing me to the good people at the Shorenstein Center, including Nolan Bowie, Edith Holway, Marvin Kalb, and Richard Parker. Several people at NPR were very helpful to me throughout the project. Chief among them are Janet Murphy (the true "power behind the throne"); Rob Robinson, NPR's talented and generous head librarian; Emily Littleton from the Communications Department; Sarah Sloan and Cindy Shea, formerly of NPR Finance; and Stacey Foxwell, who manned the telephones and e-mail systems when I tried to locate her very busy boss, Jay Kernis.

Tom Connors, Karen King, and Bob Morrow from the University of Maryland's National Public Broadcasting Archives were a huge help in terms of rounding up items from various manuscript collections and archiving my oral history interviews. A small army of people from other libraries and archives have also supported my work; they hail from the State Historical Society of Wisconsin, the University of Wisconsin–Madison Archives, and the Carter, Ford, Johnson, Nixon, and Reagan Presidential Libraries. Many, many thanks go to all of the people who agreed to give up an hour, or more, of their time to be interviewed for this book. Among these people, David Giovannoni of Audience Research Analysis deserves special mention. Dave has been one of the project's biggest supporters and toughest critics over the years, and he has patiently answered way too many of my questions about the characteristics of the public radio audience. Leslie Peters from ARA, Lori Kaplan and Jackie Nixon from NPR, Tom Thomas of the Station Resource Group, and Kristi Shepard of Wisconsin Public Radio also provided valuable insight and documentation regarding the research and strategic planning that support the industry. Greg Schnirring and Bonniejean Hutchison from WPR helped me to better understand the process of listener feedback to public radio programs, and Connie Walker provided just the right balance of friendship and editorial guidance during the year I that worked for that organization. Here in New England, Rhonda Morin of Maine Public Radio has graciously shared copies of many listener comments with me. Colleagues at the University of Maine who provided support and encouragement include Rebecca Eilers, Amy Fried, Nathan Godfried, Michael Howard, Eric Peterson, and Scott See. Research assistance on the Orono campus was provided by Christine Pardew and Patricia Turcic. Andrew Davis and Kat Taylor of the University of Maine Faculty Development Center helped with the processing of photographic images, as did Steve Anderson of Minnesota Public Radio, Randall Davidson of Wisconsin Public Radio, and Bernie Schermetzler of the UW–Madison Archives.

A number of friends and fellow scholars have read all or parts of this manuscript or have offered insightful comments through personal communications. Patricia Aufderheide stands out in this group because of her detailed and incisive comments and because it was she who introduced me to the nice people at Columbia University Press. Others who fall into this category include Robert Avery, Steve Behrens, Ronald Bornstein, William Chafe, Patricia D'Auria, Ralph Engelman, Michael Goldfarb, Robert Goldfarb, Peter Golding, Douglas Gomery, Charles Hardy, Bill Hoynes, Jay Kernis, Vincent Mosco, Donald Mullally, Adam Clayton Powell III, Jeff Rosenberg, Jeffrey Scheuer, William Siemering, Alan Stavitsky, and John Witherspoon. Heartfelt thanks also go to Michael Haskell, John Michel, Ann Miller, Ann Young, and the rest of the editorial team at Columbia University Press, whose patience, kindness, and professionalism have sustained this project for several years . . . and through three major drafts.

Though many people have helped to make this book what it is, I am, as you might expect, solely responsible for the tone and form of the final product. I have made every effort to give proper credit for the ideas and images that appear throughout, and I apologize in advance for any errors of omission.

npr

1 A LYCEUM OF THE AIRWAVES

When I first began to study the history of National Public Radio, I did not expect very much in the way of adventure. Given the civilized tone of the stories on *Morning Edition* and *All Things Considered*, I had no reason to think these shows would inspire the same level of passion as a playoff series between the Boston Red Sox and New York Yankees. Over time, though, I came to realize that NPR's news programs often *did* stimulate passionate discussions later in the day, whether at home, in the supermarket, at the gym, or in the lobby of a local theater.

William Kling, the president and CEO of Minnesota Public Radio, agrees that NPR reporters can stir up emotion when they do in-depth stories on matters of public controversy: "A commercial network will have that story over in thirty seconds. You're angry about it, but you're onto something else. NPR might spend seven minutes on it, by which time you're apoplectic, you've sent three faxes, and called two congressmen."[1] Radio is an intimate medium, one that stimulates the imagination and helps listeners feel a sense of personal connection with the people whose voices they hear. This is especially true in public radio, says NPR president Kevin Klose:

Radio is a much more open space, the way it is done in the public radio community. There's time for reflection, there's time for consideration, and there's time for people to think as they're driving to or from work, as they're patting the dog, or doing the dishes, or jogging with the headphones in their ears.... "Which way is my compass pointing today? Let me hear some interesting stories about how people's compasses are being set, or how they got reset." ... I think that's what public radio does.[2]

People who work at NPR often speak about "The Driveway Moment," which happens when someone listening to public radio on the way home from work is so captivated by the last story they hear that she or he pulls into the driveway, stays in the car, and listens until the story is over. Pity the spouse, partner, or child who interrupts this experience ... This book is an attempt to understand why NPR holds such powerful appeal for certain listeners. The people who have the strongest affinity for the network's programs are highly educated baby boomers[3] who could easily have been mistaken, at certain points in their lives, for cast members from the ABC television series *thirtysomething*.[4] America's public radio audience began to grow at an explosive rate in the early 1980s, and that growth was fueled by people who studied or worked at university campuses during the prior two decades. These idealistic boomers were imbued with the mythical American dream and a sense that their childhood communities—safe, prosperous places—could be replicated during their adult years. Many of these dreams were shattered in the 1970s, when the post–World War II economic boom came to a crashing halt. This was a time of unprecedented inflation and unemployment, one that destroyed many Americans' sense of control and direction.[5] Not coincidentally, *thirtysomething*'s characters longed for the innocent days of their youth and craved the sense of idealism and community they felt while in college. It would stretch the imagination to think that NPR News is modeled upon the same themes we can find in *thirtysomething*. It is not an exaggeration, however, to say that the American public radio industry began to soar when its leaders realized that people who were very much like this program's characters—highly educated, socially conscious, politically active—were most likely to listen to their brand of broadcasting.

The possibility of such a nationwide community of listeners is one of the things that attracted me to public radio and the task of unearthing its history. This interest was a natural outgrowth of my own career in radio, which began in December 1982 with a newswriting job at KQV-AM, a commercial all-news station in Pittsburgh. For the most part, I remained in this line of work, as a reporter, anchor, and news director, until I entered graduate school at the University of Wisconsin–Madison in the fall of 1989. As it happened, WHA-AM—a leader in the public radio industry and one of the oldest stations in the country—was located in the very same building as the School of Journalism and Mass Communication, just two floors above the office I occupied as a teaching assistant. Soon I would meet Jack Mitchell, the director of Wisconsin Public Radio and one of the first producers of *All Things Considered*. I began a series of conversations with Jack about the ways in which public radio stations were managed and was quickly impressed by the level of sophistication that he and his colleagues demonstrated. Hands down, these people knew their audiences better than any other broadcasters I had met. They were also motivated to serve listeners for reasons that went beyond the profit motive that underpins most of the U.S. radio industry.

In early 1996, stuck between limited-term student jobs, I began to wonder if the WPR newsroom could use the services of another radio journalist. When I asked Jack Mitchell if there was anything I could do for him, a series of discussions ensued that resulted in my being hired as a news anchor and reporter a few months later. Besides reading the news and running the audio console for WPR's seventeen-station Ideas Network, I reported on a wide variety of topics—from medical news to politics, from education to the environment—and produced my stories within a format that allowed much more air time than any of my former employers did. I also had the opportunity to interact with WPR's staff, management, and board of directors about my research on public radio—in effect, to analyze a company while working for it. I left Madison in July 1997 to prepare for a faculty position at the University of Maine but continued to admire Wisconsin Public Radio from afar. I often use it as a yardstick to measure how good public radio can be, especially in terms of its capacity to deliver multiple program streams (e.g., separate "Ideas" and "News and Classical" networks) to people who live in the very same community. My wife Judy and I continue to support WPR and listen to some of its fine programs on the Web.

Throughout graduate school, I read everything I could get my hands on about public radio—in newspapers, popular journals and academic volumes—on the bet that this industry would provide a fitting series of topics for a career in academic research. In the beginning, I was content to read straightforward, descriptive accounts of NPR, a network whose thoughtful long-form programs transcended the least-common-denominator feel of commercial radio. Once again, I had little idea that the public's reaction to this new kind of radio, largely unknown before the late 1970s, would be so passionate and, at times, polarized. Some people adored NPR, while othe seemed to despise it. Since the U.S. public radio industry then received, and still receives, a portion of its funding from the federal government, politicians, pundits, and activists of various stripes often questioned whether NPR was "doing its job." This was especially interesting for me, since each person's conception about what the network's job actually *was* bore some resemblance to that person's preexisting social, political, and economic views. Some conservatives, for example, claimed that NPR was a "little Havana on the Potomac," while critics on the left thought it had abandoned its essential role as a change agent in American society.[6] Why were so many people arguing about NPR, a network whose programs I had barely heard of? Was public radio really worth arguing about to this extent? The answers to these questions were not as simple as you might think.

Members of the Carnegie Commission on Educational Television—a group anointed by Lyndon Johnson for the purpose of dreaming up the contemporary public broadcasting system—thought the industry should be "a civilized voice in a civilized community," one that would "arouse our dreams [and] satisfy our hunger for beauty." In short, public broadcasting would become "our Lyceum, our Chataqua, our Minsky's and our Camelot."[7] We can find many examples, over the years, of NPR programs that have lived up to this ideal: for example, Robert Montiegel's documentary portraits of leading twentieth-century intellectuals, a thirteen-part radio adaptation of *Star Wars*, and hundreds of sparkling performances on *Marian McPartland's Piano Jazz.* Many of NPR's news and information programs have also been memorable, from live broadcasts of Senate hearings on the Vietnam War; to the expert political and legal reporting of Linda Wertheimer, Cokie Roberts, and Nina Totenberg; to award-winning coverage of the Persian Gulf wars and the aftermath of September 11, 2001. The fact that NPR has succeeded to this extent is nothing less than amazing, given the manner in which it was born and raised.[8]

Over the years, many people have criticized the network for targeting its programs almost exclusively to an audience of upscale baby boomers. Those who take this position seem to long, instead, for a national broadcaster that could offer meaningful programs for people from all socioeconomic and cultural groups—including those that are not well-served by the dominant commercial broadcasting system. This brand of public service broadcasting is common in Western Europe where most national systems, like the BBC, are funded by a license fee that is tied to the purchase of television or radio sets. By virtue of paying this fee, each European citizen has typically donated between $36 and $136 per year toward his or her national broadcasting system (compare that to a little more than one dollar's worth of federal support for each U.S. citizen). The BBC operates eight television networks, ten radio networks, more than fifty local radio and TV stations, and a forty-three-language worldwide news and information service. It also produces musical performances and children's programs and provides digital platforms for the integration of a wide variety of audio, video, and textual content. Britain's national broadcaster provides both popular programs and minority shows, with, as one observer puts it, "the former being the majority's reward for helping to fund the latter."[9]

This is a very different broadcasting system from the one that America's public radio audience enjoys. In recent years, the amount of federal money earmarked for public radio has dwindled to about 14 percent of the industry's annual budget (33 percent if you include money from state and local governments); income from private sources such as pledge drives and corporate underwriting accounts for a little more than half of the funding mix.[10] Given the heavy influence of these "listener-sensitive" funds, America's public radio system must, as a matter of survival, focus its programming and fund-raising efforts on the highly educated *thirtysomething* (now *fiftysomething*) audience that covets its programs most. It is tempting to charge, as some critics have, that NPR's financial maturation has moved the enterprise away from its funky, alternative roots and closer to the pedestrian fare of commercial radio. But, as we shall see, American public broadcasting grew up in a political culture that actually precluded most of the funk that is supposedly missing. NPR's liberal critics may also be waxing nostalgic for a kind of radio format that, for the most part, no longer exists—and has not existed for several decades. Starting in the mid-to-late 1920s, when commercial networks and their star performers became a national phenomenon, radio was a full-service medium whose local stations often provided something for everyone. But this picture began to change by the mid-1950s when, for the first time, more than half of all American households had television sets. Commercial TV, with its comedy shows, anthology dramas, and entertainment spectaculars, quickly became the country's full-service medium of choice. In order to survive, radio stations had to specialize, to move toward niche-market formats that would serve some people very well and others not at all.

Such was the fate of public radio in the United States. Born in the early 1970s, the industry lacked the coherent strategy for universal public service that its European counterparts had from the very beginning. NPR was founded because the federal government made a relatively modest sum of money available for building a ragtag collection of *educational* radio and TV stations into a national system—one that would hardly be formidable by commercial standards. Compared to Europe's national broadcasters, the U.S. public radio system has no unified sense of purpose, no firm guidelines about the kind of service that networks or local stations should provide to citizens and communities.[11] The development of NPR's civilized voice happened through trial and error—or, in the words of one long-time employee, after an initial "period of sacrificial audiences."[12] About a decade after the network's founding, its managers began to better understand how many people were listening, which kinds of people were listening, and why they chose to listen at any given time. Audience research helped public radio fuse its programs more snugly to the values, beliefs, and attitudes of the people who tuned in (and pledged their financial support) most often. The central insight to be gleaned from NPR's history, then, is not that its programs are politically biased or aesthetically tilted in one way or the other or that the network could do a much better job than it has of serving each and every American. The most noteworthy thing about this organization (and the wider public radio industry) is the remarkable job that a few talented and dedicated broadcasters have done in playing the hand they were dealt. Born of humble circumstances, NPR has blossomed into a civilized voice which serves its listeners better than any other network could.

AN OVERVIEW

This book traces the history of noncommercial radio in the United States from its roots in the educational radio stations of the early twentieth century, to the creation of a modern public broadcasting system, to NPR's development as a primary purveyor of high quality news, information, and cultural programming. Nonprofit educational stations, most of them owned by colleges and universities, were the pioneering institutions of American radio; more than 200 of them were licensed in the 1920s. But many of these stations began to languish just a few years after signing on, as university administrators failed to see the usefulness of radio beyond the sheer novelty of music and human voices that somehow, invisibly, flew into and out of speaker boxes. Regulatory decisions in Washington, pressure from would-be commercial broadcasters, and the Great Depression also took their toll, forcing more than 75 percent of these stations off the air by 1933.

Chapter 2 covers the development of nonprofit radio from its meager beginnings through NPR's first two years of existence. As commercial radio entered its heyday in the 1930s and 1940s, educational and other nonprofit broadcasters fought for their very lives. The Ford Foundation kept them

to, considering the high quality and superior depth of the on-air product. A tougher problem for me was deciding the best way to portray NPR's history. The sociologist in me understands that this network mediates information from a wide variety of cultural spheres, including politics, economics, art, science, and entertainment; in effect, it interprets and reinterprets contemporary culture for those of us who listen. And because it is so adept at reaching a certain type of person (well educated, well off, socially conscious), it often draws critical comments from those who think it should play a different role—even though the major changes in funding and industrial structure that such a new role would require are not likely to happen anytime soon.

Some of the people I consulted during my research were determined to sway me to one viewpoint or another. Most commonly, I encountered well-meaning people of the left-side-of-liberal persuasion who thought that NPR, in the course of its maturation, had turned into a safe haven for well-mannered white folks—a faint echo of its original promise as a progressive, free-ranging sphere of public communication. I spent a few years sympathizing with this position, as it seemed a natural extension of my own liberal outlook on life. Other people have flung "the L word" at me derisively, certain that their anecdotal sampling of NPR stories gave them the right to tar the whole enterprise as an irredeemable fixture of the liberal-Democratic complex. In the end, however, the main thing that motivated my writing was a sense that I could tell NPR's story in a way that most people familiar with the industry would find authentic. A wise person once said that the real test of scholarship lies in the following question: When all is said and done, can the author invite all the different kinds of people that he or she has written about into a room, look each person in the eye, and still be comfortable with what has been written? In my opinion, research is of little value unless most of its subjects can see themselves—at least in part—in the final write-up. The chapters that follow may please or displease some of the people I have written about. That said, I am comfortable in knowing they were crafted with the goal of reaching some level of common understanding.

Noncommercial radio has a rich and interesting history in the United States, one which defies easy explanation. The pioneering broadcasters who started educational radio stations in the early 1900s could not have imagined the changes this medium would go through over the next eighty years. These people, and the generation of radio professionals they trained, are the intellectual and philosophical parents of NPR, and their experiences form the heart of the next chapter. Before telling their story, however, I have two final thoughts for the reader. First of all, this book focuses primarily on NPR News. This conscious choice—an artifact, in part, of my own experience as a journalist—is not meant to denigrate the network's fine cultural and entertainment programs. Though NPR has a long history of broadcasting musical performances and other cultural fare, it is undeniable that it has always been, first and foremost, a news and information company. I apologize in advance to people who would have preferred a more extensive treatment of other programs. I also want to mention, very briefly, my method for handling names and references. When writing about important figures in NPR's history, I generally use their full, formal names on first reference; after that, I revert to the first names by which they were commonly known to others in the industry. For example, William Siemering, the network's first program director, is known, after first reference, as "Bill." This practice should not connote a sense of close familiarity with all of my sources. Rather, I want the reader to encounter each person in the very same way that he or she has been addressed by friends and colleagues. With these minor caveats out in the open, we are now ready to meet some of the people who helped build public radio into the industry we know today.

2 THE VERY FIRST BRUSH STROKES

Noncommercial stations have been part of American broadcasting from the very beginning. There is no literal connection between educational radio and Justin Morrill's effort to create land-grant colleges in the Civil War era, but for some observers, America's pioneer educational stations seemed a natural extension of Morrill's imperative to expand the reach of a modern university to every corner of its home state. The extent of early educational broadcasting is surprising, as more than seventy colleges and other institutions secured radio licenses by the end of 1922. In 1930, a group of forward-thinking broadcasters envisioned "a network of educational stations which would present better programs and compete on a more even basis with commercial broadcasters."[1] However, the rapid ascent of commercial networks in the 1920s meant that any widespread movement to organize nonprofit stations would be a long time in the making; in fact, the industry that brought us Big Bird and *Morning Edition* did not materialize in anything close to its present form until a few years after President Lyndon Johnson signed the Public Broadcasting Act of 1967. The reasons for this delay include lack of money, lack of interest, and conflicting missions on the part of various broadcasters. Given these challenges, it is a wonder that public broadcasting, and public radio in particular, managed to survive.

This chapter begins with an introduction to noncommercial radio in the United States, a field that was buffeted by political and financial pressures in its earliest years and, as a consequence, remained a marginal enterprise for decades. Trade groups and large foundations kept the industry afloat until President Johnson supplied the first dedicated programming support for nonprofit stations in the late 1960s. Not surprisingly, the Corporation for Public Broadcasting, the agency charged with disbursing government funds to stations, placed most of its support behind public *television*. NPR's incorporation in 1970 was made possible by the hard work of a few dedicated radio advocates; it was certainly not the product of any foregone conclusion. *All Things Considered*, the network's flagship news magazine, debuted in May of the following year. The remainder of the chapter is devoted to the task of getting this program off the ground. I also offer a detailed examination of the relationship between NPR's first president and its program director, including a series of creative conflicts that gave the network its original shape. As one might expect, the conflicts that obtained throughout public broadcasting's early years—in both radio and television—have left a powerful imprint on the industry we know today.

In the Beginning

Physicists and engineers at American universities first experimented with radio technology shortly after 1900. Scientists at the University of Wisconsin, who had been tinkering with "wireless telegraphy" (i.e., radio Morse code) since 1902, secured a license for an experimental station called 9XM (later WHA) in 1914. The university regents took control of the license in 1916, and the station made its first voice and music transmissions the following year. Similar developments at other universities foreshadowed the start of a radio boom in the 1920s, when more than 200 licenses were granted for educational AM stations. Many of them offered a platform for professors interested in teaching courses over the air, but instruction was not the main emphasis for educational radio stations, which also featured entertainment, public affairs programs, farm reports, and other specialty shows.[2]

Despite this promising start, educational broadcasters soon hit a wall. Some licensees backed away from radio in the mid-1920s after engineering professors tamed the technology and then lost interest; at other institutions, administrators simply did not see the educational potential of this new medium.[3] One frustrated broadcaster complained that many colleges and universities "found the notion of educating the general mass of people off campus a very foreign one."[4] Late in the decade, the Federal Radio Commission complicated matters by enacting stricter engineering requirements. These rules helped to diminish the chaos of unrestricted broadcasting, a situation in which competing signals reduced parts of the AM band to "an inferno of the unfavored . . . a place of howls and squeals and eternal misery, from which escape seemed difficult."[5] But this cleanup forced educators who could not afford the necessary technical upgrades to go out of business. Finally, other pressures came from commercial broadcasters who coveted the frequencies used by nonprofit interests. These forces, and the lean times of the Great Depression, caused a drop in the number of educational AM stations from ninety-eight in 1927 to forty-three in 1933.[6]

Early regulatory pressures on educational broadcasters were quite significant, and they deserve separate attention. The first law that covered audio transmissions, the Radio Act of 1912, did not anticipate their use for anything more than point-to-point communication between military and business interests. Thus, regulators were ill prepared in the 1920s when a variety of other applicants clamored to secure licenses for the purpose of transmitting music and the spoken word. To address the consequent crowding of the airwaves, Secretary of Commerce Herbert Hoover convened a series of national radio conferences from 1922 to 1925. Following the last conference, Hoover decreed that permanent regulation of the electromagnetic spectrum would be necessary if radio broadcasters were to avoid signal interference and other causes of poor reception.[7]

The Radio Act of 1927 marked the first serious attempt at broadcast regulation. This "emergency" law created the Federal Radio Commission and paved the way for reallocation of the radio frequencies that had been assigned to individual stations during the following year. In November 1928, the FRC reassigned 94 percent of the existing frequencies. The stations left unaffected were either commercial network affiliates located on nationwide clear channels (reserved for exclusive or near-exclusive broadcasting by the licensee) or stations actually owned and operated by for-profit networks. Policy decisions developed concurrently with this order further reduced the number of stations on the air. For instance, the commission made it possible for any prospective station owner to challenge the frequency assignment of an existing broadcaster at the end of the three-month term that was accorded each license. In many cases, the various applicants would share the challenged frequency, with the majority of broadcast hours going to the applicant that *seemed* most worthy. As a matter of policy, the FRC deemed the worthiest applicants to be those with the best technical equipment; of course, these were the people with the most capital—the operators or would-be operators of commercial stations. Thus, the commission's actions went a long way "toward determining which broadcasters would be favored in the general reallocation and which would be under constant pressure to maintain their licenses or their totals of assigned broadcast hours."[8]

By the end of the 1930s, the contours of America's commercial broadcasting system, and its weak sister in the noncommercial realm, had become firmly entrenched. The Communications Act of 1934, which established the Federal Communications Commission, made government intervention in the broadcast spectrum a permanent fixture. In passing this law, Congress also rejected the Wagner-Hatfield Amendment, which would have reserved 25 percent of all radio channels for educational broadcasters. Real progress on the channel reservation front would not come until 1940, when the government allocated 40 new frequencies in the FM band and reserved the first five for nonprofit interests. Five noncommercial FM stations were on the air at the end of World War II; in late 1949, that number increased to forty-eight. By that time, the FCC had *authorized* more than 1,000 new FM stations, but the reluctance of listeners to purchase expensive new receivers, coupled with a period of intense interest in television, meant that FM was a money loser for most broadcasters. More than 350 FM station owners actually returned their licenses to the FCC from 1949 through 1952.[9]

Educational broadcasters, who had faced a real threat of going off the air, created a trade group in 1925 called the Association of College and University Broadcasting Stations; eight years later, it became the National Association of Educational Broadcasters. This name change and related changes in the group's constitution were motivated by a basic need for survival; specifically, the group hoped to attract more support from educational institutions that broadcast their programs over commercial stations. The NAEB was strapped for cash as the 1940s unfolded but, nonetheless, managed to play a central role in the slowly developing educational broadcasting movement. In 1949 and 1950, the University of Illinois, soon to become the association's new home, hosted the Allerton House seminars. These meetings, bankrolled by the Rockefeller Foundation, marked the first time that educators, noncommercial broadcasters, and government officials had a chance to sit down with one another to discuss their hopes and dreams and assess their capabilities for producing programs on a larger scale. Soon, another powerful organization entered the picture. In 1951, the Ford Foundation began puzzling over what to do with the many requests it was getting for monetary support of educational radio and TV. Ford's trustees did not want to consider each request separately; instead, they committed a subsidiary, the Fund for Adult Education, to the task. Soon, the FAE created the Educational Television and Radio Center, an organization that, in several different incarnations, would be a force in noncommercial broadcasting until 1972. This turn of events held both good and bad news for radio broadcasters. The good news was that FAE and ETRC represented a significant infusion of outside funds; the bad news lay in the fact that these organizations would focus most of their attention on television.[10]

The Ford Foundation began to study the feasibility of a live educational radio network on the East Coast in 1960, while, at the very same time, the managers of WGBH-FM in Boston were laying the groundwork for just such a project. On April 3, 1961, the Educational Radio Network opened for business with live interconnections among six stations. Ford assumed financial support for this network on an experimental basis in July 1962. The foundation was then funding the NETRC (the acronym given to ETRC in 1959 when the word "National" was added to its name) at a level of $2 million per year and was considering whether to make a much bigger investment.[11] But, as public broadcasting veteran Donald Quayle recalls, the foundation shifted its priorities just eighteen months later.

> They made the decision, on a philosophical basis, of funding [NETRC] at $6 million, but they wanted them to concentrate specifically on the production of five hours of *television* programming. And they said, "No radio, no station relations, no instructional television. Five hours of general television for a general audience—two-and-a-half hours public affairs, two-and-a half hours cultural affairs. Everything else goes out.[12]

In making this decision, Ford was banking on television's steadily increasing popularity, relative to radio. Whatever the reason, its withdrawal from educational radio in 1963 was a missed opportunity, the likes of which would not appear again for another four years.

By the mid-1960s, educational broadcasting, both radio and TV, was still on the ropes. The sheer number of noncommercial outlets had grown significantly; between 1961 and 1966 more than one hundred educational FM and sixty-two ETV stations went on the air. Positive as this may sound, these stations were operated mainly on the local level, with a dearth of both funding and quality programs. The fortunes of the system improved somewhat in May 1962, when Congress passed the Educational Television Facilities Act. This legislation provided $32 million in matching grants for the activation of new stations and the expansion of existing stations (predictably, it ignored educational radio). But in spite of this government largesse and lavish support from the Ford Foundation, the industry seemed stagnant. Content was often perceived as dull, stuffy, or cheaply produced. The increasing number of ETV stations also began to tax the efficiency of the antiquated system through which taped programs were circulated. Finally, the authorization of funds from the 1962 act was scheduled to expire within five years. Given these pressures, educational broadcasters knew the only way they could realize their full potential was to build networks of their own.[13]

From Carnegie to CPB

The year 1964 marked the beginning of a series of coordinated efforts to build a noncommercial broadcasting system. Initial plans were set in motion at the First National Conference on Long-Range Financing of ETV, called by the NAEB under a grant from the United States Office of Education. At that conference, Boston banker and philanthropist Ralph Lowell argued that a presidential commission should be formed to study educational television's financial situation and recommend a new national policy. Lowell's support for this idea was significant as he was a gifted fund raiser and a trustee of "almost every important charitable, cultural and civic institution" in Boston. He was also a cofounder of the local educational broadcasting council that launched WGBH-FM and WGBH-TV, stations which have since risen to national prominence.[14]

Soon after the conference, Lowell and others urged President Johnson to form an ETV commission. Since Johnson had close ties to the commercial broadcasting industry (a potential conflict of interest) and since several other presidential commissions already existed, it was decided that a privately financed body would be more appropriate. Lowell and his colleagues approached the Carnegie Corporation for funding, and the Carnegie Commission on Educational Television was formed in November 1965 under the leadership of James R. Killian, chairman of the Massachusetts Institute of Technology. Members of the blue-ribbon panel came from the fields of higher education, media, politics, business, and the arts. Their mission was to deliver "an overall appraisal of educational television, a prescriptive definition of ETV's role in contemporary America, and recommendations as to how that role can be fulfilled" (absent, once again, was any discussion of radio).[15] The Carnegie Commission was given twelve to fifteen months to do its work and, in January 1967, it published a report titled *Public Televi-*

sion: A Plan for Action. The report recommended these steps, and others, for strengthening educational television:

> Efforts to improve the facilities and funding for existing stations, and to increase the overall number of stations;
>
> Action by Congress to establish a nonprofit, non-governmental entity known as the Corporation for Public Television to receive government and private funds and use them to improve programming;
>
> Provision by this Corporation for the interconnection of stations by conventional means (and, eventually, by satellite); and
>
> Provision by Congress of a long-range funding mechanism for the ETV system. This funding should take the form of a manufacturer's excise tax on television sets, and tax revenues should be made available to the Corporation through a trust fund.[16]

Mindful of the need to maintain political and editorial independence, the commission recommended that the president of the United States appoint only half of the CPB board.

Funding was the most urgent topic of debate as the Carnegie proposals worked their way through the legislative process. A decade earlier, when the Educational Television Facilities Act was introduced, opponents often cited their "fear of federal control" over the noncommercial system. As debate unfolded in 1967, the precise meaning of this phrase became more clear: funding for public broadcasting must be drawn from sources outside the commercial broadcasting and consumer electronics industries and must be structured in a way that fosters political and ideological neutrality. The excise tax and trust fund proposals detailed in the Carnegie report were nonstarters, as the Electronic Industries Association, the trade group for TV- and radio-set manufacturers, threatened to wield its clout on Capitol Hill. Commercial broadcasters sought to limit the kinds of content public broadcasters could offer, a transparent attempt to preserve maximum profits on their end.[17] Finally, a voting bloc of Southerners and conservatives in Congress promised to look critically at any program of federal aid "to a segment of the mass media that had a powerful potential for influencing public opinion and shaping public attitudes."[18] Given all these pressures, the Johnson administration decided the public broadcasting legislation it sent to Congress would contain a one-year, nine-million-dollar funding proposal. Once the system got up and running, Johnson would return to the question of long-term financing.[19]

The conference committee for this bill filed its report in October. Under the version that was sent back to the White House, the president would select all fifteen members of the Corporation for Public Broadcasting's board, with no more than eight members from one party; public broadcasters would be barred from editorializing or supporting political candidates; and programming would be defined more narrowly as that which was "primarily designed for educational or cultural purposes." This bill was a substantially weakened version of the legislation the Carnegie Commission had proposed, due largely to the fact that lawmakers in Washington had to mediate the interests of commercial networks, TV and radio manufacturers, and conservative politicians. President Johnson signed the Public Broadcasting Act of 1967 on November 7, thus bringing a brief yet rocky legislative process to a close.[20]

Though the debate about public broadcasting in Washington had focused mainly on TV, advocates of noncommercial radio had worked quietly and effectively to put their stamp on the process as well. In 1963, just before the Ford Foundation pulled out of radio, the National Association of Educational Broadcasters created a semi-autonomous division called National Educational Radio. Early the following year, Jerrold Sandler, the production manager for the University of Michigan radio station, was asked to come to Washington as NER's executive director and to study the possibility of linking institutions of higher learning with a web of various telecommunications technologies.[21] Though the job description seemed vague on the surface, Sandler says it was designed with one overriding purpose.

> It was really a cover for getting some money to study the feasibility of getting a live, interconnected, educational radio network on the air; but the feds wouldn't accept that kind of talk, so this was going to be a look at the feasibility of tying institutions of higher education together for both broadcast and non-broadcast purposes.[22]

Sandler's activities with the university project did little to further the prospects of a nationwide educational radio network, but other, related efforts began to pay off. In September 1965, seventy NER affiliates were connected live for three hours to broadcast the returns of the German national elections; this represented the first large-scale effort at interconnection for nonprofit radio stations. The old ERN—renamed the *Eastern* Educational Radio Network—also managed a few live broadcasts over eight member stations.[23] Other developments prior to the Carnegie Commission report included a nationwide survey of educational radio licensees that was spearheaded by broadcasting consultant Herman Land. The resulting report, titled *The Hidden Medium*, portrayed an industry that was troubled, yet hopeful:

> Educational radio remains virtually unknown as a communications force in its own right. Overshadowed first by commercial radio, then by television, it has suffered long neglect arising from disinterest and apathy among the educational administrators who control much of its fortunes. As a result, it lacks cohesion as a medium, its purposes are varied and often confused. Yet somehow it manages not only to survive and fill its traditional cultural role, but to move forward, innovate, experiment.[24]

The Hidden Medium supported the development of educational radio on a national scale, though at the time, the prospects of getting Congress to pay for anything other than television were not at all certain.

The fact that the Carnegie Commission failed to mention anything about educational radio was not lost on NER's Jerrold Sandler. As the commission and the Johnson administration planned the introduction of a public television bill, Sandler and his small team of radio lobbyists went to work. Three contacts were especially helpful: Douglass Cater, a special assistant to the president who helped publicize educational broadcasting within the White House; Dean Coston, deputy undersecretary of the Department of Health, Education and Welfare, who was charged with writing the actual bill; and Nick Zapple, chief counsel to the Senate Commerce Committee, who was the point man for moving communications bills through that body. Zapple lectured Sandler and Herman Land on the art of building political pressure behind their cause, and Coston helped ensure that the word *radio* was included in public broadcasting legislation—or so he thought.[25]

The day before president Johnson was to announce the bill, Sandler got a phone tip from the editor of *Television Digest* that someone had managed to remove any mention of radio. Alarmed by this report, he phoned Coston, a former colleague from the University of Michigan radio station. Sandler heard nothing more on that day, but learned exactly what happened early the following morning.

> At about 5:30 [or] 6:00 in the morning my phone rang. And what I heard at the end of the phone was a very tired Dean Coston who said, "you miserable SOB," and so on and so on—expletives deleted. He'd been up all that day and all that night working with Doug Cater and company at the White House because, in fact, *radio had been taken*

out, and they had to put it back all over again. And I have in my files a xeroxed copy of every page of the amended bill, with the scotch tape showing where they had to put radio in, you know, hundreds of times—because of all the amendments in the Communications Act.[26]

Sandler did not say who tampered with the bill but was convinced that he and his educational radio team "were about to be screwed." If not for the intervention of a well-placed acquaintance, those people who wanted to reserve all federal funds for public television would have won the day.[27]

Despite legislative approval in 1967, the Corporation for Public Broadcasting did not get up and running until late April of the following year. The fifteen new members of the CPB board had little conception of how to form a nationwide, interconnected radio system, but an early clue came in November 1968 at a planning conference in New York City. There, Hartford Gunn, an important figure in the development of educational television, delivered a paper titled "A Model for a National Public Radio System." In part, it mirrored Gunn's views for developing public TV; he envisioned a "nucleus of five to eight stations that would help determine network policies, provide production facilities," and become the system's key affiliates. He also recommended the hiring of a Washington-based staff that would provide "a service of tightly-formatted, in-depth national and international news and public affairs, with the emphasis on analysis, commentary, criticism and good talk." These early musings provide an outline of the service that NPR would offer, later on, in the form of *All Things Considered* and *Talk of the Nation*.[28]

Shortly after the New York conference, CPB commissioned media analyst Samuel C. O. Holt, a protege of Gunn, to evaluate the noncommercial radio resources that lay scattered around the country. In a sense, his *Public Radio Study* would be a detailed follow-up to *The Hidden Medium*. Holt completed his work in the spring of 1969, and the most interesting finding, he said, was the utter sense of poverty that continued to pervade the industry. He and his aides sent a questionnaire to every licensed noncommercial, educational broadcaster known to the Federal Communications Commission. When station managers were asked about the first thing they would buy after securing new federal funds, the most frequently mentioned piece of hardware was a *typewriter*. Holt made several recommendations for strengthening the system, including a reallocation of relevant radio frequencies, a strengthening or expansion of FM radio (which had not yet reached its peak of popularity), and the establishment of an advisory board of experienced noncommercial broadcasters. The last of these goals came to fruition almost immediately in the form of CPB's Radio Advisory Council, which had six members from the NER board and another six chosen by Holt and officials at CPB.[29]

In May, the corporation hired Albert Hulsen from WFCR-FM in Amherst, Massachusetts, to be its first director of radio activities. Initial expectations were modest indeed; Hulsen remembers that his "office with a window" in Washington was the sole piece of evidence the corporation really *was* involved with radio. CPB's appropriation for the 1969 fiscal year was $5 million, about one-fourth of the money that Lyndon Johnson had originally proposed for public broadcasting. Of that sum, radio received about $260,000, with a third of the money earmarked for NER's tape-distribution system. Since resources were scarce, Hulsen and his colleagues developed minimum criteria that public radio stations would have to meet in order to qualify for CPB funding: they had to broadcast at least eleven months a year, six days a week, and eight hours a day; they also needed at least 250 watts of power and a staff of three. Reasonable as these requirements may now seem, only 73 of America's 457 noncommercial stations were able to meet them. Hulsen was determined to hold fast, reasoning that CPB should spend whatever radio money it had on stations that would genuinely make a difference in the lives of listeners.[30]

The next task, of course, was to organize America's viable noncommercial stations into a national system. Hulsen and his staff traveled the country, talking with station managers and fielding a variety of suggestions. Based on this research, any notion that the new system would simply be a "remodeled" version of the old NER was quickly dismissed. In November 1969, Hulsen announced the formation of a new organization—National Public Radio. The planning board for this network gathered in San Diego in January 1970 for a session that proved to be of great consequence. It was at this meeting that William Siemering, an educational broadcaster from Buffalo, led the effort to write a mission statement titled "National Public Radio Purposes."[31] It began with the kind of soaring prose that Siemering would become famous for in public radio circles.

> National Public Radio will serve the individual: it will promote personal growth; it will regard the individual differences among men with respect and joy rather than derision and hate; it will celebrate the human experience as infinitely varied rather than vacuous and banal; it will encourage a sense of active constructive participation, rather than apathetic helplessness.[32]

The San Diego meeting was also the place where the concept for a daily news magazine, later known as *All Things Considered*, was formally introduced.[33]

COUNTDOWN TO AIR TIME

National Public Radio was incorporated on March 3, 1970, whereupon the NPR planning board became the network's first real board of directors. John Witherspoon, a widely respected educational broadcaster from San Diego, was named chairman. Other directors included Bill Siemering, Joseph Gwathmey from Austin, Texas (who would later hold key programming positions with the network), and Karl Schmidt of WHA Radio in Madison, Wisconsin. Schmidt brought with him the credibility and influence of America's first noncommercial radio station; he also presided over a network of educational stations in Wisconsin with a staff and budget that were, by far, the largest in the industry. Aside from these men and William Kling, the driving force behind Minnesota Public Radio, the board was not a luminous collection of top-level talent; at the time, most of the shining stars in public broadcasting found television more appealing. Still, the first board had a decent mix of strong managers, creative programmers, and experienced radio men. At the time, NPR was poised to become a viable producer and distributor of radio programs, a purveyor of information and culture that was not available on commercial stations.[34]

These hopeful beginnings aside, the months that followed the network's incorporation were marked by conflict. First, John Witherspoon and Bill Kling left the board for jobs at CPB; their departure stripped this body of its two most competent members. Those who remained were badly split on a number of points, including the issue of centralized program production. Witherspoon had argued that NPR should produce much of its own content, since the public radio system did not, at first, have many strong program-producing stations. Other members wanted significant contributions from local stations right from the start. The board addressed this controversy by locating a central programming staff in Washington, D.C.; the directors, all of whom were station managers, would ensure that local affiliates continued to have a say in the kinds of material produced and distributed. The board was also divided over the selection of the network's first president. Several noteworthy candidates were suggested, including broadcast-historian Erik Barnouw and network newsmen Erik Sevareid and Walter Cronkite. When the process of sifting and winnowing was through, however, two other candidates came to the fore: Robert Mott and Robert Lewis Shayon. A group of

directors considered to be part of the NAEB old guard, including Richard
Estell of WKAR Radio at Michigan State University, lined up behind Mott,
who was then executive director of NER. For the most part, Estell and his
allies simply wanted CPB to improve the kind of educational radio programming that already existed—classical music, book-reading programs, news
from the wire services, and farm and extension reports. They assumed that
Mott would become president of the new organization; after all, the existing NER tape network distributed at least 60,000 hours of programming in
1970 alone. But another group, including WHA's Karl Schmidt, prized new
beginnings over continuity. They wanted someone who could imagine and
then implement a schedule of programs that would be totally different from
anything offered by NER. With that in mind, Schmidt's group supported
Shayon, a well-known media critic.[35]

The NPR board interviewed the two candidates in May but became dead-
locked in the vote for president. Both men promptly withdrew. Interestingly, the board broke its impasse by offering the job to a man who probably
could have taken it, had he wanted to, before Mott and Shayon entered the
picture. Donald Quayle met with the NPR board in Chicago on June 29 and
was selected as the network's first president. Quayle had wide experience in
educational broadcasting, from his college days at Utah State, to management positions at educational radio stations in Ohio and Massachusetts, to
setting up a regional radio network on the East Coast. He left that work in
November 1968 to help establish an interconnection system for TV stations
funded by CPB, and that position made him a force to be reckoned with in
public broadcasting. Quayle had initially taken himself out of the running
for the NPR job since he was then working in public television and wanted
to become president of PBS. When that job was given to his former boss,
Hartford Gunn, Quayle accepted the offer from NPR. He began his new
position in September 1970 and, by the end of that month, had hired the
first four members of his administrative team. Lee Frischknecht, a lifelong
friend from Utah, would be his top assistant. Charles Herbits, a Columbia-
trained lawyer with public television experience, was chosen to head Business and Legal Affairs. An acquaintance from the Eastern Educational Radio
Network, Elizabeth Young, found a job in Station Relations. Quayle also
hired Jack Mitchell, formerly news director at WHA Radio, to make good on
a promise by NER's Bob Mott—who, like his allies on the NPR board, had
assumed that he would become the network's first president.[36]

Most of Quayle's early hires were inside choices, people whom the president knew he wanted even before job descriptions were written. He had a
tougher time choosing someone to head NPR's programming operations

but finally settled on Bill Siemering, the board member who had been the lead author of the network's mission statement. Siemering had worked in educational radio and television since his college days in the early 1950s. Before coming to NPR he managed WBFO-FM at the State University of New York at Buffalo; it was there that Siemering melded a diverse collection of influences into his own unique programming philosophy. By listening to broadcasts from neighboring CBC stations, he developed and refined an idea for a talk and information program called *This Is Radio*, which later influenced the shape of *All Things Considered*. By covering student protests in the 1960s in a manner that respected all parties involved, he made WBFO a "beacon of light, and calm, and reason" in the community. And by opening a storefront studio in a minority neighborhood, he helped residents communicate their interests and concerns to a wider audience.[37]

Siemering was clearly different from the other early managers at NPR. His strongest talent lay in translating ideas from outside the world of broadcasting—from artistic and social critics, in particular—into recommendations for the sort of programs that NPR was aiming to produce. His vision for public radio, a service that would allow Americans to "listen to the country" in all its diversity, was quite different from the existing practice of educational radio, an industry that thrived, in part, on the adaptation of book and newspaper content for broadcast purposes.[38] CPB's Al Hulsen admired Siemering's outlook, which was shared by other progressive thinkers on the NPR board.

> I think there was a whole group of people, [and] Bill Siemering stands out among that group, that said, "There are resources all over the United States that can be tapped for national enlightenment"; that ideas are not restricted to the East Coast or Europe. They're all over the world in the smallest places, in the biggest places. There are brilliant minds everywhere that could solve human problems, and put society ahead, and stop war.[39]

The decision to hire Siemering as program director was difficult, in part, because he brought a 1960s mentality to an organization whose top managers were men of the 1950s—with all that this implied about conservatism in programming. For example, his commitments to "uplift the downtrodden masses" and shine a light on the things that were not working in society would prove irksome for others at NPR. Don Quayle also had reservations about hiring one of his own board members for a key staff position but thought he could work with Siemering to transform some of the nobler aspects of the network's mission statement into compelling radio programs.[40]

Quayle played a part in hiring two more programming people—*New York Times* veteran Cleve Mathews, and Robert Conley, formerly of the *Times* and NBC News.[41] Jeff Rosenberg, an associate producer in those days, remembers that Siemering filled out the rest of the program staff with an eclectic mix of people.

> You had people who were educated but [had] never done anything. You had people with no exposure to either radio or print journalism of any sort. I think there was more of an intent to hire a sympathetic crew, people with more or less the same kind of general notion of what they were headed toward, than there was to slap it into some kind of journalism mold.[42]

Ira Flatow, Mike Waters and Rich Firestone had worked with Siemering at WBFO. Susan Stamberg had several years of experience at WAMU in Washington. Linda Wertheimer had gained some rudimentary broadcasting skills in jobs with CBS and the BBC. Jim Russell came on board after working for United Press International in Vietnam, and Barbara Newman brought print journalism experience. Stamberg remembers that NPR always had "a handful of superb workers." But mixed in with these people, she said, were others "who were literally right off the street, rookies who had never done radio before."[43]

Siemering and Quayle built their respective staffs with little regard for the procedures commonly used in human resource departments; furthermore, the kinds of people they hired were quite different. For Jack Mitchell, the disparity in age was most obvious.

> Quayle hired his old friends, who were all about 40. And Siemering was accustomed to dealing with college students at Buffalo and hired people in their 20s. It was a generational thing to some extent, because I think Quayle saw a lot of the programming staff like his daughters, who were college students.[44]

A more serious difference lay in the attitudes that each group brought to the workplace. Siemering ties this dynamic to a divergence in real-life experience between himself and Quayle. "[Don] had been in high rise offices in New York," he said, "while I was in Buffalo, you know, running from tear gas in some cases or visiting a reporter that had been injured, had his face cut in a demonstration that went awry."[45] He also remembers that most of his charges dressed more like students than corporate executives; thus, there developed a classic demarcation between "the staff" and "the suits." There was something deeper about this clash of cultures, though. A young, eclectic programming staff, possessed of widely varying experience and an attitude to boot, often grated against the psyches of people in other departments. Siemering recalls a time when, in a fit of irreverence, he responded to a question about Mike Waters's job title. "And I said, 'well, he's a first-rate editor and a great reporter. Why can't we just call him Mike Waters?'" Predictably, that comment failed to amuse his inquisitor. Public broadcasting scholar Joseph Kirkish notes that "with a staff selected on the basis of personalities rather than expertise, it would follow that Siemering's people would not work within specific guidelines." This sense of free agency on the part of the programming staff would prove destructive to the organization in years to come.[46]

Most of Siemering's personnel reported to work just one month before the debut of All Things Considered. Shortly, these people would have to gather each weekday morning to create a high-quality, ninety-minute national news magazine from scratch, a task one former producer likens to "taking a teaspoon and trying to fill in the Grand Canyon."[47] In the face of this challenge, Siemering urged his people to do things differently, reminding them that NBC and CBS News already existed and should not be simply replicated. "'We have a blank canvas,' I told the staff. 'There'll be a lot of paint put on this canvas over the years, but the very first brush strokes are critical in terms of the color and the style that we establish for it.'"[48] Members of the program staff did not lay their hands on recording equipment until two weeks before show time. When equipment was finally available, the engineering staff, whose members were experienced broadcasters, had to walk the rookies through the steps of their own jobs (interestingly, it was George Geesey, NPR's head of operations and engineering, who suggested All Things Considered as the name for the network's first program). Siemering himself lacked some of the radio producing and directing skills his employees would need to learn.[49]

In spite of these mounting tensions, the show had to go on. Don Quayle told local station representatives that NPR would be on the air no sooner than April 1971, but he did not want to push the launch date back much further. Siemering and others decided to provide seasoning for the news staff by staging a limited journalistic experiment. On April 20, the network began live, gavel-to-gavel coverage of the Senate Foreign Relations Committee hearings on the end of the Vietnam War. Then on May 3, the day All Things Considered was to debut, Siemering dispatched reporters to cover the huge May Day protest staged in Washington by angry college students and Vietnam veterans. This exercise made for compelling broadcasts as helicopters buzzed, tear gas canisters flew, and protesters were either pushed or dragged away by police. Aside from the great front line reporting experience, the May Day coverage provided badly needed audio for the first installment of the network's flagship program.[50]

All Things Considered hit the airwaves in Washington on the afternoon of May 3 and pulsed through some 12,000 miles of telephone line to more than eighty affiliated stations. The show started right on time at five P.M. Eastern, but audio tape for the first scheduled story, a lengthy report on the protest, was still being edited. Robert Conley, the program's first host, managed to ad-lib until the tape finally made its way to the control room. By most accounts, the first ninety minutes of *ATC* were quite uneven. Other stories in this inaugural broadcast included a dramatic piece from the CBC that combined antiwar poetry with songs and battle sounds from World War I and a lengthy story about a heroin-addicted nurse named Janice who had contemplated suicide. Some were excellent pieces, while others were thoroughly unpolished. And Conley's generous ad-libbing, necessary as it was that first day, became a problem almost immediately. So, too, did his sense of timing; Conley abruptly signaled the end of the first program five and a half minutes early, leaving NPR affiliates coast-to-coast with dead air. Karl Schmidt, listening at WHA in Madison, echoed the reaction of many station managers when he said, "Our child has been born, and it is *ugly*." Producer Jeff Rosenberg says this first broadcast heralded the start of a "period of sacrificial audiences," when those few people who listened "had to sit there while we learned about what we were trying to do."[51]

GROWING PAINS

In October 1971 *Variety* praised NPR as a network that was "quietly developing a distinctive programming schedule," which included twenty-four live feeds of hearings before congressional committees and audio rebroadcasts of *Firing Line*, the PBS talk program made famous by its host, William F. Buckley Jr. CPB's appropriation for the 1971 fiscal year rose to $23 million; NPR garnered about 4 percent of that sum, a little more than $1 million. The network's administrative and programming units employed nearly fifty people by year's end and the shows they produced were broadcast to more than 110 stations. This sort of growth might seem impressive to the casual observer, but comments made by some public broadcasters suggested an air of dissatisfaction with NPR. Negative reactions to *All Things Considered* included a sense of uneasiness or irritation about the new magazine-style format, the uneven quality of stories, and Conley's rambling, self-involved delivery.[52] An understandable sense of panic also developed on the part of Jeff Rosenberg and other harried staff members, who were beginning to feel the consequences of lax programming management.

> I mean, we'd go on the air at 5:00 with no tape sitting in the control room, 'cause it wasn't ready yet. It was frightening. I mean, if I hadn't been twenty-something years old, I don't think I would have had a digestive system that could have made it through most of those days, much less a circulatory system.[53]

Less than a month after *ATC*'s debut, Susan Stamberg, then a production assistant, told News Director Cleve Mathews the program needed a thorough overhaul, an infusion of "shape, form, style, and personality"; she also urged that Robert Conley be removed as host. It is important to remember that Stamberg was an experienced hand at noncommercial radio by the time she arrived at NPR. What's more, her views resonated with those of many staff members and station managers. Siemering followed up on her suggestions in July, and named Mike Waters and Jim Russell as cohosts of the program.[54]

The changes at *ATC* were clearly helpful, but any progress in this regard was soon overshadowed by Bill Siemering's inability to manage day-to-day operations. Many people associated with NPR in the early years talk of the enduring love and respect they feel for Siemering. Susan Stamberg, for example, says he did a great service in terms of "educating our ears, teaching us new ways to talk and new ways to listen."[55] But Stamberg and others, like Elizabeth Young, say their friend and mentor simply did not have the wherewithal to look after his own staff.

> Bill was, and is, a terrific idea person. If you said, "Bill, there's a problem with abused children in Keokuk. What should we do about it?" . . . he'd come up with a fantastic idea. If you said, "Hire a staff, create a salary program, create benefits," he couldn't do it. And that became more and more of a problem.[56]

Karl Schmidt agrees that Siemering was ineffectual in carrying out basic personnel functions, and offers this anecdote about a visit to his friend in Washington.

> We talked one day, and he admitted to me frustratingly that "that person over there, at that desk. I fired her three weeks ago, *but she*

won't leave." Somehow, that sticks in my head as being very typical of Bill. He wasn't interested in that sort of thing. He was interested in program[ming] and not in management, or efficiency, or in personnel management.[57]

By way of contrast, Siemering's boss, Don Quayle, could most often solve organizational problems by using his ability as an *actor*—a talent he cultivated during graduate studies at Ohio State. On some occasions, Quayle played the role of a consummate politician, taking on a "Jack Kennedy look" just before making a public speech. At other times, he could be a convincing father figure, helping an employee in need or hosting informal, family-style gatherings at his home.[58]

The problems that developed in Bill Siemering's programming staff, however, were of a kind that even Quayle was unprepared to handle. For example, Siemering's inability to delegate creative tasks left other staff members wondering exactly what *their* roles were. Deborah Emanatian, then Quayle's assistant, says this had a ripple effect on NPR's ability to serve its local affiliates. She remembers that audio tapes piled up everywhere as Siemering invested too much time in analyzing story submissions. The managers of local stations, in turn, began to wonder if NPR would ever actually *do* anything. Jeff Rosenberg concurs, noting that early broadcasts of *All Things Considered* included a great deal of soft, feature material that was part of some foggy, ephemeral programming goal he and his colleagues *failed to hit*, day after day. Speaking in his own defense, Siemering felt a loose, hands-off approach was necessary in a department full of highly creative people.[59]

These and other problems continued to find their way to the desk of NPR's president. Convinced from day one that he had problems in programming, Don Quayle looked for ways to build a supportive structure around Siemering. In the fall of 1971, he brought Joe Gwathmey back to Washington—Siemering was to generate program ideas and provide charismatic leadership, while Gwathmey would make it all work. But Quayle soon found that his program director would not allow Gwathmey to have operational control; he then told Siemering that he was "on trial" and would be monitored more closely. In February 1972, Siemering turned editorial control of *ATC* over to Jack Mitchell. Most observers agree that NPR's flagship program began to thrive under this arrangement, especially after Susan Stamberg joined Mike Waters as cohost. In spite of these developments, Quayle remained uneasy. He found that Siemering's staff was working around him and in spite of him, and says he simply didn't have the money to sustain an "in-house guru." He fired Siemering at that point, turned the day-to-day programming operation over to Joe Gwathmey, and left Cleve Mathews in charge of news and public affairs.[60]

Siemering had known about Quayle's concerns for some time, but he remains puzzled to this day about the precise reasons for his dismissal.

> I never thought, given my eight years manning WBFO, that I had a problem in management. The station was known for its innovation, for fiscal responsibility, for being part of the university—making good progress. I attracted good people and maintained them with little money. So I never was confronted with the "you're not a good manager" issue at that point. Granted, managing NPR is something else. So that's why it hit me kind of out of the blue, and was hard to deal with . . . Because I cared deeply about NPR. And I felt that we had turned a corner.[61]

Siemering offered to stay on in a diminished role, as a tape editor by some accounts. Not surprisingly, his request was turned down.[62] It is sadly ironic that within about a year of NPR's launch, top management put all the pieces in place for a successful ninety-minute news magazine—and then fired the man who got the whole thing started.

In July 1973, not very long after Siemering's departure, Don Quayle also left National Public Radio. In some ways, Quayle was made for NPR's top job; he had years of public broadcasting experience and close ties with many important players in the field. He was also a gregarious man, one who could mend fences in an organization by sheer force of personality. These skills were not lost on other key figures in Washington. In particular, Quayle caught the eye of Henry Loomis, the man picked by Richard Nixon to be the new president of CPB. The corporation focused heavily on television in those days, and Loomis was concerned about an ongoing conflict between his agency and PBS. As the two organizations fought over the scope of their responsibilities and for control of programming funds, Loomis searched for an executive to make peace between them. Convinced that Quayle was the man for the job, he asked a mutual friend, CPB Chairman James Killian, to coax him into the corporate fold. Quayle gave in to Killian's arm-twisting and joined CPB as senior vice president for broadcasting. This move took him "out of what I found to be the most exciting and creative job that I'd had in my career, and put me right into the middle of a political fight." He stayed at CPB for four years and, shortly thereafter, became vice president for administration at WETA-TV and radio in Washington, working there until his retirement in 1989. NPR veterans remember Quayle's departure with sadness since they had, in effect, lost an important father figure. His chief legacy at NPR involved the difficult work of getting the enterprise off to a successful start. By handling the necessary political negotiations, and by securing a permanent corporate headquarters for the network, Quayle amply demonstrated his concern that public radio be taken seriously.[63]

Since staying at NPR was not an option for Bill Siemering, he decided to test the level of regard that public broadcasters had for him by running for the NPR board; he won as a write in candidate. Siemering has enjoyed a distinguished career in public radio since that time, overseeing the development of *Fresh Air* and other programs at WHYY-FM in Philadelphia; winning more than twenty-five awards for his *Soundprint* documentary series; serving as a radio consultant in Europe, Africa, and Asia; and winning a coveted MacArthur Foundation Fellowship, the unrestricted $500,000 award that is more commonly known as "The Genius Grant."[64]

Many people regretted Siemering's departure from NPR, though most acknowledge the difficulties he embodied while there: high-minded principles that offered little in the way of concrete guidance for staff members and a set of philosophical statements about public radio that was so fuzzy that a wide variety of people—from progressive radio activists to commercially oriented audience researchers—now claim to be working in his name.[65] Those issues aside, one must conclude that Bill Siemering has left an indelible mark on NPR; it would be appropriate, in fact, to say that he gave the network its very soul. According to Minnesota Public Radio's Bill Kling, Siemering's impact on public radio stems from his genuine concern for every human being.

> He clearly would have been talking about celebrating the culture, the diversity [of our nation] . . . of helping people *understand* through the development of the common culture. And I think that part of the *Federalist Papers* and Bill Siemering's papers were very much in sync; that you, as a white male, ought to hear a lot about minority females and every other kind of minority, so to better understand each other. You get the richness of what every part of the country has to offer. You get the great performances—not just the symphony orchestras, but the Indian tom-tom. And all of that is drawn together in a way that feeds the mind and expands the horizons. And Bill believed all of that.[66]

Long time staff member Jeff Rosenberg thinks that listeners who feel a sense of ownership about the network do so because of the emotional weight that Siemering placed on crafting "the NPR sound."[67] Even Don Quayle agrees that Siemering has left his mark on the network.

He is a very humane and a very sensitive individual in terms of his colleagues, in terms of his space on this earth, his relationship to others,
wherever they might be . . . men, women, black, white. . . . He is one of
the most equitable persons I have ever met. And that communicated
through his philosophy . . . into what he wanted NPR to create. And
that, as far as I was concerned, was the basis of the programming that
we were all trying to do.[68]

WHAT WE HAVE WROUGHT

Public broadcasting has certainly made its presence known in the years since
1967, as millions of people now watch and listen to programs on PBS and
NPR each week. Yet in another sense, these organizations, and the legislation that helped create them, have spawned a legacy of institutional weak-
ness. Public broadcasting in the United States was designed as an entity that
would not threaten the profits of commercial broadcasters or the sensibilities of conservative politicians; as a consequence, there are still no workable
mechanisms for political insulation or long-range public financing. During
NPR's early years, noncommercial broadcasters in the United States were
still plagued by many of the problems and questions that had troubled them
before 1967. Should the center of programming control be at the local or national level? Should programs reach out to specific minority groups, or will
these groups be adequately served in the course of regular programming?
Should the system aim for large audiences in its own right, or forever be
mindful that commercial broadcasting is America's primary service?[69]

The Public Broadcasting Act helped mitigate these tensions for only a
short time; in fact, the process of crafting this law caused some harmful long-
term side effects. First and foremost, the selection process for the CPB board
has made the organization vulnerable to co-optation by presidents and federal lawmakers who want to use it for their own political ends. The early
1970s were a scary time for public broadcasters in this regard because of the
antipathy that Richard Nixon felt for the industry. *Paranoia* is a fair word
for describing the president's fear that noncommercial broadcasting (mainly
PBS) would somehow ruin him because of its "Eastern liberal bias." Nixon
and his aides—including Supreme Court Justice Antonin Scalia, who then
worked for the White House on public broadcasting policy—tried to foist an
ethic of "localism" upon the public television community, reasoning that stations whose programming decisions were rooted in local communities might
be more immune to liberal taint. Having enjoyed little success in that effort,

Nixon vetoed the reauthorization of The Public Broadcasting Act in June 1972, sending shock waves through the industry. Funding remained stagnant for a time, and a CPB board dominated by Republicans sacked the chairman and president of the corporation, replacing them with political allies. These maneuvers effectively curtailed the programming independence of PBS.[70]

Frightening as this episode was, it did not affect NPR directly, since the public radio system was then small, virtually unknown, and nestled comfortably beneath the radar of Washington politics. But some at NPR felt a prescient twinge of anxiety about future funding threats and efforts to influence news content. In 1985 Sonia Landau, a Reagan appointee to the CPB board, locked horns with the corporation's president, Edward Pfister, about his proposal to send a delegation of public broadcasters to Moscow—noting that CPB's statutory independence from Congress meant that it should not be influenced by the Kremlin either. Another Reagan appointee, Richard Brookhiser, feared the trip might lead to programs based on "wonderful Soviet ideas on their own history or something." Brookhiser agitated for content analyses of public broadcasting programs by a conservative media research center, a move that led to a spate of additional studies and allegations of liberal bias in Congressional hearings. Such displays of crass political influence continued through the 1990s and into the new millennium (see chapter 4). At best, these acts of partisan bickering are a significant waste of time. Such was the case in July 2002, when industry executives went to Capitol Hill to discuss digital broadcasting technologies but spent most of their time deflecting charges of biased programming. At worst, these conflicts take their toll in both economic and human terms. Following conservative attempts to cut public broadcasting funds in the summer of 1995, NPR's management team—mindful of the need to create a "glide path" for the organization—cut nine of the network's cultural programs and twenty related jobs. These episodes make little empirical sense, as surveys have consistently shown that Americans find public broadcasting to be politically balanced, credible, and a wise use of taxpayer dollars.[71]

Setting all political considerations aside, the key determinant of NPR's fate during the period covered by this chapter was the personal interplay between the its first president and program director. Since Don Quayle built up NPR's physical body and Bill Siemering gave the network its soul, the departure of both men in short order was traumatic for the organization on at least two levels. One important conflict that ensued was a philosophical rift between those staff members who advocated a hard news focus and those who wanted more "soft" content, such as cultural programming. Siemering wanted the network's program schedule to strike a balance between the two, but that was much easier said than done. Funding for NPR programs, from the federal government and other sources, was dangerously thin until the early 1980s; thus, clear priorities were needed as to which programs would be well supported. Until *Morning Edition* came along in 1979, *All Things Considered* was widely viewed as *the* program at NPR—it clearly garnered the lion's share of resources. NPR's documentary, artistic, and dramatic programs were also very good. Prime examples include Josh Darsa's "Man with a White Cane," a sound-intensive documentary about a seventy-five-year-old blind man who fell off a subway platform and was nearly killed by a train; a taped musical performance series called *Concert of the Week*; live concerts by jazz artists Carmen McRae and Herbie Hancock; and dramatic presentations from the BBC, CBC, and WHA Radio in Wisconsin. Despite the quality of these programs, their intermittent scheduling precluded the development of a regular audience. As a result, producers who wanted to get significant airplay for any sort of content had to realize that *ATC*, with its reliable daily presence, was the primary venue for doing so.[72]

Herein lies a related problem. In spite of Siemering's wishes, *All Things Considered* never could offer a thoroughgoing blend of news and cultural content. Audience research has shown that people tune in to their favorite stations because they offer a certain discrete genre of content, whether it be music, news, or something else. To the extent that *ATC* has content that is consistent with a station's overall format, it will help that station (and NPR) to develop a loyal audience. If, on the other hand, this program embodied an ever-changing array of disparate program elements, audience attention would become fleeting and transitory. Philosophically speaking, NPR was supposed to rise above these worldly considerations, to fuse all aspects of human knowledge and creative expression in such a way that listeners might come to understand themselves on some deeper level. But in the early and mid-1970s, the network was far too susceptible to a number of pressures, both internal and external, for this to happen in any significant way. The disquieting forces that define this period are the first topic of the chapter that follows.

3 THE PRICE OF FAME

The people who worked at NPR in the summer of 1973 had every right to wonder what their network might actually become when it grew up. This chapter charts the transition from the network Don Quayle bequeathed to his top assistant in 1973 to a completely revamped organization that emerged less than four years later. The corporate makeover became necessary, in part, because of a lack of leadership skills on the part of NPR's second president, Lee Frischknecht, but even more important was the growing influence of another force in public broadcasting—Bill Kling of Minnesota Public Radio. Kling was a driving force in Frischknecht's ouster from NPR in 1977 and in the creation of a new network that was shaped, to a greater degree, by the managers of powerful stations. These people wanted the public radio system to grow beyond its highly centralized, Washington-based hub, and they cast their fortunes with a brash new chief executive by the name of Frank Mankiewicz.

Mankiewicz would transform NPR from a tiny, "alternative" network into a major international news organization. Known for his political acumen and promotional—often *self*-promotional—skills, he secured more federal funds for public radio (at the expense of public television), presided over the launch of a new satellite distribution system, started *Morning Edition*, and, in the process, put the network on the map in Washington as it never had been before. At the same time, Mankiewicz dismissed Bill Kling's effort to build another sort of public radio system, one that honored the ever-increasing capability of member stations to produce and distribute their own national programs. The relationship between Kling and Mankiewicz was the most important dynamic during NPR's adolescent years. Both men wrestled with the potential loss of operating funds from the federal government; in the process, each devised plans for profit-making activities that would ward off downsizing and ensure future growth. Mankiewicz's plan for expansion proved to be part of his own undoing in the spring of 1983. His visceral dislike for Kling's brand of public radio—indeed, for any organization other than NPR—accelerated the process and, ironically, cleared the way for member stations to gain much more influence in the system. This state of affairs now seems natural to public broadcasters, but during the late 1970s and early 1980s, NPR's top management had few, if any, thoughts about sharing its wealth and power.

A CHANGING OF THE GUARD

As Don Quayle left NPR for his new job at the Corporation for Public Broadcasting, he recommended that Lee Frischknecht, his lifelong friend and second in command, be appointed to succeed him. Frischknecht claims he did not have the slightest interest in the job; he decided to offer his name for consideration, however, because he thought the other candidates were not up to the task. If the truth be told, NPR's new president lacked some of the important qualities a chief executive should have. He was not the outgoing, decisive leader that Don Quayle had been; he also lacked his old friend's ability to work a party and manage external relations on Capitol Hill. Frischknecht preferred to stay behind the scenes, to sit alone and weigh administrative options with great care. His presidency would lack the paternal, even feudal tones of the Quayle years and this proved disappointing for subordinates.[1]

Some people remember the early days of Lee Frischknecht's presidency as a life-threatening time for NPR. There were several reasons for this perception, and, to be fair, some of them were simple byproducts of organizational growth. First, the network moved to new facilities near Dupont Circle, right across the street from the CBS News Washington Bureau. Though the move to a legitimate headquarters building was badly needed—at first, the staff of *All Things Considered* had to sit on broken chairs or on the floor—it

contributed to a small deficit in 1973. Also, people who worked in programming during NPR's first few years generally encountered difficult conditions and low pay. In 1974, the pay scale for the network's top hosts and reporters ranged from $16,250 to $24,375 per year. By 1976, most NPR reporters earned between $18,000 and $20,000, with *ATC* host Susan Stamberg pulling down $22,500 that year. These journalists knew their peers in commercial broadcasting made substantially more money and were none too happy about it. Finally, Frischknecht got off to a rocky start because he inherited an organization in which few people paid attention to policies, procedures, and all the other trappings of business administration. NPR was, after all, trying to invent a style of radio that virtually no other U.S. broadcaster had attempted before.[2]

In 1975, Frischknecht made the first of his two major attempts at corporate reorganization. He split the network into two units: a corporate division consisting of himself, the board and the business affairs department, and a programming division, which included all other functions. One important offshoot of this move was the founding of a National News and Information Bureau that was headed by journalist Robert Zelnick, who later enjoyed a distinguished career with ABC News. NPR management had become increasingly concerned about the uneven quality of news reporting, and Zelnick's job was to even things out, to coordinate the efforts of reporters, edit their work, and ensure that the product that went on the air was worthy of national attention. By most accounts he was quite successful at these tasks, but his presence also had another effect: it legitimized the goals of hard-nosed reporters like Linda Wertheimer and Nina Totenberg, who wanted NPR to focus on the conventional brand of news reporting offered by the Big Three networks.[3]

As one might imagine, this exacerbated the friction between NPR's journalists and those employees who favored a more eclectic mix of information and cultural fare. Jack Mitchell says this disagreement was rooted in two different interpretations of the network's mission.

> It was pretty much common understanding that what public radio was about was to be an *alternative*. And Zelnick, not by statement, but by action, was saying "you can be an alternative *by doing a better job of what the other guys do*, rather than doing something different." . . . He was the only one that I would say was really a competent journalist of all the people in the news area. And he was just really, really very bright—but disruptive to the organization, because he knew "exactly what ought to happen" and set out to do it.[4]

Naturally, Frischknecht began to pay close attention to office politics at NPR headquarters.

In the meantime, many people who worked in public radio began to cringe at the way NPR was faring in the so-called Level 2 negotiations with CPB. In these talks, NPR and PBS haggled over what percentage of the federal money earmarked for public broadcasting should go to each organization. Since 1973, public TV had managed to win about 83 percent of these funds, with the rest going to radio. The managers of NPR-affiliated stations were dismayed by this split, since the public radio system was in desperate need of funds to start new stations, stimulate program ideas, and hasten the development of satellite interconnection. PBS officials were upset for a different reason: they wanted to keep even more of the money for themselves. The Level 2 negotiations in August 1975 were especially difficult for Lee Frischknecht. First, the radio team at these talks consisted of spokesmen from both NPR and a rival organization that had been founded to represent the interests of individual stations—one whose history is detailed later in this chapter. This division of labor need not have been troublesome, but representatives from the two groups made it so by failing to coordinate their efforts. To make matters worse, the public television lobby presented a highly unified front under the leadership of PBS Chairman Ralph Rogers. In the end, the public radio team was not able to increase its share of federal money. This infuriated station managers and heightened the perception that Frischknecht was not providing sound leadership.[5]

In response to the many internal and external pressures he faced, Lee Frischknecht made his second attempt to reorganize National Public Radio in early 1976. The process began with an organizational analysis by consultants Al Engelman and Steve Symonds, both from the Antioch College branch campus in Baltimore. According to Symonds, it soon became apparent that NPR's president did not have control of the company. He and Engelman launched into an ambitious schedule of interviews and meetings with NPR employees and board members and, eventually, with representatives from the Corporation for Public Broadcasting. Many who took part in this process say it was confrontational and sometimes vulgar—so much so that Engelman came to be known as "Lee's Rasputin." Jim Russell, then a news reporter, said the interview process felt to him like a bicycle ride, with Engelman and Symonds trying to dismantle the bike in midstream.[6] Susan Stamberg recalls the trauma that resulted.

> It was a bloodletting. We were this tiny little band of people. We were desperately trying just to get an hour and a half [of *All Things Consid-*

ered] on the air every night . . . and along came these folks who made individual appointments with all of us. And so we all sat and sort of poured our hearts out and told all the things that were really on our minds—and in the best faith. And it ended up being used against us.[7]

Symonds says the abrasive style that he and Engelman employed was a necessary part of the study design, since the NPR staff had become polarized into warring tribes. The consultants felt this approach might force people to talk more honestly about their feelings.[8]

On April 14, Frischknecht briefed the NPR board on the results of the study and announced the corporate reorganization plans that he and his consultants had developed. The most controversial item was a decision to merge the functions of Bob Zelnick's National News and Information Bureau with those of cultural and special interest programming.[9] Zelnick resented this move deeply.

> I covered Washington. Nobody said, "Go to the Supreme Court and do a piece on Chief Justice Burger's taste in chamber music." I was supposed to do an incisive report, in a five minute spot, on the Supreme Court. When Linda Wertheimer was on Capitol Hill nobody said, "Go up to Capitol Hill and do a piece on mysticism." They wanted her to cover politics insightfully and dig deeper and be more analytical than a journalist could be in a one or two minute report.[10]

Soon after learning of the reorganization, an outraged Susan Stamberg shared the news with two other staff members. Word spread quickly through the building, and throughout the public radio system. With Jim Russell leading the way, fifteen members of the National News and Information Bureau threatened to resign.[11]

Frischknecht's study was designed to ease communication problems between himself and the rest of the NPR staff. In the process, however, he and his consultants discovered that the real problem lay at a deeper level. Engelman detected a mismatch between the network's stated mission and the newsroom's day-to-day performance; he clearly identified with the desire of some employees to blend news and information programming with softer genres. His opinion was undoubtedly an important factor in Frischknecht's decision to rein in an unruly news staff and make it conform more closely to the words Bill Siemering had penned in 1970.[12]

After the reorganization was announced, Bob Zelnick was asked to take a demotion and a substantial cut in pay. When he refused, he was issued a severance check. Jack Mitchell was offered a chance to stay on in a supervisory role, but he objected to the new chain of command and moved back to the Midwest to head Wisconsin Public Radio.[13] In hindsight, Mitchell feels that Frischknecht's study and the chain of events it caused were natural consequences of his introspective nature and overall lack of confidence.

> Lee never could figure out what he was supposed to be doing. He was always looking for somebody to tell him, you know. Quayle wasn't there to tell him. And I was working directly for him on the research side . . . he was expecting *that* would tell him. And then he was essentially looking for Al Engelman to tell him.[14]

BILL KLING AND APRS

Halfway across the country another radio executive continued to build his own empire, the roots of which predate our modern public broadcasting system. In the mid-1960s, Bill Kling had dreamed about starting a classical music station, the kind of service he could not find on the radio dial at his home in Collegeville, Minnesota. Father Colman Barry, a history professor at St. John's University, was also intrigued by the possibility of a campus station and encouraged Kling, then one of his students, to explore this opportunity by pursuing graduate work in communication. Kling did just that, and following his studies at Boston University, he returned to St. John's to build the very station he had first envisioned. In 1967, he and a handful of associates began broadcasting on KSJR-FM.[15]

Though quite young (he was only twenty-four at the time), Kling was soon recognized as a leader in the talent-thin field of noncommercial radio. Karl Schmidt, a friend and fellow station manager, says Kling's vision for public radio was not inhibited by the "depression scars" that most other educational radio operators had, following decades of meager financial support. Over the next few years, he took advantage of extraordinary opportunities to get in on the ground floor of a newly revitalized industry. In 1967, St. John's University received permission from the FCC to build a second station and to boost its signal in the Twin Cities. One year later, SJU Broadcasting—the new corporation that had formed to operate Kling's budding network—announced plans for a third station in the Fargo-Moorehead market. Innovative programs began to find their way into the schedule; for example, Kling and one of his KSJR colleagues provided live coverage of the Humphrey-McCarthy debates at the 1968 Democratic National Convention.

That same year marked the beginning of a first-of-its-kind audio service for the visually disabled. Broadcasts on KSJR and sister station KSJN were apparently well-received by listeners, as basic membership rates rose from twelve to eighteen dollars per year. In 1969, St. John's turned its broadcasting facilities over to Minnesota Educational Radio, an independent organization that Kling developed for the purpose of running his first two stations and others that would join the network in the future.[16]

Kling left Collegeville that year to work for Al Hulsen as CPB's associate director of projects for radio and also served briefly on NPR's planning board and first board of directors. During his East Coast travels, he developed a working relationship with Hartford Gunn, who then headed WGBH-TV in Boston. Gunn disdained the traditional university stations that had long dominated the field of educational radio and television. He sought, instead, to promote an entrepreneurial brand of community-based broadcasting—one in which universities and other organizations would contribute resources to stations but leave decision-making responsibilities to broadcasting professionals. He turned WGBH into an independent force with a broad base of community support, especially among Boston's well-to-do families. Kling took that vision with him to CPB, NPR, and, eventually, Minnesota Educational Radio. He never wanted the singular, Washington-based production center that NPR had become; instead, he and other like-minded colleagues wanted to build the public radio system upon a skeleton of powerful regional production centers. Not coincidentally, he thought that one of these centers, a regional news operation, should be located in Minnesota.[17]

Having taken part in all the major policy decisions that shaped public radio, Kling left CPB in 1971 to put the things he had learned into practice. The two years that followed his return to Collegeville were a time of mixed success for the noncommercial industry. Though NPR had swung into operation with *All Things Considered*, the wider public radio system was still a very marginal operation. In 1972, nearly 80 percent of all public radio stations failed to meet CPB's minimum requirements for general financial support; because of this, the corporation developed a supplemental grant program to encourage more stations to pass muster. A Lou Harris poll conducted in the same year showed that public radio signals were available over less than half of the country's land mass. It should come as little surprise that Minnesota Educational Radio went through a period of financial difficulty at roughly the same time; at one point, the tiny network was saved from bankruptcy by a $1,200 foundation grant.[18]

One of Kling's first major successes was the attraction of five grants that helped MER open new studios and a regional news and public affairs center in St. Paul. He soon enjoyed other breakthroughs, as the Minnesota network put its third and fourth stations on the air and began a fine arts program service called *Music Through the Night*.[19] Kling and other top regional broadcasters noted that NPR was not making similar progress; this quickly became a problem, since the managers of local affiliates sent the network a portion of their hard-earned money for that very purpose. In response, Kling set out to build a second public radio organization, one that would lobby on behalf of all program-producing stations for a share of the federal money that had heretofore been directed to NPR's Washington headquarters.

> A number of us felt that National Public Radio couldn't fairly represent the needs of the stations and its own needs to Congress. And so we said the logical way to do this is to have an organization that goes to Congress and says, "Here's the case for public radio. Include in that NPR and anybody else that's a part of the system, and then make a decision as to how money ought to be distributed—whether you build stations, build other programming resources, or whatever."[20]

In May 1973, Kling, Ronald Bornstein of Wisconsin Public Broadcasting, and other station managers formed a group that would later become the Association of Public Radio Stations. In theory, this group would stick to lobbying while NPR handled programming concerns. That arrangement might have even worked, had Bornstein and Kling not remained quite upset, over the next few years, about Lee Frischknecht's failure to develop new shows, make NPR more visible, and connect member stations more effectively for the real-time transmission and reception of public radio programs.[21]

Board members from NPR and APRS were still smarting from the shabby treatment the industry had received at the recent Level 2 negotiations when, in August 1975, they gathered for a series of business meetings in Grafton, Vermont. There, they discussed the possibility of forming a single organization to govern public radio and present a united front to Congress and the CPB. Talks continued throughout the year, and the two organizations retained consultants to examine the merger idea more closely. NPR and APRS joined forces the following year because of a desire for more effective lobbying, a demand by APRS that Lee Frischknecht be replaced, and a perceived need to further decentralize the public radio system. In reality, APRS—led by the likes of Kling and Bornstein—had engineered a takeover of National Public Radio, with the board of directors of the new company dominated by members of their own group. The confluence of tensions that characterized NPR in 1975 and 1976 had paved the way, then, for a new and improved public radio network.[22]

Getting Ready for Prime Time

The new NPR made its formal debut on May 4, 1977, when station managers from NPR and APRS, under the watchful eye of Ron Bornstein, voted overwhelmingly to combine the two organizations. The new board of directors chose Edward Elson, a wealthy Atlanta businessman and public member of the APRS board, to be chairman; Patrick Callihan, a Michigan businessman and former public broadcaster, became interim president. Elson, Bornstein, and a handful of others formed a search committee and set out to find a new CEO. More than 370 people applied for the job, including Lee Frischknecht, Sam Holt, APRS president Matthew Coffey, and Thomas Warnock, then CPB's radio chief. Committee members had narrowed the list of applicants to about ten when they realized that none of the finalists had the high energy, creativity, or public presence they felt necessary for guiding the organization to greater prominence. But just when they seemed to run out of leads, Elson's political connections began to pay off. The new chairman had strong ties with the Carter administration; in fact, Bert Lance—who ran the Office of Management and Budget—was his best friend and next-door neighbor. Elson went to the White House for advice on filling the NPR presidency and found a list of people who had unsuccessfully sought jobs in the new administration.[23] The resume of Frank Mankiewicz stood out from the rest.

> If you remember, he was Bob Kennedy's Press Secretary. He was George McGovern's campaign manager. He was, of course, the son of a very famous motion picture family. He was *everything*! He was a lawyer, journalist, politician. And I said, "My God, if we had to go to central casting and find the perfect vitae for this job, it would be Frank Mankiewicz."[24]

Elson quickly summoned Mankiewicz to the Washington hotel where the search committee was meeting. One thing that gave some board members pause was the fact that Mankiewicz knew nothing about NPR.

> Yeah, I certainly didn't know. As a matter of fact, the search committee asked me at one point, "If you became president of NPR, what's

the first thing you would do? What do you think's the most important?" And I said, "To do whatever was necessary so that people like me would have heard about it."[25]

The committee held several more meetings. Though Mankiewicz was a popular choice, some board members were suspicious about the selection process. Elson and the rest of the search committee decided to present Mankiewicz as the one and only candidate—"vote him up, or down." Some people resented this tactic, but Elson and Bornstein persisted, as they only had confidence in one candidate.[26]

The first thing Mankiewicz noticed about NPR was a sense of edginess among the news and information staff.

> At the board meeting where I was elected, Linda Wertheimer, whom I had never met, came up to me and said, "Hi, I'm Linda Wertheimer. I'm the shop steward. We're striking you next week." And I had talked to the search committee about that. They had said that they had this problem with the union and that they were refusing to meet with the union . . . I said, "You can't do that. That's called an unfair labor practice." The morale was terrible. The first thing I did was sit down with the union and negotiate a contract.[27]

NPR's rank-and-file employees greatly appreciated the prompt consideration they got from the new boss. Mankiewicz was a different kind of manager than his predecessor; for one thing, he clearly identified with network's news operation. Soon after starting his new job, he visited the newsroom on a regular basis to chat, to make suggestions about sources, and, often, to see if anyone was free for lunch. NPR's journalists now had a leader who would value their work, raise their pay, and actively promote their product to a wider audience.[28] Neal Conan, who produced *All Things Considered* earlier in his career, remembers that Mankiewicz was a godsend for the staff of that program.

> What we started getting with Mankiewicz was *resources*. We started getting reporters. I don't think people remember that our primary White House coverage in those days was [from] Tom Ottenad of the *St. Louis Post-Dispatch*. Primary economics coverage [came from] Harry Ellis of the *Christian Science Monitor*. These were wonderful, informed people, but we didn't have our own White House person and we didn't have our own economics person. [When] we ended up covering the [Iran]

hostage crisis, we didn't have any foreign staff members. . . . And that's simply *not* being a primary news source.[29]

Mankiewicz initiated a series of projects that would make NPR better known to listeners and policy makers alike. In 1978, he arranged live coverage of the contentious Panama Canal debates in the Senate. This sort of coverage had never been done before, and Mankiewicz had to seek special enabling legislation to make it happen.[30]

There were internal obstacles to overcome as well. Jim Russell recalls that some reporters and producers were hesitant to tackle this assignment, since it didn't seem consistent with the "NPR style"—meticulously recorded and heavily produced pieces that were as artistic as they were factual.

> The response from many of the NPR-types was, "We can't do that."
> Frank said, "Why not?" And the answer is, "We don't have 100 micro-
> phones." I mean, can you imagine a mind set [of] "no-can-doism?"
> And Frank had to overcome that, and he did immediately. He basically
> said to the assembled people, "I tell you what. I'll be back in half an
> hour. And [you will] either have resolved how we're going to do it . . .
> or have your resignations on the table." It worked.[31]

The decision to cover the Panama Canal hearings gavel-to-gavel for thirty-seven days was a master stroke. NPR won a prestigious duPont-Columbia award for its coverage, anchored by Linda Wertheimer. These broadcasts softened partisans on both sides of the debate and left them feeling that NPR had portrayed competing points of view in a manner that was quite fair, even complementary. Most important, they paved the way for future broadcasts from the floors of the House and Senate.[32]

Another important bit of external work lay in the task of bettering NPR's fate at the Level 2 negotiations with CPB. In 1977, public radio received only 18 percent of the federal money available for noncommercial programming. Mankiewicz immediately set his sights on 25 percent and achieved that goal in 1981 by having it written into the CPB authorization bill. This made him a hero at NPR—and a villain at both PBS and CPB, where television was the number one priority. Some pundits and broadcasting insiders felt that Mankiewicz's biggest asset was his ability to attract publicity. *Fortune*, for example, published an article with a picture of him throwing a baseball, and a *People* magazine spread showed the Mankiewicz family sitting around a pool. These articles clearly raised awareness about NPR, though critics felt they had little or nothing to do with public broadcasting. Scott Simon remembers that his former boss was sometimes viewed as a "Hollywood sharpie." He tended to rub the managers of affiliated stations the wrong way, treating them, in the words of one employee, as "a group of people to be coaxed and massaged" into accepting his views. One glaring example was his decision to spend money on gavel-to-gavel coverage of the 1980 national political conventions—another showcase for the talents of Linda Wertheimer, but one in which very few stations chose to participate.[33]

Robert Siegel also recalls a dark side to Mankiewicz's habit of visiting and dining with members of the NPR news team.

> I liked the fact that I could walk into Frank Mankiewicz's office any time of day and tell him what was on my mind. But to be quite honest about it, the fact that I was doing that, and that a few other people were doing that, meant that a whole chain of command was routinely being bypassed in terms of the management of the organization. And all of those lunches that we had together, with Nina [Totenberg], and Linda [Wertheimer], and Cokie [Roberts] and me were all, in a way, also cutting out people who in theory were Vice President and Executive Vice President. . . . And I think that those vice presidents became kind of nominal "yes men" over the course of time.[34]

The fact that Mankiewicz was quite partial to NPR's journalists would become a problem later on, especially since he had little taste for the business side of the network or, in fact, for anything other than the newsroom.

A LITTLE COMPETITION ON THE PRAIRIE

When NPR's new president arrived in 1977, Bill Kling had already been running Minnesota Public Radio (the name that MER assumed in 1974) for a decade. Most people who know Kling agree that he learned better than anyone else about the ways in which the U.S. public radio system could be built with optimum speed, efficiency, and self-support. He built his regional network upon a web of relationships with colleges and universities in Minnesota. These institutions provided funding and facilities for the stations of MPR, as well as a body of students who might later become employees. They also came to trust that Kling's management skills would provide them with the best means of achieving their objectives in broadcasting. The radio organizations that Kling has founded over the years are noteworthy for their strong boards of directors, composed largely of influential public members—not station managers, as NPR's model of governance dictates. Strong market-oriented directors fit perfectly with Kling's guiding principles for building a public radio system. First, he thought that only one station per geographic market should be given the right to run a particular program. This would avoid the ceaseless duplication the National Public Radio system would later produce when multiple stations in the same area ran *All Things Considered* at the same time, every day. Contrary to the assumptions of the old educational radio system, Kling felt that *public* radio need not sustain every tiny station that could find an open frequency. The system he developed was based on the transformation of strong, existing operations into income-generators through aggressive underwriting and development work—and, later on, through business endeavors that would support the stations' nonprofit missions.[35]

Over time, MPR's statewide news service became one the best in the nation. This part of Kling's operation was every bit as strong as his fine arts programming, but since it was only available in the upper Midwest, it did not become widely known elsewhere. The more famous part of his network, then, lay in its homegrown music programs and other cultural fare. Since 1969, Kling had nurtured the career of a young writer and disc jockey named Garrison Keillor, who then hosted *The Morning Show* on MPR's original stations in Collegeville and St. Paul. The two men developed a concept for the show that was quite different from the classical music that occupied much of the network's schedule. Keillor's musical selections ranged from the Beach Boys, to jazz, to the marches of John Philip Sousa. Between songs he told stories about people named "Old Scout" and "Mr. Fist," forerunners of the fictitious characters he would later become famous for. Keillor left the program, and returned to it, a number of times over the next decade. Eventually, it came to be known as *A Prairie Home Morning Show* (named after "A Prairie Home," a cemetery Keillor had seen while traveling near Fargo, North Dakota), with a Saturday version called *A Prairie Home Companion*. Though live audiences were initially small for the weekend show—fifteen people on the first day—it soon drew a large and loyal crowd. *PHC* was broadcast for the first time to a nationwide audience in 1979; that same year, Keillor staged a two-week tour of live shows in the upper Midwest. Soon, a million or so listeners could tune to their favorite public radio station each Saturday for his broadcasts from the World Theater in St. Paul, complete with tales from the mythical Lake Wobegon and music from the Powdermilk Biscuits Band. Kling had a hit on his hands and the time seemed ripe for expanding *PHC*'s national audience.[36]

By 1979, the number of full-service public radio stations in the United States had reached 200. Those stations garnered from 1 to 3 percent of the weekly national radio audience; stated inversely, between 97 and 99 percent of all radio listeners did not listen at all. At the very same time, however, the fortunes of Minnesota Public Radio continued to rise. MPR purchased a commercial AM station in the Twin Cities and converted it to a news and information format, and CPB honored the network for the high quality of its public service programs. The most important factor in its future success, however, was the construction of public radio's satellite distribution system. Prior to its deployment, NPR sent its news and music programs to affiliate stations over telephone lines—well before the days of crystal clear fiber optic links. CPB aimed to improve the quality of program transmissions in 1977 by arranging a $32.5 million satellite financing package. Bill Kling had been the dominant force on an NPR/APRS technology committee that worked out the final details of the system. He and other APRS members wanted, once again, to uplink their own programs for national distribution; however, initial plans called for only four satellite channels—two stereo pairs—that would originate in Washington and carry NPR's programs exclusively.[37]

[So we] came to CPB and we said, "We have a plan, and it's a 24-channel system. We want a full transponder. And we want uplinks, at least 16 uplinks around the country." They said, "No, we can't stop now and design it that way." And we said, "then, we don't want it. It's not worth the money if it's going to be two stereo pairs feeding from Washington."[38]

After much haggling, CPB gave Kling and his allies thirty-six hours to develop a blueprint for the system they wanted.

Amazingly, no one else in the world of public radio knew what satellite uplinks were or what benefits they could provide for local stations. As Kling recalls, there was no fight over the uplinks; to the contrary, he and his partners on the technology committee had to call other station managers and ask, "Wouldn't you take one?" Minnesota Public Radio got an uplink, of course, as did the home station of every other committee member.

Having done that, it changed the whole nature of the public radio system. Because it meant, then, that there could be other program entities developed elsewhere in the country, that there were enough channels for there to be more than the NPR program on at any given time. And it opened up the highway to what would eventually become [Public Radio International], and independent producers, and station[-based] producers, and all of the rest that's happened since then.[39]

Minnesota Public Radio was riding high as the new system came closer to fruition. The network kicked off its first capital campaign with a $750,000 lead grant from The Saint Paul Foundation and *A Prairie Home Companion* continued to draw attention on the national level. *PHC* seemed a natural candidate for wider distribution via satellite. For a short time, however, other circumstances in Washington would prevent this from happening.[40]

Morning Edition and *PHC*: Vying for the Nation's Ears

National Public Radio had a few achievements of its own to be proud of in the late 1970s. The opening of a London bureau was one sign the network was on its way to becoming a serious player in international radio news. However, the crowning achievement during the Mankiewicz years was the launching of a news and information program in "morning drive," the time of day when most people listen to radio. Since 1971, NPR had cast its fate with *All Things Considered*—abandoning, in the process, any potential audience that might exist between six and eight A.M. Some of the network's managers thought their flagship program should be launched in morning drive time instead of the afternoon slot it has always occupied, but that idea proved impractical from the standpoint of logistics and finances. Early morning news programs require round-the-clock staffing (or something close to it) to ensure that fast-breaking stories from distant parts of the world can make their way into the show. The network's modest budget in the early 1970s would not permit this level of staffing, but the budget grew by some 50 percent during the first eighteen months of the Mankiewicz regime. Suddenly, NPR was ready to build a serious morning show.[41]

To get this program off the drawing board and onto the air, Mankiewicz hired Barbara Cochran (then Cohen), an ambitious young journalist who had recently been named managing editor of the *Washington Star*. Cochran came to NPR in March 1979, just four months before the date when Mankiewicz had promised to put his new morning show on the air. The tasks that lay ahead of her were quite formidable; in fact, she could not get the program ready in time for its originally scheduled debut. One reason, says Cochran, was that she and Mankiewicz had to convince many station managers that a morning show would actually attract a significant audience. Some had requested such a program for years, one that would feature a variety of breaks so local stations could insert their own material. But Cochran says many other stations were simply "classical music jukeboxes" whose managers thought that no news and information program on Earth would draw an audience larger than the one they already had. To win them over, Mankiewicz hired audience researchers and dispatched them coast to coast. Using numerical data for each station, they persuaded one skeptical manager after another that a high-quality news magazine, specially designed to complement the hectic schedules of morning listeners, could help them retain a healthy audience throughout the day.[42]

Cochran also had to convince some members of her own Washington-based staff that a morning program would be worth doing. She and Mankiewicz knew the NPR News team operated like a short-order kitchen, with just a few people turning out an immense amount of product. Still, they thought the time was right to expand. Lawrence Lichty, then NPR's director of audience research, asked about Susan Stamberg's availability as morning host. Stamberg was not interested, and, at first, top management vetoed the idea of using her afternoon partner, Bob Edwards. Cochran then hired two commercial radio producers who, in turn, hired journalists Mary Tillotson and Pete Williams as cohosts.[43] Soon after these deals were struck, Jay Kernis—the arts producer for the new show—sensed trouble. He claimed the program's producers knew commercial radio well enough but did not respect the unique sound and mission of public radio. As a consequence, they produced some terrible dry runs just twelve days before the program was to air in November 1979. Some say the *Morning Edition* pilots lacked depth and analysis; others say they were too perky and "smelled of bubble gum." Ten days before air time, Tillotson (who later worked for CNN) and Williams (who landed at NBC News, by way of the Pentagon) were fired, along with the producers who brought them in. Shortly thereafter, Kernis, Frank Mankiewicz, and others gathered at Barbara Cochran's house, where they decided to take Bob Edwards away from *All Things Considered* for a thirty-day trial run and to make Kernis the senior producer of the morning program.[44]

Kernis had to rework the staff and get the program on-air in very short order. *Morning Edition* debuted at five A.M. Eastern time on Monday, November 5—just one day after followers of the Ayatollah Ruhollah Khomeini seized the U.S. Embassy in Teheran, taking seventy-one hostages in the process. Bob Edwards recalls that he and his staff (including Barbara Hoctor, who cohosted with him for about six months) were so unprepared for this event that the hostage story did not even make it onto the program's "rundown sheet" of scheduled stories. But Jackie Judd featured the story prominently in her newscasts, and the ongoing hostage crisis literally fueled the new program during its first year. Edwards, of course, never returned to *ATC*, and that put Susan Stamberg in the difficult position of working with "musical co-hosts" on the afternoon show for months. For a time, *Morning Edition* also put extra pressure on NPR's small staff of about thirty reporters and producers. Despite these tensions, the network's investment in the new show began to pay off quickly. Just one week after *Morning Edition*'s debut, about half of NPR's 222 affiliate stations signaled their intention to carry at least some portion of the program; about 90 percent of them were carrying all or part of the show within a year. As a result, most of these stations experienced a substantial increase in listening.[45]

In the end, says Scott Simon, *Morning Edition* made NPR a different kind of company.

> Up until that point, doing *All Things Considered* every night, we were content to be an organization that said, "Well, people can get the news elsewhere. We're mostly devoted to *analysis*." Analysis and perspective are clearly still an important part of what we do, but I think [now], we're a news organization. We've got to get there "firstest with the mostest." And *Morning Edition* threw our hat over the wall that way. It made us shorter [and] punchier, but more to the point and more pertinent—more relevant. It turned us into a *news organization.* [46]

Amidst all the jubilation over *Morning Edition*, however, Frank Mankiewicz and his management team had failed to acknowledge Bill Kling's growing impact on the public radio system. Disbelief at the success of *A Prairie Home Companion* was part of the problem; another part was Mankiewicz's belief that public radio was entirely synonymous with NPR. Kling tried to sell *PHC* to NPR's National Program Service for about $250,000 per year— the program, which cost $600,000 to produce, already had some corporate underwriters. But Mankiewicz, himself, became a significant obstacle to the idea.[47] NPR was theoretically bound by its mission to seek out and broadcast the best programs (including cultural programs) from public radio stations all over the country. But with a flourishing news operation, a hit program of his own, and a genuine dislike for Keillor's show, Mankiewicz decided to take a rain check.

> I knew it was a yuppie program. I didn't like it. I don't like it now. I think it mocks the values of middle class America. It's for people who like country and western music, but are ashamed of it. So it mocks the values of the people who create it. I thought it was the *Laverne and Shirley* of public radio programs.[48]

Kling wanted NPR to offer greater support for *A Prairie Home Companion* because the costs of production, marketing, and distribution were becoming too great for the Minnesota network to handle. However, Mankiewicz felt the asking price for the program was too high, and both he and his programming executive, Sam Holt, apparently felt that Keillor's humor would not find a large national audience. For Kling, this standoff was the latest in a series of affronts that NPR had committed against the managers of large regional stations.[49] He says tensions over this issue peaked at an NPR board meeting in Phoenix.

> We went to Frank Mankiewicz and we said, "Frank, now that the satellite system is in place and we've had ten years of support from CPB, some of the stations are able to produce national programs. The next time that you get a chunk of money from CPB to expand the programming of NPR, we would like you to [ask] what our ideas might be for that money, before you choose to tell us how you're going to spend it on your own productions."[50]

Kling was stunned when Mankiewicz flatly rejected this request, and he retreated to a nearby restaurant with a handful of other station managers to sort things out. As individuals, none of them had the money to distribute programs on a national basis, but Kling began to solve this dilemma by drawing on his intimate knowledge of NPR's new satellite system.[51]

> Obviously we have a system, now, able to distribute programming from places other than NPR, but no money to do it. We need to form another entity which will be able to raise [money] for our ideas, which will be able to distribute programs that are *our* programs. And while we're doing it, let's make it the opposite of National Public Radio.[52]

In 1981, Kling joined with the managers of four other major stations in forming American Public Radio Associates, a marketing and distribution arm of Minnesota Public Radio that offered Keillor's program, and others, to stations willing to pay additional fees (APRA became an independent for-profit company called American Public Radio, or APR, the following year. Later, in 1994, the name of this firm was changed to PRI—Public Radio International).[53] APR would be a distributor, funder, and packager of programs, but would not, at least in the beginning, produce programs of its own.[54]

Though this new company would focus on artistic programming, and NPR on news and information, Mankiewicz, his top aides, and some board members became "apoplectic" at the very thought of a rival organization. NPR's president described American Public Radio as "a minor irritant," a one-program network that would go out of business if Garrison Keillor got sick. To this day, a number of current and former NPR employees question Kling's motives; some, for example, feel that APR was formed with the express intent of destroying the Washington-based network. Whatever the case, Frank Mankiewicz and others at National Public Radio saw this brash upstart as one of several obstacles that would have to be overcome in the early 1980s.[55]

PROJECT INDEPENDENCE

One of Mankiewicz's biggest problems came when a fellow broadcaster ran against Jimmy Carter in 1980 and won the first of his two terms in the White House. Initially, he thought NPR might escape close scrutiny by Ronald Reagan, but he soon learned otherwise. Following the conservative tradition of the Nixon administration, Reagan's transition team reportedly became so upset with the "liberal" output of public broadcasting that it wanted to abolish CPB by 1983. Mankiewicz never considered this a serious possibility, knowing that his industry had strong support from the upper-middle-class do-gooders that populated both the Democratic and Republican parties. But the Reagan camp was prepared to inflict *some* damage. In February 1981, the Office of Management and Budget recommended cuts of up to 50 percent in federal support for arts and humanities programs; it was estimated that CPB would face a cut of 25 to 28 percent. Mankiewicz, with his flair for all things promotional, seemed exhilarated by the chance to fight for his network's honor. He did so publicly at the end of March, telling a National Press Club audience that Reagan's proposal to rescind funds already appropriated for CPB would force his network off the air by the first of October. These comments were, in all likelihood, a finely crafted exercise in hyperbole, designed to boost private fundraising; yet the argument also rang true in one important way. Any significant drop in funding was bound to weaken CPB's ability to act as a heat shield between the federal government and public broadcasters themselves.[56]

The cuts that did materialize in 1981 were not as deep as anticipated. The Reagan administration left CPB's appropriation for 1982 intact, while cutting 1983 funds by 20 percent. This blow was painful to NPR, but Mankiewicz, ever quick with a slogan, vowed that public radio would wean itself from congressional funds and be "off the fix by '86." In May 1981, he mulled the possibility of delivering radio programs to home audiences via cable TV. In November, he announced a sweeping new effort to raise nearly half the network's revenue from the private sector; in the process, he said, NPR would be prepared "to enter almost any profession except the oldest one." His three-part plan, called "Project Independence," was widely publicized in newspaper and magazine articles. First, Mankiewicz would explore a variety of new methods for raising funds from corporations and other private sources. With the help of programming chief Sam Holt and conservative publicist Peter Hannaford (a former partner of Reagan aide Michael Deaver), he developed a plan to sell "shares" in NPR News and Performance Funds. A corporation could buy one of these shares for a quarter million dollars; in return, it would get brief on-air credits throughout the day. This mechanism would provide an alternative to the program-specific support that was common in public television (e.g., ExxonMobil's support for *Masterpiece Theatre*). Mankiewicz also set up fund-raising task forces in New York, Chicago, and Los Angeles. These efforts were part of an overall plan to secure millions of dollars worth of nonfederal grants and contributions during the 1983 fiscal year.[57]

A new program service called "NPR Plus" constituted the second part of Project Independence. NPR Plus was initially launched as a response to Classicsat, a satellite music service that Bill Kling planned to offer through American Public Radio. The cost of NPR's round-the-clock classical music service was first pegged at $700,000. By July 1982, the project had expanded to the extent that it would nearly triple the network's programming output; by December, the price tag for this service—which now included thirty-six hours of jazz programming and hourly newscasts—rose to $1.7 million. Member stations would have to pay for all this new content, which was organized into two twenty-four-by-seven program streams, but management thought it could make the numbers work if 150 to 200 stations bought in.[58]

Finally, Mankiewicz proposed a separate for-profit subsidiary called NPR Ventures. It would include partnerships with private businesses that, for the most part, would exploit the excess channel capacity of the public radio satellite system. NPR had already begun to do business with other companies that wanted to rent transmission capacity, including Muzak, the Mutual Broadcasting System, and NBC Radio's "Source" network. The management team held talks with other firms as well and developed plans for six new business ventures. Three of these projects would draw NPR into the development of paging and high-speed data transmission technologies, along with satellite-based systems for the private, in-home recording of public radio programs. Agreements for these ventures had been struck even before the NPR board formally approved its new money-making subsidiary in January 1983, and they went forward in spite of the fact that neither NPR, nor any of its prospective partners, had enough money to finance them. Another difficulty lay in the fact that NPR had not yet received permission from the FCC to actually use its excess satellite capacity for some of these initiatives.[59]

Tom Warnock, now executive vice president, outlined National Public Radio's fundraising plans at the industry's national conference in 1982. Confident the Ventures program would succeed, he said the network would ask CPB to decrease the amount of its annual contributions to NPR and increase the sum that went directly to stations. NPR would take significant cuts in 1984 and, by 1988, would get no more than $4.7 million; federal support might be ended at that point if income from other funding sources was sufficient. In summary, Warnock told station representatives that 1983 was the year that NPR would brave the "unfamiliar, risky territory of private enterprise, despite the loss of more than $2 million in aid from CPB. If this sounds a bit schizophrenic to you," he said, "it is."[60]

Many at NPR felt that if anyone had the clout and connections to pull off this financial sleight-of-hand, it was Frank Mankiewicz. After all, the network had attracted more listeners, member stations, and income under his tutelage than ever before. But some of his plans for making money also raised eyebrows. In February 1982, five members of the NPR board voiced their skepticism about Project Independence, in light of the anticipated drop in federal funding. Mankiewicz generally brushed these comments aside. In response to one query, he said that just because federal dollars were going down, the board should not assume the network would go down with them.[61]

The perception of a rapid increase in spending at NPR also began to trouble the programming staff. For Susan Stamberg, it seemed that Mankiewicz and his team raised new money, and spent even larger sums, right from the start.

> All of a sudden we were getting credit cards; you know, it started feeling like *Downtown!* We were checking into a nice hotel—not staying with friends—in fancy cities. And there were lunches for groups of us. All of a sudden, it looked like there was this *budget*. And that's when I certainly got concerned. I thought, "Where is this coming from?" I mean, I certainly loved it, but I had some concerns about it.[62]

Jeff Rosenberg says many of NPR's employees began to question the explanations their bosses gave to justify these new spending habits.

When you used to hear about people buying equipment, it was like, "Bill it to NPR Plus," you know. Computers were rolling in here; people were buying stuff like it was Going Out of Business Day at Filene's. And, you know, if you put two and two together, you could pretty easily see that . . . there couldn't have been the revenue to match it. 'Cause there just wasn't the revenue coming out of NPR Plus.[63]

Indeed, the network began to spend money in the winter months of 1982 and 1983 as if the goals of Project Independence had already been met. Aside from new credit cards and equipment purchases, the overall size of the NPR staff increased by 17 percent during that time.[64] Robert Siegel took note of these developments from his post at NPR's London bureau. He remembers that managers in Washington were considering a major corporate expansion while, at the same time, they seemed to have great difficulty with the fundamental tasks of day-to-day business.

At one point, Barbara [Cochran] described to me what was going to happen to NPR. And here I was in London—by that time, three years in London. My paycheck had been misdirected any number of times. Envelopes addressed to me would be sent surface mail all the time. Within a year I was getting *freelance checks* that I was returning to NPR. This was not a big-league business. And I remember telling Barbara, "You mean that this company which has not figured out how to put an air mail stamp on an envelope is, within a year, going to be a global communications conglomerate?" And she laughed a great deal, and said "Yes, that's right."[65]

THE DEBT CRISIS

In early 1983 National Public Radio probably seemed, to the casual observer, a dynamic business poised on the brink of success. For one thing, the size of its audience had been growing at a brisk pace for three years. The board of directors also went full-speed ahead with NPR Plus and formally approved the bylaws and articles of incorporation for NPR Ventures. Finance chair Steven Meuche told his colleagues that the network had undergone "a clean audit without qualifications" and the board approved his report unanimously. But management soon got some terrible news about money, details that should have been known months earlier but, for some reason, seemed to come out of the blue. On March 11, Meuche told his fellow directors about

a deficit estimated at nearly $2.8 million. Talk of budget cuts began imme-
diately, and a special committee was organized to study the problem. Word
of the deficit spread quickly through the media, with the trade publication
Current reporting that it would likely result in thirty to forty layoffs. Frank
Mankiewicz claimed that he, too, was surprised by this turn of events. After
a quick review of the problem, he blamed it on the reluctance of underwriters to support public radio during an economic recession, a variety of
problems with NPR Ventures, and greater-than-anticipated expenses from
NPR Plus. Public television officials expressed concern, since any effort to
bail NPR out of trouble would surely affect the amount of federal money
available to them.[66]

It would be months before employees fully understood the severity of the
deficit. In late March, *Current* reported that NPR's Performance Programming division would lose about a dozen employees and about a quarter of
its 1983 budget. NPR Plus was, indeed, losing money; without proper fiscal
correction, it would probably overspend its current budget by $300,000. In
mid-April, management said the size of the deficit would likely increase to
$5.8 million. That news marked the passage of NPR's debt from a momen-
tary problem to a full-blown crisis. It would have been possible to cut $2.5
million from the budget, but the only way to save $5.8 million would be to
close the network down. Mankiewicz told the NPR board he did not consider this problem to be an actual deficit, but rather a near-term shortage of
cash. He suggested the network cover part of it by imposing a $2.5 million
fee on member stations. That statement proved quite unpopular with managers throughout the NPR system, few of whom realized the deficit was still
growing when they traveled to Minneapolis for the 1983 Public Radio Conference. Mankiewicz survived two no-confidence votes at this gathering but
soon resigned under pressure. Shortly thereafter, some members of the NPR
board began to look for an interim executive who could stop the network's
financial hemorrhage.[67]

To carry out this difficult task, they turned to Ron Bornstein. By then,
Bornstein had served on the boards of NPR, APRS, and PBS while, at the
same time, holding a series of administrative positions at the University of
Wisconsin and the Corporation for Public Broadcasting. He once conducted
a painful reorganization and downsizing at CPB, but says he had never encountered the sort of mess he faced this time around.[68]

> Anywhere you turned, there was trouble. Anywhere you turned, there
> was no answer. And we decided, the team that I aggregated and I, that
> we would just "do the right thing." We all knew that we were in there

for the short-term, and none of us would stay in terms of a lengthy relationship with NPR. And we really went in to fix it the very best we could. But it was truly overwhelming.[69]

Bornstein would serve as NPR's top executive on a part-time basis for six months. His hastily assembled team of advisors included Jack Mitchell from Wisconsin Public Radio, Steve Symonds, now working at CPB, and George Miles from WBZ-TV in Boston. He also hired the accounting firm of Coopers and Lybrand to perform a crash audit, to get a fast, accurate picture of NPR's assets and liabilities and recommend a course of action. In June, the auditors reported that NPR's financial management was a "sorry mess" and warned that the network might be forced to shut down. Coopers and Lybrand estimated the deficit at $6.5 million and found that certain finance employees had tried to offset part of it with $850,000 in tax money withheld from paychecks.[70]

The human toll from the debt crisis also began to mount, as management announced the cutting of another eighty-four jobs in late May. At the time, it was thought the network would lose a total of 131 people; ultimately, it lost 157. Management did not think it could make enough cuts to balance the current budget; it could scale operations back to an affordable level in the following year, however, while borrowing enough money to survive until then. Resignations came from executive vice president Tom Warnock and board chairman Myron Jones. Jones did not want to leave and became furious when Bornstein told the board that Riggs National Bank, a potential source of bailout funds, considered him an impediment to ongoing discussions. Quite understandably, Riggs found it difficult to lend a large sum of money to any organization whose board chair and finance chair remained in place, despite serious lapses in financial oversight and leadership during their watch. Jones asked for a vote of confidence in either himself or Bornstein, and the board obliged—voting overwhelmingly to keep Bornstein. Steve Meuche resigned as finance chair, but remained on the board. Circumstances were clearly not as difficult for two other figures central to the debt crisis. Frank Mankiewicz became executive vice president of Gray and Company, a Washington public relations firm, and news VP Barbara Cochran landed a management job at NBC.[71]

The daily lives of NPR staff members were anything but pleasant in the spring and summer of 1983. Scott Simon, who had just returned from El Salvador, became the network's in-house reporter on the crisis, covering his own company in stories that would air on *Morning Edition* and *All Things*

Considered. Simon remembers a predicament he found early one morning while preparing one of these reports.

> I remember coming in to type up my notes, *and there was no paper.* We'd run out of paper and hadn't ordered any more. And I said on the air, "Not to be too dramatic about it, Bob, but I came in here today and couldn't type up anything because there's no paper left!" And the two of us laughed. And CBS heard that. [They] were then right across the street from us, in the old days, on M Street. They brought over some paper. And I think Cokie Roberts was getting stopped that day on the Hill. And people were giving her note pads and that kind of thing, and saying "Give it to him," you know.[72]

If that story comes as a fond remembrance, it must be balanced with the profound sense of low morale that developed at NPR, where more than 150 employees were discharged by the Fourth of July. The vaunted news and information staff would lose twenty people, including seven reporters. Barbara Cochran warned that this move would impair the network's ability to cover fast-breaking stories, but other sources say the cuts merely brought the news staff back to its originally authorized level of spending. Bornstein and his emergency management team implemented strict controls on all spending, a move that prompted widespread dissent. A staff that had begun to enjoy some of the trappings of inside-the-Beltway journalism began, by one account, to feel like a group of Belgians in occupied Europe. Gallows humor poured freely from office doorways and through the halls of NPR headquarters. On June 22, Clem Taylor, one of the reporters let go during the crisis, gained one final bit of consolation by winning an office pool on the size of the deficit. There was not enough money to offer Taylor an actual prize; instead, he received a collage of photocopied business cards used by NPR's former finance managers.[73]

By mid-June, the projected deficit peaked at $9.1 million and talks began in earnest with CPB to arrange a bailout loan in that amount.[74] Donald Mullally, manager of WILL Radio at the University of Illinois, became chairman of the NPR board following Myron Jones's departure. Mullally began to analyze the assets of the company that one could put up as collateral.

> And the fact of the matter was *there were no assets.* The equipment was used broadcasting equipment and, you know, that's worth practically nothing. So we looked at the question of, "how are we going to keep

meeting payroll?" Because clearly there was no cash. The cash flow was, in fact, *negative* cash flow. And there was a point at which the staff said, "if we don't get paid next week, we walk out." So that was the first in a series of crises that we had to deal with.[75]

CPB had already provided a short-term loan of $500,000 to help the network meet its payroll. Bornstein also secured a credit line of $1 million from Riggs National Bank and, shortly thereafter, a majority of affiliated stations voted to help out with a $1.6 million dollar fund transfer.[76] But those fixes were only temporary. NPR would have to hold more talks with CPB if it wanted long-term relief, though Mullally wondered what the corporation would want in return.

It became clear in relatively early conversations that they wanted more control of NPR, which we felt was an inappropriate kind of thing, considering the fact that CPB was, even then, a very political organization. And NPR, as a journalistic enterprise, had to have a certain freedom form external control to be credible. NPR was owned by the stations, and I didn't feel that we had the right to give up something that the stations had worked for just as a condition of bailout.[77]

Mullally and Bornstein developed a strategy for playing hardball with NPR's major creditor. Knowing that CPB was mandated by Congress to support public radio programming, the two men drew up bankruptcy papers and threatened to shut the network down if suitable conditions for a loan could not be worked out. Negotiations continued through June and July, as NPR wobbled in and out of solvency. *Broadcasting* reported that on Wednesday, July 27, the network had only $20,000 in the bank to meet a $500,000 payroll that Friday—and was also behind on rent. Fortunately, the two sides agreed to the terms of a bailout the very next day: an $8.5 million loan to cover the bulk of the expected deficit, with CPB forgiving another $600,000 of debt. The corporation also advanced enough money for NPR to make one more payroll. Member stations would have to guarantee the loan package and a panel of high-level trustees would oversee the network's satellite equipment until all the money was paid back.[78]

The terms of this bailout were excruciatingly difficult to achieve. The sticking point was CPB's demand that NPR surrender the title to its satellite equipment until its debts were repaid—a condition that, once again, was unacceptable to the public radio negotiating team. The impasse was broken during a final marathon bargaining session with the following compromise: three citizens of sterling character (former Attorney General Elliott Richardson, telecommunications policy expert Henry Geller, and former CPB board member Virginia Duncan) would temporarily hold the title to the satellite equipment in trust; the operation of this equipment would be guided by the majority vote of the network's member stations; and NPR staff would continue to manage it, as before. It took the constant threat of bankruptcy, a twelve-hour negotiating session, and some last-minute arm-twisting by Tim Wirth (a Colorado Democrat), then chairman of the House Subcommittee on Telecommunications, to achieve the final bargain. In fact, Wirth spent much of the night in a car parked outside CPB headquarters, periodically phoning Chairman Edward Pfister to pressure him into a deal. When talks concluded, Ron Bornstein limped into a local bar, ordered an Amstel Light, and drank what he considers to be the most satisfying beer of his life.[79]

Negotiations with CPB marked the bottoming out of NPR's financial crisis. The loan agreement was announced on the final day of a national, on-air fundraising effort called "The Drive to Survive." One hundred or more of NPR's member stations took part and, in the process, they raised more than $2 million. The bailout agreement was signed in early August, and, the following month, NPR officials indicated they might not have to borrow the full amount. Budget controls and money-raising efforts by Bornstein and his team had cut the size of the deficit by a million dollars or more. This optimistic news was tinged with a hue of caution, though. In September, the board adopted a new budget of $18.8 million, down about 30 percent from the spending plan that almost drove the organization out of business.[80]

As the interim management team continued its clean-up work, a search committee began to look for a new full-time president. Don Mullally was deeply involved in the process.

> You've got to think about who in their right mind would become the president of an organization that is essentially bankrupt, that has no assets particularly, that has just the very beginnings of a positive cash flow, that is owned, in fact, and controlled by a group of stations that are as fractious as public broadcasters tend to be . . . and, especially, where you have strong unions and you have a group of *prima donnas* as the key staff people, all of whom feel terribly cheated by the fact that this whole thing has come to pass. So, it was clear that we needed somebody that was really special, and somebody that had the courage to deal with a not-for-profit corporation that was really screwed up.[81]

Mullally and his colleagues wanted someone with broad administrative experience—not necessarily in broadcasting, but in some role that required great political skill. In late October they announced that Douglas Bennet, a seasoned hand in Washington, would be the man to lead NPR out of the woods. Bennet had handled a number of assignments for top politicians and had recently held an administrative post in the State Department. His appointment signaled the start of a long, slow climb back to solvency, and to a time when NPR employees could begin recovering from the psychic scars left by their brush with corporate extinction.[82]

AFTERMATH

In early 1984, the General Accounting Office presented its report on the debt crisis at a six-hour hearing called by the House Subcommittee on Oversight and Investigation. The agency found that NPR's financial woes were the result of several unfortunate circumstances: unrealized projections for grant revenue and other contributions; overspending on NPR Plus and other operations; unreimbursed spending on NPR Ventures; and financial management software that had ceased to function, thus rendering the company inauditable. For starters, NPR's management team was counting on the receipt of $7.2 million in nonfederal grants and contributions in 1983, yet waited until just six weeks before the start of that fiscal year to hire a vice president of development. This fundraising executive, Jane Couch, was not able to meet the goal, which represented more than twice the amount of grants and contributions NPR had ever secured in one year. Couch said she was told, at the time of her hiring, that NPR's development goal for FY 1983 was $5.3 million. Even if *that* goal had been reached, it would not have been sufficient to cover the network's expenses. NPR tried to meet most of its fund-raising goals by seeking a couple of three-year foundation grants—one for $4.5 million, the other for $5 million. By September 1982, however, one foundation said it was not interested, and formal talks with the other had not yet begun. Executive vice president Tom Warnock thought that any resulting shortfall in revenue would be covered by profits from NPR Ventures.[83]

As it happens, the Ventures program got off to a rocky start. The network bankrolled it with regular operating funds; no dedicated seed money or other venture capital was involved. Thus, management put itself in a position where *all* of its for-profit ventures would have to pay off in a short period of time—one year, by some accounts. In early 1982, a consulting firm warned NPR that the private partners it sought to do business with had little in the way of money or operating experience. And the trouble did not end there—especially since NPR failed to gain timely approval for the use of its excess satellite capacity. CPB actually stalled this initiative by filing a challenge before the Federal Communications Commission. The corporation questioned the wisdom of using government funds to support NPR's satellite-based ventures, owing to a concern that they might technically interfere with radio reading services for the visually impaired. Because of these circumstances, and others, only one of NPR's high-tech business ventures was still functioning by the time of the GAO audit. In the case of NPR Plus, the program committee of the network's board of directors approved final cost estimates in December 1982, despite the relatively small number of stations that had signed on. By July of the following year, only 101 stations had bought in—leaving NPR 50 to 100 stations short of the number it would need to break even.[84]

Ron Bornstein later added that the corporate review done by his interim management team uncovered several prominent examples of faulty judgment and corporate mismanagement. For instance, NPR was spending money at an annual rate of $30 million at the start of FY 1983, while money flowed into the network's coffers at a rate of roughly $20 million.[85] To be fair, the network's financial problems began long before 1983. Bob Goldfarb came to NPR from the Harvard Business School in 1979, to help Tom Warnock monitor the Finance Department. He says that prior to his arrival, the budget system was practically nonexistent.

> It was described to me as . . . some people would sit down one day—just a small group of people sitting around a table—and would take the CPB funding that was known for the following year and allocate it, department by department, line-item by line-item. And they'd keep the coffee pots percolating. They worked late into the night and produced a budget document in time to submit to CPB. There was even some sense of frustration with having to do *that* much, because the sense was that CPB was making life difficult for NPR—that NPR should just get the money and be done with it.[86]

In addition, says Goldfarb, NPR's financial reporting systems were not well suited for the radio business. In radio and TV organizations, he says, financial managers must learn the goals of different groups of employees and then mediate their competing worldviews. Some employees, like those in the news and information area, value the *product* above all else and consider administrative matters to be of secondary importance. Other employees do not have expertise in programming, but do, ideally, know how to keep a company solvent.[87]

During his six years at NPR, Frank Mankiewicz did little to bring the news staff to a point of closer understanding with his financial team. As a former journalist, he clearly prized his role as the leader of a news organization. In fact, says Ron Bornstein, Mankiewicz tried to buy the love and admiration of his journalists by letting them have pretty much anything they wanted, even when the money was not available. We can see, then, that NPR's financial operations were a disaster waiting to happen. To be sure, Mankiewicz inherited an organization that was already growing so fast its financial control systems could not keep pace. But he presided over an even bigger period of expansion which happened, unfortunately, at a time when federal funds began to decline.[88]

Finally, Frank Mankiewicz's disdain for Bill Kling, *A Prairie Home Companion*, and anything related to Minnesota Public Radio contributed to NPR's financial misfortune through a complex web of causes and effects. In the summer of 1982, for example, Mankiewicz and NPR board chair Maurice Mitchell sent a letter to the trustees—not the managers—of the five stations that had formed American Public Radio Associates. It was designed to give the licensees of these stations a bit of "background information" about APRA—in other words, to ensure that these people fully understood the effect their station managers would have on NPR by virtue of their support for this new organization. Included with each letter was a copy of a brief article written by the manager of an NPR member station, explaining his distaste for APRA and his decision to remove *A Prairie Home Companion* from the airwaves. Mankiewicz and Mitchell took this action without the knowledge of the station managers in question and with no advance warning to anyone else on the NPR board. Later that month, five board members called for their resignations. Mitchell "took the bullet" for his president by stepping down immediately, and that marked a very bad turn of events for NPR. Mitchell was a well liked and extremely well qualified chair with top-level experience in education, publishing, and nonprofit institutions. Myron Jones, the man who succeeded him, was also well liked; however, the bulk of his professional experience had been in local social service agencies. Jones did not have the sort of experience that would adequately prepare him for the exercise of stringent financial oversight at NPR. It would be grossly unfair to blame any significant portion of the debt crisis on him. That said, a lack of leadership at the board level may be part of the reason why others at NPR did not learn of a $1.5 million working-capital deficit—which had accrued by September 30, 1982—until just before the larger debt crisis became obvious some five months later. Had everyone been apprised of this situation in a timely manner, it is conceivable that NPR Plus and NPR Ventures would have been put on hold, or at least reined in a bit.[89]

NPR's history from 1977 through 1983 may best be understood in terms of the decisions that Frank Mankiewicz and Bill Kling made in response to the changing circumstances of the day. More important, the essential view that each man formed about his place in public radio helped to determine the success or failure of these decisions. Frank Mankiewicz passed through National Public Radio on his way to greater fame and fortune. He fantasized about other high-profile jobs and was once mentioned as a candidate for commissioner of Major League Baseball; later, he assumed a powerful position at the Hill and Knowlton public relations firm. Mankiewicz was a gifted publicist who knew nothing of NPR when he came there but led the network to much greater visibility than anyone else had been able to. His single biggest achievement was the launch of Morning Edition, a program that captivated early risers and gave them more reason to stay with NPR throughout the day. Mankiewicz's competitive nature would not allow him to scale back his news operation in the face of dwindling federal support; instead, he developed ambitious, even audacious plans for raising money from other sources. Today's public radio leaders generally agree that his ideas were sound, though a little bit ahead of their time. Some at NPR will never forgive Mankiewicz for the 1983 debt crisis, yet others feel his overall influence on the organization was quite positive. After all, he transformed the network from "the best-kept-secret in America" to the New York Times of the airwaves—all in the space of six years. In that time, NPR realized a fourfold increase in budget, a near-tripling of its staff, and a substantial increase in the number of affiliated stations.[90]

By way of contrast, Bill Kling earned his fame and fortune more gradually. Kling had worked in noncommercial radio before the modern public broadcasting system was born. Building upon a foundation of fine arts programming, he turned a single station in central Minnesota into a large regional network with significant news and program-production capabilities. Always uncomfortable with the power of NPR's Washington-based operation, he built other organizations that would give individual public radio stations a better way to sell their wares nationally. Kling was certainly no angel when it came to fund raising and interorganizational politics, but his conviction that public radio's for-profit activity should always support its public-service mission has served him well. While NPR tried its hand at risky ventures, Kling and his colleagues stumbled upon the idea that a catalog business featuring program-related items could yield a profit—which could then be plowed back into their broadcasting operation. Soon, their Minnesota-based enterprises would pose a serious challenge to NPR's self-image as *the* public radio network in the United States.[91]

Because of these developments, the managers of local stations would one day have the power to select programs from a wider collection of vendors. Many broadcasters now agree that this sort of competition was healthy for public radio in the long run. In the days that followed the debt crisis, however, this shifting field of relationships proved to be traumatic for the Washington-based network that considered all things for a growing number of curious listeners.

4 PHOENIX RISING

National Public Radio badly needed a dose of stability after the debt
crisis, and it came in the form of a new president. Douglas Bennet
was a career civil servant who, like his predecessor, knew little about the
business of public broadcasting. However, he did have a doctorate from
Harvard, excellent political connections, a hard-nosed business sense, and
a conviction, heretofore lacking at NPR, that member stations were important clients. This chapter begins with the ways in which Bennet worked to
right the network's financial ship and to ensure that it developed compelling
new programs for the audience. During his ten-year term, a variety of forces
also pushed the public radio system into a new way of doing business—an
arrangement through which the federal government would come to direct
almost all of its radio funds to local stations. Doug Bennet was masterful
in helping his network adapt to these changes. But the real story here is
the creative interplay between himself, other public radio executives, their
friends and inquisitors in Congress, and a handful of influential researchers
and consultants.

If more funding was to go directly to stations, NPR would simply have
to become more sensitive to their needs. Increased acceptance of audience

research, once considered heretical in public broadcasting, helped the net-work and its member stations become even more attractive to a highly edu-cated audience whose income level made commercial broadcasters drool with envy. Rival organizations and producers also found new ways to fund and distribute their programs. The chapter concludes with a brief survey of the job done by Bennet's successor, Delano Lewis. Entrepreneurial hunger, political intrigue, and another spate of soul-searching over public radio's mission were the hallmarks of his presidency—which helped to determine the shape and trajectory of the network whose programs are now heard by more than 20 million people each week.

DIFFERENT STROKES . . .

If Frank Mankiewicz brought visibility to NPR, Doug Bennet brought a somewhat different set of qualities to the network in the fall of 1983. As one staff member put it, Bennet knew "how to raise money, how to deal with Congress and how to work with the 280 [member] stations." He developed strong political skills as former head of the U.S. Agency for International Development, and in staff positions with Vice President Hubert Humphrey and Senators Abraham Ribicoff and Thomas Eagleton. During the Carter administration, he also took part in talks that led to the signing of the Pana-ma Canal Treaty. The troubling events that happened in the months before Bennet took office at NPR guaranteed that his political skills would be put to a test. Representative John Dingell (Democrat from Michigan), chair of the House Energy and Commerce Committee and one of public broadcast-ing's most ardent supporters, had pledged to increase federal funding for the industry just prior to the debt crisis. When the shortfall became public knowledge, it also became an embarrassing obstacle for the congressman. At a committee meeting in June, Dingell and Rep. Timothy Wirth (Dem-ocrat from Colorado) had to fight off Republican colleagues who, armed with sordid tales of mismanagement, tried to take money away from public broadcasting. The committee finally approved a bill to increase the amount of CPB's authorized funding over the next three years, but it also passed an amendment that gave the corporation much more authority over NPR's af-fairs. CPB would no longer be allowed to fund the network unless its man-agers developed sound budgetary practices and made their financial records continuously accessible. When Bennet and company could show that their house was in order, the amendment would expire.[1]

Unfortunately, a number of key players in Washington were still annoyed about Frank Mankiewicz and the debt crisis.[2] Public radio consultant Tom Thomas recalls that Mankiewicz's habit of "riding roughshod" over customary CPB practices—when, for example, he made a backdoor maneuver to secure 25 percent of the corporation's program funds for public radio—created a series of strained relationships that lingered into the Bennet years.

> Beyond any prior history, I believe [CPB Chairman] Sharon Rockefeller was deeply, deeply angered at the straight facts of the matter of the debt crisis at NPR itself, and saw what had happened as a betrayal of public trust, an abdication of fiscal responsibility that should go with the leadership of an organization of that sort, of just patent irresponsibility . . . and was genuinely angry at those who had let that happen on their watch. And I believe that would have been the case even if the prior relationship had been one of great cordiality and friendship.[3]

Doug Bennet fully expected extra attention from CPB, which served simultaneously as "a heat shield, a grant maker [and] a creditor" for his network. He regretted that the two organizations spent "hundreds of hours battering each other on issues of procedure and doctrine," while the origins of this combat were rooted in the period before his arrival. Heavy CPB scrutiny—and, as a result, tighter controls on newsroom spending—contributed to a serious morale problem at NPR, whose employees felt they were "being nibbled to death by accountants." In a move that *Variety* called "the worst-kept secret" in Washington, staff members convinced Walter Cronkite, Judy Woodruff, Bill Moyers, and other media luminaries to go public with their concern about budget cuts and firings, calling themselves "Friends of NPR." Network officials were caught off-guard when they first saw advertisements by the group in the *Washington Post* and *New York Times*.[4]

Eventually, the General Accounting Office found that CPB's oversight procedures were straining the network's management resources at a time when greater support in that area seemed appropriate. In response, CPB established a committee to ensure that NPR officials had "a single point of contact within the Corporation" when it came to money matters. But this was not the only financial issue that needed attention. Doug Bennet's corporate-development team feared that its hands might be tied in terms of national fund-raising since the NPR board, which consisted largely of station managers, had implemented a rule barring on-air pledge drives by the Washington-based staff. Fortunately, ninety-seven stations circumvented that rule just prior to his arrival by collaborating with the network in the "The Drive to Survive"—raising more than two million dollars in the process. Following that precedent, about 200 stations took part in NPR's second national on-air fundraiser in April 1985. Listeners contributed $6 million this time around, more than enough money to help member stations recoup a $5.4 million assessment that Bennet had levied on them the year before as an initial strategy for debt retirement. [5]

CPB helped *Morning Edition* and *All Things Considered* stay afloat in 1985 with a grant of more than $900,000, but member stations, and some friends in unlikely places, would have to make additional contributions in order to solve yet another problem. When the corporation refused to give NPR enough money to save *Weekend All Things Considered*, a popular program that first aired in 1977, management told the show's producers that operations would be suspended . . . unless they found additional resources. Concerned staffers began to roam the halls of NPR headquarters, looking for leads on potential funders. Producer Jeff Rosenberg had been talking the situation over with his father around that same time. He learned that the elder Rosenberg—a real estate agent in Fort Lauderdale—had sold a house to, and become friendly with, H. Wayne Huizenga, the cofounder of Waste Management, Inc. (and, later, the CEO of Blockbuster Entertainment and owner of the Miami Dolphins, Florida Marlins, and Florida Panthers). Huizenga was reportedly a devoted NPR listener, and following a rapid series of discussions, Waste Management provided $100,000 in the first of several grants that would help *WATC* stay on the air. Inspired by this remarkable bit of luck, NPR raised the rest of the necessary funds.[6]

These events gave NPR some breathing room, and its managers and journalists responded eagerly to the challenge of expanding their menu of programs. No major new programs had gone to air since *Morning Edition* in 1979, and stations had begun to ask for a sixth day of that program on Saturdays.[7] Robert Siegel, who became NPR's news director following the debt crisis, was the person who had to answer these demands. He says the stations simply wanted a "Best of *Morning Edition*" show, hosted by Bob Edwards,

> and as News Director, I took and twisted that demand into a demand for a new program that would be on Saturdays, that would be a complement to *Morning Edition*, and that would be at a different time, and have a different name, and have a different host. . . . And the reason it was so important to me was that we had, a year earlier, come through this financial crisis. And there was a widespread belief that NPR was dead and that it no longer had any creativity in it.[8]

Siegel knew this program would have to be great from the start, and he enlisted Bill Siemering (then chair of the NPR board's program committee) and audience researcher David Giovannoni to help conceptualize it. Then, he asked the network's best producer, Jay Kernis, and his best host-in-waiting, Scott Simon, to get everything ready for air.[9]

Kernis had played an instrumental part in the success of *Morning Edition*, and he saw a tremendous opportunity to attract new listeners on Saturday. He wanted the show to continue NPR's tradition of excellent news coverage, but do it in a way that spoke to the somewhat different needs of weekend listeners—with more stories about books, theatrical performances, health, and sports, for example.[10] Kernis recalls that Simon left his mark on the new program, called *Weekend Edition*, even before the first broadcast.

> He said, "*I want this show to stand for something.*" It basically stood for respecting the intelligence of the audience, understanding that the audience is insatiably curious about the world and wants information . . . and, given that information, would be more involved in [political] decisions. I mean, that's what Scott's about, and was about, and still is about. And that was my job, to make sure that Scott could do that every week.[11]

The program debuted on November 2, 1985, and soon became popular because of the special bond that Scott Simon has always been able to form with listeners. Its success helped pave the way for *Weekend Edition Sunday* in 1987, hosted by Susan Stamberg.

A New Way of Doing Business

While launching new programs had become a priority for Doug Bennet, the retirement of NPR's debt remained, of necessity, a more central focus. Bennet was instrumental in developing short-term solutions, such as the solicitation of funds via direct mail and the recruitment of more corporate sponsors. But the long-term strategies that helped NPR retire its debt and rethink its place in the public radio system actually had roots in public television's formative years. As the educational television system faded away in the early 1970s, the Nixon administration began to view the Public Broadcasting Service, the network that replaced it, with increasing suspicion. Nixon was especially upset by the creation of public TV's first news operation, the National Public Affairs Center for Television, and feared that it might generate politically hostile coverage. By insisting that local stations drive the process of deciding which programs to air—news, entertainment, and otherwise—Nixon and his aides helped create the very shape of today's PBS, which has no capacity to produce programs of its own. Most federal support for public television flows directly to local stations, which buy programs from outside producers or, in some cases, make their own. Consultant Tom Thomas suspects that some of the people who operated public *radio* stations in the early 1970s viewed this funding arrangement with envy. Since theirs was a comparatively small (and largely unknown) industry, however, the government did not press for "decentralized" programming in similar fashion. Thus, CPB steered virtually all of its radio programming dollars to NPR for the first sixteen years of its existence.[12]

Flashing forward to the early 1980s, one can find other reasons for the eventual movement toward a different kind of public radio system. First, the National Federation of Community Broadcasters began to complain on Capitol Hill that its member stations, most of which did not belong to NPR, were getting little or no financial help from the federal government. As we have seen, a handful of major program-producing stations also wanted more help from CPB so they could distribute their own programs nationally. NPR had a similar appetite for expanding its production capabilities and found that the amount of money it was getting from the corporation was insufficient for the task. Finally, CPB was open to fundamental changes in the system. During negotiations over the NPR bailout, the corporation (and some members of Congress) had favored the idea of splitting its radio funds between NPR and all of the noncommercial stations that qualified for federal aid. This marked the first tangible movement toward the major restructuring of public radio's finances that later came to be known as the "NPR Business Plan." The network's board of directors took another small, tentative step in this direction when, in November 1983, it formed a committee to study funding issues. Doug Bennet said its main purpose was to show Congress and other potential funders that NPR was capable of "cleaning its own house." But station managers, independent producers, and other interested parties were determined to move beyond superficial fixes. They wanted to remind NPR that it did not fully represent the dreams and aspirations of everyone who worked in the public radio system.[13]

The following summer, fifteen managers from major public radio stations gathered for an ad hoc meeting in Texas. The group—which included Minnesota Public Radio's Bill Kling, Susan Harmon of KERA-FM in Dallas, and Wayne Roth of KUOW-FM in Seattle—was concerned about the overall direction of the industry following the NPR debt crisis. In particular, these people felt that forces beyond their control were steering the system and that the welfare of local stations was not a top priority for anyone in Washington. Tom Thomas attended the meeting, where managers "moaned and groaned about the state of the world" for a couple of days. As the festivities came to a close, each of them pledged $1,000 to hire someone to lobby on their behalf in Washington. They approached Thomas about the job since he and Terry Clifford, his wife and fellow radio consultant, had just stepped down as copresidents of the National Federation of Community Broadcasters. Thomas said yes, and when his efforts began to yield positive results, the station managers decided to continue their association and to invite another dozen or so colleagues to join them. The group maintained a loose structure until September 1987, when it incorporated under the name its members had informally assumed. In time, the Station Resource Group would become widely known as a think tank and advocacy organization for public radio stations across the country. More immediately, it would play an important role in discussions about a complete overhaul of the system.[14]

In February 1985, NPR chairman Donald Mullally proposed a new five-year business plan that would have the Corporation for Public Broadcasting send all of its radio money directly to local stations; the stations would, in turn, be free to buy programming from NPR or any other vendor. The board proposed a fee structure for member stations that would cover the cost of programming, lobbying, and other services, and it said these fees should be calculated as a percentage of the total revenues of NPR stations. Shortly after the release of NPR's proposal, the Station Resource Group responded with a position paper of its own. It rejected the notion of tying member dues to industry-wide revenue growth and proposed, instead, that NPR craft a detailed budget each year; this budget would then be submitted to the entire public radio system for approval. SRG's idea prevailed in the final draft of the business plan, as station managers feared that NPR, with its appetite for programming expansion, might overcharge them when calculating dues. These stations also wanted to *unbundle* NPR's program content—to disaggregate the entire schedule of its programs and make them available to stations in piecemeal fashion. Many stations thought they could trim expenses through this sort of arrangement by avoiding payment for programs they did not want or use. Stations that belonged to SRG, or distributed programs through American Public Radio, also felt that unbundling would enhance their prospects for competing in the national programming marketplace.[15]

These divergent viewpoints notwithstanding, station representatives overwhelmingly approved a new NPR Business Plan in May 1985, with its provisions taking effect at the start of the 1987 fiscal year. This version did not include any notion of unbundled programs, and serious discussions about that topic continued. In fact, APR threatened to file an antitrust lawsuit, charging that NPR's distribution policies "posed a significant barrier to entry for other program producers." Finally, in December 1987, the NPR board approved a proposal that would let stations choose from morning news, evening news, and cultural performance packages. Another point of contention, the calculation of dues for NPR member stations, was not so easily resolved. The debate on this matter continued well after Doug Bennet left office.[16]

One additional, and less publicized, feature of the business plan was the development of CPB's competitive Radio Program Fund, which opened for business in 1986. The proposal for this fund, which offers both seed and expansion money for promising programs, was originally resisted by NPR but was later inserted into the plan at the behest of many stations. Under the direction of CPB's Rick Madden, it supported station-based productions such as *Fresh Air* (WHYY-FM, Philadelphia) and *Soundprint* (WJHU-FM, Baltimore), independent cultural programs such as *Afropop*, and NPR's *Talk of the Nation*. Madden, the corporation's vice president for radio, became well known for the peer-review panels he convened to meticulously screen all proposals and for the quality and depth of his advice to radio producers throughout the country. In general, the Radio Program Fund helped local stations and independent producers feel more welcome within the larger public radio system. Some people whose proposals failed to pass muster resented Madden's seemingly ironclad authority. Still, most public broadcasters came to regard the fund as a primary force in getting new programs on the air.[17]

As one might expect, APR—the program distribution firm that later changed its name to Public Radio International—benefitted from the NPR Business Plan and the new provisions for unbundling. Of the more than 400 hours of programming that PRI distributes each week, one may find a variety of station-based productions such as *Michael Feldman's Whad'Ya Know* (Wisconsin Public Radio), *This American Life* (Chicago Public Radio), and *World Café* (WXPN-FM, Philadelphia). A long-time supplier of classical music and other cultural fare, PRI sought to fill a gap in NPR's news coverage when it began to distribute *Marketplace*, public radio's premiere business program, in January 1989. It also built up a stock of foreign-news offerings and, in 1996, entered the program-production business with *The World*—an international-news magazine aired in cooperation with the BBC and WGBH-FM in Boston.[18]

Doug Bennet, board chairmen Don Mullally and Jack Mitchell, and, eventually, Sid Brown (who came on board as NPR's chief financial officer in

1986) developed and implemented the new business plan as a way of making peace in the public radio system—while also preserving their conception of NPR as the industry's primary player. In the process, they made great strides toward getting the company back into the black. By the spring of 1986, the network had reduced its debt to about $226,000 and indicated that it would pay that sum off ahead of schedule. NPR retired the debt completely in 1988, ending the fiscal year with a surplus of nearly $2.8 million. Better accounting systems, the accumulation of working capital, and increased donations of various kinds were all important parts of this economic revival. The new business plan meant that *stations* were now covering a larger portion of NPR's expenses; yet more and more of them found value in affiliating with the network (over one hundred stations became members from the time of the debt crisis through September 1988). In an article about this fortunate turn of events, the *New York Times* noted that NPR had gotten by "with help from its friends."[19]

GUYS IN SUITS WITH CHARTS

One of the remarkable things about NPR's financial rebirth is that it happened at a time when the funding mix for public broadcasting was changing dramatically. The significant budget cuts proposed by the Reagan administration in the early 1980s never materialized. But public broadcasters took stock of the political winds in Washington, along with their future needs, and began to look for other ways to raise money. From 1983, the year of the debt crisis, through 1993, when Doug Bennet left NPR, the growth in public radio revenue from listeners and business underwriters (*listener-sensitive* funds) outstripped the growth in *tax-based* funds (from governments and public universities) by about seven to one.[20] How were listeners, and the businesses they might frequent, convinced to pick up more of the tab? Simply put, the public radio industry learned much more about its audience and then put this knowledge to good use. Through the 1970s, modest annual growth in the number of listeners came as a result of system expansion—bringing new stations into the fold, putting more of them on the FM band, and expanding their hours of operation. The main reasons for audience growth since that time are compelling programs, tightly focused formats, and stations that are, because of these things, much easier to listen to. This movement toward *accessible* programming helped lay to rest the old theory that public radio should deliver programs that "listeners just had to hear"—with the person behind the microphone having little knowledge about things that happened simultaneously in the minds of those listeners. Audience researcher Tom Church once noted that "many stations could completely fulfil their mission statements without anyone ever actually listening." This sort of broadcasting had no conception of people being affected by programs, finding their stations important, or using the knowledge they gained from radio to make a difference in their communities.[21]

Audience research would become a key factor in the process of matching public radio programs with the actual preferences of listeners. Some observers think NPR began to focus on this sort of research in 1986 when it formed the Audience-Building Task Force. One of the goals embraced by this group was the doubling of public radio's average quarter hour audience[22] by the spring of 1990. The task force succeeded in drawing attention to the audience and to a variety of practical methods that could be used to help it grow. But according to Jack Mitchell, then chairman of the NPR board, it actually represented "a quick game of catch up on the part of NPR, attempting to assume 'leadership' of a process that was well underway elsewhere in public radio."[23] Audience research had, in fact, been conducted in noncommercial broadcasting since the 1920s. But for a variety of reasons, including a general lack of interest and financial support, these efforts were of marginal value to the industry for five decades. When educational radio began changing into the modern-day *public* radio system, audience studies often became objects of suspicion. Garrison Keillor once mocked the people who did this work, calling them "guys in suits with charts and pages of numbers."[24]

Undaunted by critics, CPB began to provide public radio stations with ratings estimates from Arbitron, the dominant radio-research firm, in the spring of 1973 (though it took three more years to make them fully comparable with the data used by commercial stations). The corporation also tried to ease skepticism about the value of research by supporting three major initiatives later in the decade. From 1978 through 1981, it funded a series of seminars around the country in which expert practitioners assured station managers that the proper use of audience data would lead to better programming—and more productive pledge drives. A study done by the University of Wisconsin's Lawrence Lichty in 1978 demonstrated the dearth of listeners to public radio in the morning hours; in fact, it helped justify the start of *Morning Edition* in 1979. That same year, Lichty's graduate teaching assistant, David Giovannoni, came to NPR for the purpose of designing the Public Radio Audience Profile. PRAP helped the network track the listening habits of nearly 300,000 Arbitron survey subjects, and it was the first computerized system designed to study audiences on a scale that was larger than a local radio market. It could tell a station manger how many people listened to a particular program each week, how long they listened, what their demographic characteristics were, and how they actually came to listen to the program (e.g., directly tuning in, listener flow from a previous program, etc.).[25]

Dave Giovannoni has certainly not been alone in studying the public radio audience, but it is arguable that no one else has done more to promote the notion that listeners are valuable components of the system—and should be treated as such by the managers of NPR and its member stations. Tom Thomas says that Giovannoni, his friend and colleague, was "the first persistent, consistent, disciplined voice" to say that public radio programs may not always affect listeners in the ways that radio professionals think they do.[26] He developed

> notions about program appeal and accessibility . . . which was just something that had not been much on the minds of NPR and much of public radio in its early days. We were all deeply imbued with our notions of public service and the content we wanted to bring to the airwaves—"unheard voices that needed to speak." But we were remarkably unsophisticated in our knowledge of how to be successful in broadcast terms, and what the underlying dynamics [were] of how people use the radio, *including us in public radio* [emphasis added].[27]

In time, many of the industry's leading figures learned that this researcher, who collected antique audio equipment and had loved the medium since childhood, could help them understand who was listening, and why, better than ever before.

In 1985, Giovannoni released the results of a CPB-sponsored study titled "Public Radio Listeners: Supporters and Non-Supporters." This so-called "Cheap 90" study found that only 10 percent of all listeners supported their local stations financially; not coincidentally, these people were more likely than anyone else to say that public radio was an important part of their lives. The study also found that a station's programming—especially news and information programming—was the most powerful factor in explaining why these listeners actually chose to make financial contributions. The following year, when Giovannoni left NPR to focus on his own consulting business, he teamed up with Tom Thomas, Terry Clifford, and Linda Liebold to work on a larger study that would later be known as "Audience 88." This study used cutting-edge market-segmentation software to better understand what kinds of people listened to public radio and how their listening experiences were actually related to the programming practices of local stations. One of its major conclusions was that public radio could only hope to serve a specific portion of the American radio audience: people who were highly educated and socially conscious and who, in most cases, enjoyed a mix of high-quality information programming and classical music. The researchers noted that a handful of stations located in one geographic area could enhance the overall diversity of local programming—the very stuff of mission statements—if each of them targeted a highly specific audience of its own. They cautioned that no public radio station should try to serve multiple audiences all by itself, a common practice in the days of educational radio. One important consequence of "Audience 88" was the gradual abandonment of *checkerboard* programming, a something-for-everyone strategy that seemed lofty in principle but actually tended to drive listeners away. Public radio formats are now much more seamless, as one can tune to almost any station and expect to hear consistent programming at key times of the day.[28]

Throughout the 1990s, Giovannoni's firm, Audience Research Analysis, developed a variety of analytical tools and terms that are now widely used throughout the industry. One such development was the measurement of program *appeal*, the quality of a radio show that attracts certain listeners and repels others. This concept was significant for station managers in terms of helping them choose which programs were suitable for their particular audiences. ARA's crowning achievement, however, was the completion of "Audience 98," the largest research project in public radio history. A key finding of this study was that "public service begets public support"—that is, when people feel well served by the programs they listen to, come to rely upon them, and consider them to be important, they are more likely to help pay for them as well. People listen to public radio, said the authors, because its programming resonates with their interests, values, and beliefs. *Morning Edition* and *All Things Considered* resonated deeply with many listeners, as one-third of all the money pledged to their favorite stations came in response to these programs. Some of the study's findings seemed counterintuitive to program directors; take, for example, the observation that most members of the public radio audience valued news over classical music and nationally distributed shows over local fare. Nonetheless, Giovannoni and his team argued that stations whose daily schedules reflected the lessons of "Audience 98" could expect their pledge and underwriting income to rise.[29]

How did the industry benefit from this body of research? Public radio's national weekly audience increased steadily from 1.3 million listeners in 1971 to 5.3 million in 1980, a period in which the addition of stations and transmitters to the system was largely responsible for its growth. Between 1980 and 1983, a time when stations began to take the lessons of audience research more seriously, the audience jumped to 8.7 million listeners, a gain of 63 percent. In the decade that followed, a time of even stronger programs and formats, weekly listening to public radio increased by an average of more than 8 percent each year. Because of their efforts in audience building and public service, Dave Giovannoni, Tom Church, Tom Thomas, Terry Clifford, and the late Rick Madden (who funded much of their research) have all received CPB's Edward R. Murrow Award, the public radio industry's highest honor.[30]

NPR's Stars

All the hard work that Doug Bennet and others did to make NPR healthy again had one very positive side effect; it helped to focus public attention more consistently on the network's lineup of award-winning programs. *Morning Edition* and *All Things Considered* have long been NPR's most powerful one-two punch in terms of attracting listeners, and they are still the favorites of public radio's core audience, the people who spend more time listening to noncommercial programs than any others. But a network cannot live on two hits alone; thus, NPR set out to make, or distribute, another set of popular shows. In 1987, just two years after the launch of *Weekend Edition*, the programming lineup was further expanded through agreements to distribute *Car Talk* and *Fresh Air*. Hosted by MIT-trained mechanics Tom and Ray Magliozzi (once described by *The Washington Post* as "Boyz Under the Hood"), *Car Talk* first hit the airwaves in 1977 on Boston's WBUR-FM. The show evolved from an initially formless state—when, as the brothers joke, they answered about three questions in an hour-and-a-half—into a well-produced program that showcased their advice and humor, phrased in an endearingly (for some, annoyingly) thick Boston accent. Robert Siegel, Jay Kernis, and producer Gary Covino all claimed credit for discovering *Car Talk* and bringing it to the attention of their bosses in Washington. Whatever the case, it has become NPR's number-one entertainment show, with "Click and Clack" earning a prestigious George Foster Peabody Award for distinguished radio programming in 1992. *Fresh Air* is another of NPR's Peabody winners. Host Terry Gross began her radio career in 1973 by working on several shows at WBFO-FM in Buffalo including *This Is Radio*, a program conceived by Bill Siemering. Gross, whose interviewing style has been described as "a remarkable blend of empathy and warmth, genuine curiosity and sharp intelligence," moved to WHYY-FM in Philadelphia two years later to produce and host a live, local version of *Fresh Air*. A weekly thirty-minute edition of the program debuted in 1985, and NPR began distributing the current hour-long version two years later. Originally designed as a lead-in to *All Things Considered, Fresh Air* is also used by many stations as a bridge between afternoon news programs and musical presentations in the evening.[31]

Some members of NPR's news team also gained stature during Doug Bennet's time at the network. This is noteworthy since in the early 1970s, it would have stretched the imagination to think that "the network of dead air and 28-minute stories" would produce any radio personality who could rightfully be called a star. Susan Stamberg and Bob Edwards had already risen to that stratum by the time *Weekend Edition* built its own devoted following in the mid-1980s. Its host, Scott Simon, left the Saturday morning show in August 1992 to cohost the weekend *Today* programs on NBC but returned to NPR fourteen months later. He was one of several NPR reporters who, mindful of their comparatively low salaries, tried their hand at commercial network news—either full or part time (John Hockenberry, Deborah Wang, and Nina Totenberg also fall into this category). Perhaps the most famous practitioner of network hopping is Cokie Roberts, who came to NPR in the Mankiewicz years and developed a reputation for incisive commentary on the world of politics. Roberts began working as a political analyst for ABC News in 1988 and cohosted *This Week* on Sunday mornings from 1996 until 2002. Now involved in several broadcast and print journalism projects, she continues to work for NPR as a senior news analyst.[32]

To many of her colleagues, Roberts was also known as part of a powerful newsroom "troika" (along with Linda Wertheimer and Nina Totenberg) that wielded considerable influence at NPR. The three were good friends who often socialized with each other.[33] But they also had strong reporting skills and political connections—and, on occasion, used the leverage of their positions to influence various practices and decisions at NPR. Jay Kernis remembers that the three women, whose desks were located in the same corner of NPR's former headquarters, joked one day that their part of the building should be called "The Fallopian Jungle."

> I mean, that's what it was known as. And they were formidable. . . . There was a famous yellow ochre couch in that area. When you were summoned to sit on the couch, you knew that either you were going to be lectured, or that they were gonna discuss strategy, or they were gonna discuss the company's future. And I think, rightly so, they took it upon themselves to make sure that whoever was managing the company, they were managing it well.[34]

The three reportedly influenced the rise and fall of Adam Clayton Powell III (who became news chief after Robert Siegel moved to *All Things Considered* in 1987) and made certain that Linda Wertheimer had the chance to apply for a cohost position on *ATC*, which she held from 1989 to 2002. Kernis argues that Roberts, Totenberg, and Wertheimer were more often right than wrong in their opinions about NPR and says their input was important, given the vacuums of leadership that have sometimes bedeviled the network.[35]

NPR also gained notoriety in the 1990s for some of the high-profile stories its reporters worked on. Such was the case with Nina Totenberg when she and Timothy Phelps of *Newsday* broke the story of Anita Hill's allegations of sexual harassment against Supreme Court nominee Clarence Thomas. The network also made the front pages when it announced plans to broadcast commentaries from a Pennsylvania prison by convicted cop-killer Mumia Abu-Jamal—a decision that was quickly rescinded by top management following complaints by the police union in Philadelphia. But nothing the NPR news team had done before provided the sort of visibility that came with its coverage of the first Persian Gulf War in early 1991. The network spent $1.8 million on its war coverage (a paltry sum by commercial news standards) and rapidly parlayed the investment into a dominant position among broadcast news organizations.[36] Neal Conan knew NPR's presence in the Gulf was something special when he first reached the pool of network reporters stationed in Saudi Arabia.

I realized as I walked in that room and looked around at the other people, of which I had been in awe all of my life . . . *that we were bigger than they were and better than they were.* I was in Dhahran. We had Scott Simon, Deborah Amos, Deborah Wang, all in Saudi, which was more people than any other radio organization had, plus Jacki Lyden and a number of other people on the periphery. It wasn't a contest! We were outstripping these people in quality and quantity. And I realized at that point that we were the biggest radio news organization in the United States. And I was astonished.[37]

NPR earned high praise for its richly textured coverage of the war, an approach most evident in stories that aired on *Weekend Edition*. Author Mary Collins recalls with special poignancy the report in which Scott Simon observed young soldiers eating Fruit Loops out of paper cups and wondered whether children's food would be enough to fortify them for battle. Deborah Amos delivered the typical repertoire of war reporting and political analysis but also mixed in personal stories about Persian Gulf residents "who washed dishes, drove the children to school, ate dinner and worried about the future."[38]

Correspondents like Sylvia Poggioli, Linda Gradstein, Mike Shuster, and Anne Garrels were all part of NPR's Gulf War effort, and they have made significant contributions to the foreign desk ever since. Poggioli, whose reports embody a rare combination of authority and lyrical tone, covered European reaction to the war from London. Now based in Rome, she has also earned critical acclaim for reports on ethnic cleansing in Bosnia and NATO's air war against Yugoslavia. Gradstein, a devout Jew and mother of three, has often covered stories in dangerous parts of the Middle East—sometimes while pregnant. Though each side in the Israeli-Palestinian conflict has accused her of favoring the other in certain reports, Gradstein strives to make a positive contribution to the region by balancing the tone and content of her coverage over the long run. Shuster covers the diplomatic beat but has also served NPR's bureaus in London, Moscow, and Los Angeles. In addition, he has reported from such far flung locations as Iran, Uzbekistan, and the Congo. And Garrels—a former premed student who turned to journalism after taking a Russian course—has also distinguished herself in a series of difficult high-profile assignments since 1991. All of these people played central roles in the network's coverage of September 11, 2001, and the second Persian Gulf war, and I will say more about those exploits in the next chapter.[39]

FROM TWEED JACKET TO PINSTRIPED SUIT

In his ten years as president, Doug Bennet guided NPR from the brink of insolvency to a position of undisputed leadership in American radio news. The network had 283 member stations in 1983; a decade later, it had 460 and had attracted more than 6 million new listeners. Income from listeners and businesses increased during this period, and the NPR Foundation was established for the purpose of creating an endowment and funding new projects. And accolades for NPR programs continued to pile up. In 1992, the network won top honors in three categories at the Society of Professional Journalists's awards competition, and early the following year, it won a Golden Baton, the top prize for overall news excellence at the duPont-Columbia Awards. Soon afterward, satisfied that his work was largely done, Bennet announced that he was leaving public radio for a position at the State Department. Two years later, he returned to his home state of Connecticut to become president of Wesleyan University.[40]

Given the increasing importance of private sector funds, the NPR board began to search for a new president who was entrepreneurial in spirit and capable of tapping corporations and foundations for additional support. This person would also need good lobbying skills, a solid grasp of new media technologies, and enough administrative savvy to run a complex, multifaceted organization. The board announced in August 1993 that Delano Lewis, president and CEO of Washington's Chesapeake and Potomac Telephone Company, would be the man to fill Doug Bennet's shoes. A long time associate of Mayor Marion Barry, Lewis became the first African American to head a public broadcasting network. He had worked with the Justice Department, the Equal Employment Opportunity Commission, and the Peace Corps, and had been a legislative assistant to Senator Edward Brooke of Massachusetts. He served on the boards of Colgate Palmolive, the Chase Manhattan Corporation, and Geico and had strong ties to Washington's philanthropic community. The board also hoped that Lewis's familiarity with the telecommunications industry would help him guide the network into an age where radio transmissions might be augmented, then supplanted, by new methods of content delivery.[41]

Much like his predecessors, Lewis found a corporate culture at NPR that was unlike anything he had seen before. On one hand, this noncommercial network had replaced CBS as the leader in U.S. radio news, becoming in the process an "unofficial bulletin board" for presidents, congressmen, lobbyists, and journalists. In spite of this, many of the network's employees felt a sense of foreboding when looking toward the future. Lewis called this phenomenon "the legacy of '83"—a lingering fear that NPR would, for some unknown reason, go belly up.[42] He had no idea why this bleak view persisted and also failed to understand certain idiosyncrasies of corporate structure.

> The chain of command here was a flat chain of command, with everybody reporting to the president. I also found that there was no human resource system that would begin to [address] not only affirmative action and diversity, but get at some basic stuff about benefits, about promotions, about "how do I move from one area [of the company] to the next?" And there was a hierarchy here that was not conducive to productivity.[43]

Lewis was not, by any means, the first person to notice that the network's internal culture lacked a bottom-line sensibility; despite the success of Public Radio International and other program vendors, some managers felt (and still feel) that NPR had no real competition. For all these reasons, Del Lewis vowed to instill in his troops a sense of corporate hunger. In early 1994, he told the *New York Times* that three of his major goals were to get more financial support from corporations that did business in areas that NPR News covered; to create new program genres; and to attract new listeners, especially minorities and young people. If these goals were met, they might soothe the fears of critics who thought the network would, in a more "corporate" form, focus on stronger ratings at the expense of creative programming.[44]

Lewis's attention was soon diverted from these matters, however, when he and other public broadcasting executives encountered another wave of politically motivated anger toward their enterprise. In many ways, this anger was an extension of complaints that had circulated among conservatives for a decade or more. A 1985 Heritage Foundation report asked, for example, whether the American taxpayer should continue to support NPR, a network that was—in the author's opinion—riven with ideological and political biases, dubious taste, and public affairs programming "on fringe elements in American society." It is difficult, if not impossible, to find these traits through systematic content analyses of NPR programs. Nonetheless, conservative groups railed about a few high-profile stories in the 1980s and 1990s that offended their strongly held values. In 1981, the group Accuracy in Media objected to comments from a *Pacifica Radio* call-in show, later rebroadcast by NPR, in which a female listener said John Hinckley Jr. should have "finished the job" when he shot President Reagan. Nina Totenberg came under heavy criticism a decade later when she helped break the story about Anita Hill's allegations of sexual misconduct by Clarence Thomas—a story that took off rapidly following the leak of a secret FBI report.[45]

Historically, conservatives who complained about stories like these had a tough time mustering enough political clout to cut government funds that were earmarked for public broadcasting. In the fall of 1994, however, the center of political power in Washington began to shift rapidly. Republican majorities surged to power in the House and Senate, giving public broadcasting's most vehement critics a dose of renewed vigor. House Speaker–elect Newt Gingrich (Republican of Georgia) and Larry Pressler of the Senate Commerce Committee (Republican of South Dakota) wasted no time, talking openly in December of their desire to end all federal support; Pressler even wrote CPB president Henry Cauthen about the need to defund and privatize the corporation. Two Republican lawmakers, Dan Miller of Florida and Peter Hoekstra of Michigan, brought the Gingrich/Pressler agenda to the House of Representatives in July 1995 when they pushed for a legislative amendment to eliminate forward funding for CPB. NPR's National Affairs office urged station managers to complain to their representatives in Washington, and the leaders of other public broadcasting organizations followed suit. Their efforts paid off, with the amendment losing in the House by a margin of better than two to one. The federal government appropriated $275 million for public broadcasting in 1996. This was considerably less than the $425 million that had been authorized for CPB, and the amount also reflected a rescission of $37 million by Congress. Be that as it may, public broadcasting had survived another threat to end its federal funding entirely.[46]

The budgets for NPR's top news programs actually grew during this period of tight finances, and *All Things Considered* expanded its daily run from ninety minutes to two hours. But anticipated drops in state and federal support forced cutbacks in some of the network's other operations. In the summer of 1995, NPR dropped nine of its twenty cultural programs, including *Afropop Worldwide*, *Bluesstage*, and *E-town*—eliminating twenty jobs in the process.[47] Del Lewis regretted the loss of these programs but said their small audiences attracted little in the way of badly needed private funds.

> If you're going to solicit money from corporations or foundations . . .
> they are interested now in your reach. They're interested in the audiences that you serve, and the returns that they may see from reaching those audiences. And many of the programs that we're talking about that may appeal to underserved audiences may not have as much universal appeal. So you may need special funds in order to reach those audiences.[48]

Over the years, NPR's arch-rival—Minnesota Public Radio—had been much better equipped to sustain a variety of cultural programs because of a series of shrewd business deals that helped insulate the company from the vagaries of government funding. MPR developed a corporate structure that allowed it to engage in "social-purpose capitalism"—the use of for-profit entities to generate income and endowments for public service endeavors. The most important example of this financial arrangement is Greenspring Company, a for-profit subsidiary of MPR's parent firm. Until 1998, Greenspring owned the Rivertown Trading Company, which, in turn, operated the *Wireless* and *Signals* online catalogs. Rivertown—which began seventeen years earlier as a way of selling posters for *A Prairie Home Companion*—was sold in March of that year for $120 million, with $90 million of the net proceeds going to Minnesota Public Radio's endowment fund.[49]

With passage of the new public radio business plan, and a concomitant boost in local stations' ability to choose their own programs, another of MPR's children—Public Radio International—also continued to thrive. Del Lewis became enamored of PRI's self-appointed board of directors, which raised money far more effectively than his own board could. New initiatives at NPR had often moved at a slower pace because most of its board members were station managers—whose personal interests could impede the building of consensus with colleagues scattered around the country. A consultant had once likened NPR to the UN General Assembly, whose organizational structure was quite appropriate "if paralysis is the preferred ultimate outcome." Lewis was cognizant of this point and tried repeatedly to separate NPR's programming arm from its traditional membership organization. Those efforts failed, as did a series of merger negotiations with PRI. Talks broke down when the two sides could not agree on a governance structure for the new company. Even if they had, NPR's member stations feared the creation of a larger public radio organization that might, one day, send its programs directly to listeners via satellite or the Web—completely bypassing them in the process.[50]

In time, Del Lewis's desire to run NPR like a for-profit business alienated some important members of the NPR News team. Nowhere was this more evident than in his relationship with Bill Buzenberg, a veteran editor and correspondent who became vice president of news in 1990. Buzenberg was, and still is, an emotional, highly energized advocate for the best qualities of broadcast news—thorough yet artful reporting and the maintenance of editorial integrity in the face of all attempts to co-opt the journalistic process. He left NPR in January 1997 and later commented that neither Lewis, nor his chief operating officer, Peter Jablow, fully understood "the mission of public service journalism or the business of public radio." Public statements made at the time of Buzenberg's departure indicate the move was based on a mutual agreement with top management, but others familiar with the story confirm that Lewis edged Buzenberg out of his position, probably for a number of reasons. First, Buzenberg was known to push aggressively, and constantly, for additional resources in the news department. He also may have been the "fall guy" after a handful of discrimination lawsuits were filed by disgruntled members of his news staff (some minority employees later said these suits were related to an ongoing culture of cronyism in hiring and promotion, not to anything Buzenberg said or did personally). Finally, and, perhaps most important, many at NPR thought Buzenberg fell out of favor because he was not a prototypical corporate manager. Whatever the case, he would be sorely missed by his colleagues. One staff member told the trade newspaper *Current* that "any way you look at it—quantity and quality—news went up on his watch. And frankly, Bill's got a big contribution to make in the rest of his career, for some lucky place." That place was Minnesota Public Radio, where Buzenberg became senior vice president of news.[51]

Susan Stamberg, one of NPR's earliest
employees and longtime host of
All Things Considered.
Source: NPR. *Photo Credit:* Lisa Berg.

Minnesota Public Radio president William Kling, standing near the transmitting equipment of one
of his stations. *Source:* Minnesota Public Radio, used by permission of Bill Kling.

William Siemering, NPR's first program director, on a visit to Gobi-Wave Radio in Southern Mongolia. *Source:* Bill Siemering. *Photo Credit:* Ollmedekh Dorjsuren.

Donald Quayle, NPR's first president.
Source: Papers of Jim Robertson,
National Public Broadcasting Archives,
University of Maryland.

with money, and good with people." The Bennet years are also remembered as a time when NPR and its member stations began to rely more heavily on research about the programming tastes and purchasing habits of listeners. Research, in the view of its purest practitioners, is a neutral enterprise; still, some critics rued the thought that ratings reports might lead the network to *sell* its programs to businesses, who would, in turn, peddle their wares to listeners. Fears about the marketization of NPR became even more acute after Bennet left and a genuine corporate executive moved into the president's office. Del Lewis had all the credentials any organization could want, yet he never translated his knowledge and experience into a management style that the network's highly independent news staff could accept. In seeking his replacement, the board wanted someone with one foot planted firmly in the world of journalism and the other in the ethical realm of public service. This executive would have to extend the NPR brand through a variety of new venues including Web commerce, Web radio, and, eventually, direct satellite-to-car broadcasting. And, as always, this person would have to operate in a way that pleased a critical mass of station managers.[54]

Del Lewis's move to corporatize NPR also failed to bring the network many of the financial rewards he sought. Throughout his tenure, Lewis considered several ventures designed to extend the NPR News brand and raise money in the process. Talk of major corporate deals abounded, but neither the PRI-merger proposal nor a brief flirtation with Liberty Media (a subsidiary of cable giant TCI) brought any tangible benefits. Following the lead of NPR's rival in Minnesota, the board of directors resolved in 1996 to examine for-profit ventures that were rooted in public-service values and, therefore, would not compromise the network's mission. Many small projects were hatched, including the marketing of CDs and the deployment of promotional kiosks at Borders book stores. None of these efforts produced much revenue, though. Eventually, Lewis was forced to admit the dearth of "low-hanging fruit," or natural, easy ways to leverage NPR's products into significant profits. He also faced an external funding environment that was not as friendly as the one that Doug Bennet came to enjoy. CPB funding for public radio dropped by more than 17 percent from 1994 through 1998, and the amount of money the system got from the business sector dropped by nearly 8 percent.[52]

There were positive signs, to be sure, as the average quarter-hour audience for NPR member stations jumped by more than 6 percent a year. The network was also able to move from its old headquarters near Dupont Circle to brand new digs on Massachusetts Avenue, just north of Washington's Chinatown district. This move, overseen by financial executive Sid Brown, signified a big step toward a future of digital editing and program distribution at NPR. In spite of these outward signs of success, many employees could not bring themselves to forgive Lewis's corporate overtures. They never accepted the management practices and conventions he tried to introduce, including "multitudinous task forces" and motivational experts. In Lewis's defense, a consultant who surveyed NPR employees detected a "culture of complaint" within the organization that was tied, in part, to a long history of intradepartmental communication problems. Lewis, himself, found it difficult to maintain an entrepreneurial spirit since he had to constantly balance the ambitions of NPR News against the realities of the marketplace—and the hopes and dreams of a diverse collection of station managers. He left NPR in the summer of 1998, ostensibly to spend more time with his family. President Clinton made him the U.S. ambassador to South Africa late in the following year. Lewis remained in that position until July 2001, when he moved to New Mexico to open a communications consulting firm.[53]

Many people who work at NPR today have fond memories of Doug Bennet and the late Sid Brown—the rare financial manager who was both "good

Garrison Keillor of *A Prairie Home Companion.*
Source: Minnesota Public Radio.

Former NPR president Frank Mankiewicz, founder of
Morning Edition and a central figure in the network's
1983 debt crisis. *Source: Current*, the newspaper about
public radio and television.

The late Red Barber, sports commentator and frequent Friday-morning companion to Bob Edwards. *Source:* NPR. *Photo Credit:* Beverly Frick.

Bob Edwards, the original host of *Morning Edition*. *Source:* NPR. *Photo Credit:* Cable Risdon.

Bob Edwards, broadcasting from the studios of his new employer, XM Satellite Radio. *Source:* XM Satellite Radio. *Photo Credit:* John Harrington.

Veteran public broadcaster Ronald Bornstein, a close colleague of William Kling and NPR's chief operating officer during the debt crisis. *Source:* Wisconsin Public Radio and Television.

Jack Mitchell, an early producer of *All Things Considered* and longtime NPR Board member. *Source:* Wisconsin Public Radio and Television.

Audience expert David Giovannoni conducts a research presentation for NPR. *Source:* David Giovannoni, Audience Research Analysis.

Douglas Bennet, who guided NPR back to solvency after the 1983 debt crisis. *Source:* Wesleyan University. *Photo Credit:* Bill Burkhart.

NPR producer (and puppet maker) Barry Gordemer and friends, during the twentieth anniversary celebration for *All Things Considered. Source:* NPR. *Photo Credit:* Tom Lowery.

Senior national correspondent Linda Wertheimer, a former *ATC* cohost. *Source:* NPR. *Photo Credit:* Antony Nagelmann.

ATC cohost Robert Siegel.
Source: NPR. *Photo Credit:* Antony Nagelmann.

Noah Adams, national correspondent and
former *ATC* cohost.
Source: NPR. *Photo Credit:* Antony Nagelmann.

Talk of the Nation: Science Friday's Ira Flatow in Antarctica, with a group of rather frosty interview subjects. *Source:* NPR.

NPR legal-affairs correspondent
Nina Totenberg.
Source: Michael Geissinger.

NPR senior news analyst and
ABC News correspondent
Cokie Roberts. *Source:* ABC
Photography Archives.

Senior news analyst Daniel Schorr with Scott Simon of *Weekend Edition Saturday.*
Source: Current newspaper.

Scott Simon takes a joy ride with Tom (right) and Ray (left) Magliozzi of *Car Talk*. *Source:* NPR.

Click and Clack demonstrate alternative uses of auto repair equipment. *Source:* Richard Howard.

Former news executive William
Buzenberg, now with Minnesota
Public Radio. *Source:* Minnesota
Public Radio, used by permission
of William Buzenberg. *Photo
Credit:* Eric Melzer.

Former NPR president Delano Lewis.
Source: Current newspaper.

NPR's president and CEO, Kevin Klose.
Source: Current newspaper.

Senior programming vice president Jay Kernis.
Source: Current newspaper.

All Things Considered cohost Melissa Block.
Source: NPR. *Photo Credit:* Steve Barrett.

Another *ATC* cohost, Michele Norris.
Source: NPR. *Photo Credit:* Jason Miccolo
Johnson.

Foreign correspondent Anne Garrels, one of the few Western journalists who reported live from Baghdad during the fall of Saddam Hussein. *Source:* Minnesota Public Radio. *Photo Credit:* Eric Melzer.

Terry Gross, host of NPR's *Fresh Air*. *Source:* Will Ryan.

Tavis Smiley, former host of a one-hour
newsmagazine program from NPR West, the
network's Southern California production center.
Source: Current newspaper.

Alex Chadwick, host of *Day to Day*.
Source: NPR. *Photo Credit:* Antony Nagelmann.

5 A CIVILIZED VOICE IN A NEW MEDIA ENVIRONMENT

In surveying the history of National Public Radio, one gets the sense that something has always been missing. From the very beginning, the U.S. public radio system had no unitary sense of mission; it is small wonder, then, that the two most important figures in NPR's early years struggled so hard to find *their* place in the broadcasting food chain. A vacuum in leadership developed following this period, prompting a hostile takeover at first and, later on, bringing the threat of financial ruin. In time, the network made amends with people who felt burned by its performance, whether funders, lawmakers, or station representatives; it also dabbled with a corporate model of administration—a clear break from a personality-driven management style that is better suited for social service agencies than for broadcasting companies. Sincere as the authors of these circumstances were, they were ultimately unable to develop a complete package of dynamic leadership and forward-looking strategy—one that would pass muster with the station managers and journalists who truly owned the enterprise.

NPR's board of directors swung for the fences when selecting a leader for the new millennium. This chapter begins with a look at the current chief executive, who brings strong journalistic chops, high-level management experience, and a belief that public radio is a vibrant and necessary part of the American democracy. It is easy to document Kevin Klose's achievements thus far in terms of increased financial support and the extension of "the NPR brand" through new programs, e-commerce, and other multimedia endeavors. That said, he will have to monitor the public broadcasting environment carefully for the challenges that will certainly follow from new developments in technology, funding, and listening patterns. Klose and his management team must protect the NPR brand in the face of competition from other players in the public radio field, collaborate with those same players when appropriate, and manage the migration of public radio content to technologies like Web and satellite radio. They must also work to keep NPR's current audience happy, while pondering whether groups of people who have not listened much in the past can be persuaded to do so now. Above all, they must handle each challenge in a way that maintains the noncommercial values of a radio service that millions of Americans have come to rely upon.

I conclude this chapter, and the book, with some observations based on my own experience of studying, and listening to, National Public Radio over the last ten years. The trials and triumphs of this network parallel certain developments in my own growth as a citizen and scholar. At one point in the journey, I came to realize that I had a lot more in common with the well-educated, socially conscious baby boomers who produce, and listen to, public radio than I had ever been willing to admit. All delusions of grandeur aside, the future success of NPR News depends on the ability of its leaders to better acknowledge the multiple pathways through which people like me receive and process information from the media as we try to fulfill the responsibilities that come with citizenship and democracy. By honoring the ways in which audiences increasingly monitor or sample vast stores of information—always looking for the nuggets they need—NPR can ensure its continued relevance for a growing number of Americans who prize quality news and cultural programming over the increasingly debased fare of commercial broadcasting.

PRESENT-DAY TRIUMPHS: STRENGTHENING THE NPR BRAND

In November 1998, NPR announced that Kevin Klose would be its new president and CEO. Klose had worked for twenty-five years at the *Washington Post*, including assignments as Moscow bureau chief and deputy national editor. He had been president of Radio Free Europe and Radio Liberty, and later headed the International Broadcasting Bureau, the U.S. government agency that runs the Voice of America. He had experience with large budgets and had also worked with Congress on broadcasting issues. To top it all off, radio had always held a special place in his heart. Klose's parents were radio producers and writers in the 1940s and once ran a live call-in program from their farmhouse in Red Hook, New York. At his initial news conference, he told reporters that "if I had been anywhere in my life and had the opportunity to lead NPR, I'd have taken it."[1]

From the standpoint of management theory, Klose took the reins at NPR at a very interesting time. Following a period of mismatched egos atop the company during the Lewis years, the board of directors had trouble distinguishing its responsibilities from those of the chief executive. Jack Mitchell, who then served on the board, claims that in years past, NPR's directors often became so involved in operational details that they failed to provide useful strategic guidance to management. Newspaper columnist Paul Delaney, a public member of the board, picked up on this dynamic as well; he questioned whether NPR could formulate its own unique vision for the future when station managers, the end-users of the network's programs, actually ran the show. He also wondered if Kevin Klose was prepared to explain the antics of this "dysfunctional family" to federal lawmakers and private corporations when asking them to cover part of its bills. Of course, many station managers saw things differently, and wanted the new president to "treat them as partners, not as problems or adversaries or simply customers."[2]

Given this interesting set of pressures, Klose began to spend a fair amount of time on the road, visiting station managers and trying, when possible, to respond quickly to their concerns. Klose wanted to expand NPR's audience by distributing its programs via satellite and Web radio, a plan that raised fears throughout the system. But the new president said he wanted to use these technologies in concert with local stations, to help them reach audiences that were presently not tuning in. He wanted to audition programs on Web and satellite radio, since many new shows are slow to gain acceptance from the ratings-conscious people who run public radio's terrestrial stations. He also wanted to create new programs for minority audiences, children, and college students and to do these things with content that was scrupulously nonpartisan in tone.[3]

Apart from his work with station managers, Klose would also need to monitor the audience for the network's existing programs. The number of people who tuned in to NPR programs each week had increased steadily in the years prior to his arrival, but some critics began to wonder if this growth was sustainable. In their view, NPR's news operation, built upon the narrative styles of *Morning Edition* and *All Things Considered*, was growing stale.[4] One such critic, journalist Brian Montopoli, felt the network had become a victim of its own success.

> If you listen to a lot of NPR, you realize how similar it all sounds: no mat-
> ter who is talking, or what they're talking about. There's a simple reason
> for the homogeneity: The drive time shows, the 800-pound gorillas of
> public radio, have become so successful that the sensibilities of their in-
> fluential hosts and correspondents have come to dominate all other NPR
> programming. Susan Stamberg, Nina Totenberg, Bob Edwards, Carl Kas-
> sel, and their peers have a tight grip on the sound of NPR.[5]

This sort of criticism, along with a lineup of relatively weak midday shows, argued strongly for the need to reevaluate NPR's programming strategies and to vest more responsibility in a single programming executive. This person would play a central role in creating new programs but would also take a more active role in quality control.

With all of these things in mind, Kevin Klose created the position of senior vice president for programming. The first person to fill it was Bill Davis, who formerly managed WUNC-FM at the University of North Carolina. Davis wanted to freshen-up NPR's programs by tapping the skills of producers and reporters scattered throughout the country, not just in Washington. A research project completed just prior to his arrival had also convinced him, and other top managers, to pay closer attention to audience feedback about *Morning Edition* and *All Things Considered*. In particular, listeners wanted NPR to curtail the length of stories that had no compelling appeal, reduce the number of times that stories might be repeated throughout the day, increase coverage of health and science issues, and balance the network's overall news coverage more evenly in terms of both geographic and political orientation. Unfortunately, family considerations prompted Davis to resign after less than one year on the job—well before he could address the results of this study. He soon resurfaced as president of Southern California Public Radio, a Pasadena-based news and information service founded by Minnesota Public Radio's parent company. The move made sense for Davis and his wife, who have roots in the Los Angeles area, but it left a vacuum at NPR where a new round of discussions about programming strategy was underway.[6]

Klose solved this problem in the spring of 2001 when he brought long time public radio producer Jay Kernis back into the fold as his new programming chief. Kernis had entered the radio business in 1969 as a sixteen-year-old high schooler, with a $1.75-per-hour job at New York City's WRVR-FM. There, he worked on promotional messages and documentaries and wrote news for Adam Clayton Powell III, who would later become news chief at NPR (Robert Siegel and Neal Conan also worked there at the time). After graduating from the University of Maryland in 1974, Kernis was hired as NPR's first full-time audio promotions coordinator. He began to attend the daily planning meetings for *All Things Considered* in order to gather information for the twenty-nine- and fifty-nine-second promos he would later have to write. Soon, he took on similar responsibilities for all of NPR's programs.[7]

It was a lot of work, but . . . it was a remarkable education in public radio for me, because I got to hear almost every show, or pieces of almost every show. So very early on, I was able to detect what was really good, and exciting and worthwhile, and what was sort of mediocre.[8]

Kernis went on to produce the weekly arts magazine *Voices in the Wind* and (as detailed in Chapter Three) was named Senior Producer of *Morning Edition* just prior to its debut in 1979. He later helped to develop and produce NPR's weekend news magazines and, in 1987, moved to CBS News to work on shows such as *60 Minutes*, *CBS This Morning*, and *Eye to Eye with Connie Chung*. All of these experiences, coupled with his abiding passion for public radio, made Kernis an ideal choice to head NPR's programming effort.[9]

Any grand designs that Kernis had for changing NPR's programming would have to wait for several months, as the network's normal mode of operation changed abruptly on the morning of September 11, 2001. The entire nation was caught off guard when two airplanes crashed into the World Trade Center, leaving two smoldering piles of rubble heaped against the backdrop of a magnificently sunny New York day. At first, NPR was slow in responding to the story. The first plane struck the towers shortly before nine A.M., and it took the news team the better part of an hour to begin unfolding its plan for crisis coverage. Since *Morning Edition* was then hosted by a single journalist, Bob Edwards, the network was tied that morning to a format that is not well suited for fast-breaking coverage. NPR also lacked an electronic means of preempting the broadcast of its programs to member stations in order to make way for important breaking news (a technology that other broadcast networks had used for more than twenty years).[10]

Edwards began to relay developments to listeners by breaking into a prerecorded story with brief mention of the incident in New York. His words were followed by a question-and-answer session with a local reporter, an eyewitness account about gaping holes in the two skyscrapers (and people leaping out of them), and a talk with correspondent Jacki Lyden, who watched the crisis unfold from her apartment in Brooklyn. Lyden filed reports for Edwards for more than two hours before getting an old bicycle out of her basement and pedaling to Manhattan to continue her work. By that time, Jay Kernis had decided that NPR would cover the crisis around the clock, and it did so for the next two-and-a-half days. *Morning Edition, Talk of the Nation*, and *All Things Considered* expanded their hours immediately, with Neal Conan and Scott Simon anchoring the network's programming through the night.[11] The quality and variety of reports that listeners could hear over the next several days was nothing short of amazing—a fact that my wife and I can attest to personally. Judy and I were flying to the Midwest to visit her ailing mother on the morning of September 11 and were in the air over Chicago when the first plane hit Manhattan. We became stranded in the Midwest for five days and then borrowed a twenty-five-year-old pickup truck so we could drive back to Maine. Before, during, and after that drive, we heard gripping reports about the human, economic, political, and military implications of the crisis. The things that impressed us most were the constant updates, a transatlantic talk program with hosts and listeners in the United States and Great Britain, overnight broadcasts from foreign capitals via the World Radio Network, and the somber, methodical recitation of the victims' names.

Reports we did not hear in real time—but are now available on the NPR Web site—informed listeners about the impact of the disaster on the New York Stock Exchange and the insurance and real estate industries, and the ways in which ministers across America planned to modify their sermons to fit the circumstances of a country under siege.[12] Moments that were especially poignant include an eyewitness account from inside the stairwells of one of the Trade Center towers, the running of a makeshift morgue in a Brooks Brothers storefront, and the tale of a Brooklyn firehouse that lost twelve of its members. Horrific as some of these stories were, NPR also offered tales of uncommon heroism, appropriate bits of poetry, and calm, reasoned dialogue by voices that were trustworthy and familiar—giving listeners a respite from the often-hysterical tone of the major cable and television networks. In all, NPR devoted 182 hours of programming to the tragedies and aftermath of September 11, "enabling audiences to be informed and to mourn and reflect upon those unsettled days." For these very reasons, the network won a coveted George Foster Peabody Award.[13]

After meeting the challenges of this crisis, Kernis returned to the task of freshening up *All Things Considered* and *Morning Edition*. Other public radio executives recall that NPR's initial coverage of important breaking news such as the 1993 Branch Davidian confrontation in Waco, Texas (and, later, the Columbia space shuttle disaster and the massive power blackout of

2003) was decidedly unimpressive. "When I got back to NPR," said Kernis, "it became clear that NPR's news presentation needed to change. It was no longer acceptable to be late on a story and call it analysis. It was no longer acceptable to miss a major story or not cover it in depth." Fixing these problems is a complicated matter, however, since the reverence of this network's journalists for the fruits of their own labor—and their deep suspicion of change—is legendary. If management wants better coverage of breaking news, fears begin to circulate that NPR might "go CNN" . . . with twenty-four-by-seven coverage of news headlines and a gradual abandonment of in-depth reporting. Kevin Klose is quick to point out that greater financial resources and new editorial leadership (more on these factors in a moment) now make it possible for the network to cover a larger volume of stories in a manner that is both faster and better. But back in 2001, when the latest makeover of NPR News got underway, no one was prepared for the adjustments that were necessary to get the ball rolling.[14]

In his first twenty-one months on the job, Kernis pulled off a series of changes that had major effects on the people who worked at NPR and, eventually, on station managers and listeners. In December 2001, the network announced that Linda Wertheimer would take on a new assignment as senior national correspondent after thirteen years as cohost of *All Things Considered*. Noah Adams took leave from the program three months later to write a book; when he returned, he, too, was reassigned to other duties. Some listeners protested these moves, but NPR management felt it was time to bring in fresh, new voices with different ideas—people who might liven up discussions with their guests and comment more frequently on the work of journalists and other experts who appear on the show. NPR veteran Melissa Block was the first person to join Robert Siegel on *ATC*; soon afterward, the network hired former ABC correspondent Michelle Norris to complete the program's triumvirate of rotating hosts. Later, in March 2004, NPR announced that Bob Edwards would leave *Morning Edition* to fill yet another senior correspondent position—a move that was made for similar reasons, and one that Edwards clearly opposed. This decision brought angry responses from thousands of devoted listeners who did not understand why anyone would make such changes to one of America's most popular radio programs. Many station managers were incensed by the timing of the move as well, since their on-air pledge drives were scheduled to begin shortly after the news became public. Among other things, management reportedly wanted this change because it favored a two-host setup that would improve coverage of breaking news. Some managers said Edwards fell out of *Morning Edition*'s future plans when he insisted on remaining as the program's only host—an assertion Edwards vigorously denies. In late July 2004, XM Satellite Radio announced that Edwards would join its stable of program hosts with a new morning interview show to debut in October. I say more about the implications of this move later in the chapter.[15]

In addition to the moves at NPR News, Kernis also began to revamp the network's cultural programming. This was a response to dissatisfaction throughout the public radio system with arts coverage that was "overly worshipful" and certain music programs that had simply failed to captivate many listeners. In February 2002, the *Washington Post* reported that an internal strategy paper authored by Kernis was generally critical of NPR's opera, jazz, and classical music programs; at the same time, a survey of station managers ascribed the highest value to—you guessed it—*Morning Edition* and *All Things Considered*. In April, NPR cut forty-seven cultural programming jobs, inviting those affected by the move to apply for thirty-one newly configured positions. Most of the cuts came from the staff of *Performance Today*, which, oddly enough, remains the single most popular classical music program on public radio. Interview and commentary segments were cut from this program, with the new version focusing mainly on recorded performances. Executive Vice President Kenneth Stern was quick to point out that in spite of these changes, NPR would now offer more hours of classical music programming each week than it had before. The following year, it added the Classical Public Radio Network (CPRN), a twenty-four-hour program stream created by broadcasters in Colorado and California, to its list of cultural offerings.[16]

Some critics felt the positive spin that NPR put on these changes was nothing more than window dressing, since the old format of *Performance Today* was gutted and the distribution of a twenty-four-by-seven stream of classical music was hardly a substitute for the creation of fresh content. But these moves kept NPR in the cultural programming business at a time when stations could well have switched to some of Public Radio International's music and entertainment shows. On balance, these programming adjustments—in both cultural and information programming—have yielded positive results for NPR. In March 2002, the network announced that it was reaching "the most listeners ever," with 19.5 million people tuning in each week. A year and a half later, that number rose to more than 20 million.[17]

EXTENDING THE NPR BRAND

Many listeners would abhor the term "branding" when used in connection with their favorite noncommercial medium. Yet managers at National Public Radio now speak of brands quite freely; after all, NPR is the number-one brand—or signpost, or symbol of quality—in the public radio industry. To understand the ways in which the network trades on the success of such programs as *Morning Edition* and *All Things Considered*, we first need to explore the terms "brand equity" and "brand loyalty." From the perspective of the consumer (or listener), a product (or program or network) has brand equity if it seems familiar and conjures up strong, favorable, or unique associations when its name is mentioned. Equity in public radio programs goes hand-in-hand with loyalty; since *ME* and *ATC* consistently meet the needs of public radio's core listeners, these people are likely to listen in the future. By crafting programs that appeal to the values and beliefs of its baby boom audience, NPR has been able to "make its brand a cause . . . and its cause a brand."[18]

If we can agree, for the sake of discussion, that NPR's featured programs have strong brand equity and foster a significant amount of loyalty, we can see why the network's managers try, in a variety of ways, to *extend* the brand. When new programs communicate a sense of "NPR-ness" to audience members, they take on a seemingly automatic sense of legitimacy—and strengthen listeners' good feelings about *ME* and *ATC* as well. We have already seen how this can happen when spin-off programs such as *Weekend All Things Considered* and *Weekend Edition* are introduced. This "halo effect" may also amplify the success of content partnerships with other like-minded organizations. A perfect case in point is *Time to Choose: A PBS/NPR Voter's Guide*, which aired just prior to the fall 2000 elections. *Time to Choose*, which originated from the studios of five public television stations, brought voters, journalists, scholars, commentators, and campaign surrogates together for a live, three-hour multimedia session. Other collaborations include the development of hourly NPR newscasts for PBS and the sharing of reporters on programs such as *NOW*.[19]

New content platforms, both high- and low-tech, are an important part of NPR's brand extension efforts. The network has made its signal audible in virtually every part of the world through NPR Worldwide, which utilizes two satellites, 140 radio stations, and other cable and shortwave outlets. Listeners in Europe, Africa, and the Middle East can also connect with NPR through WorldSpace, an international satellite radio provider. Back home, the network's own multimedia efforts began, in earnest, with the launch of npr.org in 1994. This Web site features a rich collection of links to news stories, special reports, individual program pages, and other information. By January 2001, it was attracting 350,000 visits and more than a million page views per week; by the summer of 2003, listeners were downloading between 5.5 and 7 million audio files each month. Npr.org also includes a live audio stream, a digital archive of past programs, a "station finder" search engine, and a link to *All Songs Considered*, a Web-only music program. The NPR Shop (shop.npr.org) went online in December 2000, offering music, books, and branded merchandise (such as *Morning Edition* latte mugs). Other multimedia projects include a deal with Audible.com to market downloadable program content; NPR Inflight, a news and information presentation for Delta Airlines passengers; and agreements to distribute NPR content to people who use cell phones and other wireless handsets.[20]

In 1999, the network created a corporate division called NPR2 to distribute programs via satellite to car stereos and other specially equipped receivers; that same year, it struck an exclusive distribution deal with CD Radio, which later changed its name to Sirius Satellite Radio. Confident about the prospects for NPR2, the network started two satellite program streams—NPR Now and NPR Talk—and hired Melinda Wittstock, a former ABC and BBC television anchor, to host a brand-new morning news program. But Wittstock left NPR several months later, and, soon afterward, NPR2 halted its experimental transmissions. Technical difficulties, the slow rollout of compatible receivers, and the hesitancy of consumers to spend money on a completely new technology all helped to dampen this project's debut.[21]

Since then, however, satellite receivers have become cheaper and more plentiful, and Sirius and its chief competitor, XM Satellite Radio, have wooed customers with new channels, multiyear subscription discounts, and other premium services. Having navigated its initial obstacles, National Public Radio has put both of its dedicated satellite radio streams back into service. NPR Now features a combination of news, information, and entertainment shows plus several programs from local stations and independent producers. NPR Talk was designed to carry some of the best call-in programs from around the public radio system; in general, though, its lineup represents a somewhat reshuffled version of the NPR Now schedule. (PRI programs its own "Public Radio Channel" on Sirius with an entirely different lineup of shows, while it and Minnesota Public Radio's parent firm have distribution agreements with XM.) Initially, NPR's satellite radio deal drew criticism from people who generally fell into two camps: First, some observers doubted whether subscription-based satellite radio would succeed in the United States and, if so, whether NPR had contracted with the right distribution company. Industry analysts now paint a positive picture of satellite radio's future; thus, there is reason to hope that NPR's affiliation with Sirius will pay off handsomely for the network and its member stations in years to come. Also, a group of nervous station managers suspects the network got into satellite radio with the intent of bypassing their own terrestrial stations and appropriating at least part of their current revenue streams in the process. Because of this fear, NPR has agreed, for now, to withhold *Morning Edition* and *All Things Considered* from both of its Sirius channels.[22]

NPR's low-tech, Earth-based news operation continues to strengthen the network's brand by expanding the number of places from which its journalists file reports. By early 2004, the network was gathering and producing the news from thirty-six locations around the world, with more bureaus slated to open over the next two years. Undoubtedly, NPR's excellent coverage of major international stories, such as the second Gulf War and the ongoing Middle East conflict, pleases the network's managers and listeners alike. NPR won another prestigious duPont–Columbia University Silver Baton Award for its reports on the most recent war, which included more than 250 hours of coverage over the first six months of 2003. Anne Garrels was one of only sixteen U.S. journalists who remained in Baghdad when the U.S. military began to attack that city on March 30. She painted a memorable picture for listeners of Saddam Hussein's distraught appearance on Iraqi television following the attack and of the deadly impact of an alleged coalition air strike on a marketplace in a poor Shiite neighborhood. NPR also won an Overseas Press Club award in 2002 for Mike Shuster's week-long series on the history of conflict between Israelis and Palestinians—from the first Zionist Congress in 1897 through the recent uprisings in the West Bank and Gaza.[23]

Closer to home, NPR maintains bureaus in New York, Cleveland, Atlanta, Los Angeles, and San Francisco and stations its reporters at seventeen other locations. The most significant domestic expansion has focused on the western United States—and rightfully so. Speaking in the summer of 2000, Kevin Klose noted that his network did not originate any programming from the west; an unacceptable situation, since nearly half of his audience, at the time, lived west of the Mississippi River. He was especially troubled that NPR's live coverage of the fall 1998 national elections had ended at 2:00 A.M. Eastern time, or 11:00 P.M. in the Pacific time zone.[24] Soon afterward, he promised a group of California broadcasters that he would make things right.

> We are going to cover the 2000 election till the damn thing ends. . . . We're going to hand off the show to the West coast. Scott [Simon is] going to be in LA. . . . As that election result sweeps across the country, we're going to be right there with it until it comes to an end. That seems to me to be what National Public Radio has to get to, if it deserves the term *national*.[25]

Within a few years, Klose would demonstrate an even greater commitment to his Western audience.

The groundwork for NPR West, the network's first major production center outside of Washington, D.C., was laid in the spring of 2002 with the purchase of a 25,000-square-foot building in Culver City, California, from the Welk Group—the holding company for the interests of the late bandleader Lawrence Welk. The price tag for NPR West came to nearly $13 million, with the network footing half of the bill and the other half coming from a group of charitable foundations. This new facility opened with great fanfare in November by producing special programming for *Morning Edition* and *Talk of the Nation* and by hosting NPR's live coverage of the 2002 congressional elections—anchored by Scott Simon and Neal Conan. It would soon become home to the *Tavis Smiley Show*, a new one-hour news magazine, and *Day to Day*, a midday show hosted by Alex Chadwick.[26]

Thus far, the payoff from NPR's brand extension efforts has been substantial. The network's total unrestricted revenues in 2002 came to more than $112 million, with more than $68 million in net assets on hand at the end of the fiscal year. NPR programs are now carried by more than 770 stations, compared to the paltry 78 stations that qualified for CPB support in 1970. About four million people tuned in to NPR programs each week in 1977; now, the audience is more than 20 million strong. This increase in audience size is quite impressive when compared to the stagnant or, in some cases, declining number of people who have listened to commercial radio over the past several years.[27]

The public radio industry has remained healthy overall, in spite of significant financial challenges in recent years. First, of all, trickle-down reductions in federal aid have translated into cutbacks in state and local government support for public broadcasting, along with budget cuts at state-sponsored universities that own public radio stations. The dot-com bust, the ensuing recession, and the deepening economic doldrums after September 11 also contributed to the industry's woes. Many listeners undoubtedly lost money in the stock market or, perhaps, even lost their jobs. Their cautious spending habits, in turn, prompted many of public radio's corporate sponsors to reduce the size of their underwriting budgets. NPR suffered a 40 percent drop in corporate underwriting revenue between 2000 and 2003; amazingly, though, the network's total revenues during that same period fell by only 6 percent. Steadily rising fee payments from NPR member stations helped make up some of the difference, but increased income from charitable donations also played an important role. For example, the John D. and Catherine T. MacArthur Foundation provided NPR with two major grants in 1999 and 2003, bringing the total amount of its contributions to more than $31 million. A portion of these grants was transferred directly to the NPR Endowment Fund for Excellence, a pool of money that generates interest income to support new initiatives.[28]

The size of this fund took a quantum leap in November 2003 with the news that Joan Kroc, heiress to the McDonald's hamburger fortune, had bequeathed more than $200 million to NPR—a move that prompted a round of fast food lunches in Washington and made one employee think, just for a moment, about changing her name to Susan *McStamberg*. The size of this gift (about $225 million, in the end) came as a surprise to everyone at NPR, though Kevin Klose had worked hard to cultivate it. Kroc, an avowed NPR News connoisseur, directed that $190 million be placed into the network's endowment fund. Some of the remaining money, along with interest income from the endowment, will be used to bolster the network's operating reserves and help NPR member stations offset increases in program fees. The most exciting impact of this gift, however, is the announcement of a $15 million program to expand news operations. Over the next three years, NPR will add forty-five reporters, expand the staffs of some key programs, and increase the number of its news bureaus. The network has also hired William Marimow, a Pulitzer Prize–winning journalist, to improve its national and investigative news coverage and will expand its menu of training opportunities for young journalists and those who work at local stations. Reflecting on this program of expansion, and the generous gift that made it possible, Kevin Klose mused that NPR has "always been a lean news group that does more with less." Now, he says, the network "will be able to do better with more." In spite of all the economic ups and downs it has faced over the years, NPR now enjoys greater financial stability than at any other time in its history.[29]

NPR's CHALLENGES—NOW AND IN THE FUTURE

As NPR and the wider public radio system look toward the future, they face a series of challenges—some that are already being addressed and others that promise to change the industry as profoundly as radio's shift from AM to FM or the development of NPR's business plan.

FINDING AND NURTURING STRONG LEADERS

We may begin with a challenge that has bedeviled the U.S. noncommercial radio system throughout its existence: the cultivation and training of dynamic leaders to serve at the national level. Chapters 2 and 3 of this book offer ample support for the argument made by Bill Kling of Minnesota Public Radio that the industry's first-generation managers were "the greatest ragtag collection of oddballs," people who succeeded almost in spite of themselves.

> We had a democracy made up of people who had a combination of talent, but no experience . . . on down through the people who were put in charge of the radio station because it fell under the audiovisual department of the university, where some professor who had tenure and couldn't teach any more had been assigned. And, literally, those people were the people who came to the meetings and who debated the policies. So [public radio] took 20 years to get where it should have gotten in two years.[30]

Operating without a unified purpose, or the need to meet some financial bottom line, public radio became vulnerable to the turf battles and other petty squabbles that characterized much of its existence from 1970 through 1983. The leadership vacuum of those early years allowed managers who were reared in the old *educational* radio system to keep doing what they did best: deciding amongst themselves which programs the audience *should want to hear*. In contrast, many of today's public radio leaders honed their craft at stations that had a healthy respect for listener preferences and for the reliable, systematic measurement of those preferences through audience research. When strategic discussions focus on hard evidence about "what works and what doesn't," the tendency to spend time fighting over irrelevant issues is greatly reduced. And when *that* happens, a station becomes better-equipped to serve its community of license.[31]

If the best managers from public radio's first two decades succeeded in spite of their colleagues, today's managers have stood very profitably on their shoulders, making noteworthy contributions in the process. Laura Walker, for example, is the first nonmayoral appointee to manage WNYC-AM and FM in New York. She has raised millions of dollars to purchase the stations' licenses from the city, establish the WNYC Endowment, expand live-concert programming, and improve the stations' news and documentary units. Mark Handley of New Hampshire Public Radio has added four new stations and three translators to his statewide network, built a sixteen-person news staff, and developed underwriting and membership programs that are among the best in the industry. Maxie Jackson has fostered a supportive environment for the training of student broadcasters at Morgan State University's WEAA-FM, maintained the high quality of the station's jazz programming, and, in the process, helped make WEAA the most popular public radio station in Baltimore. And in his first three years on the job, Stewart Vanderwilt of KUT-FM in Austin increased station revenues, decreased the length of on-air fund-raising drives, launched an award-winning news department, and revamped the station's Web site and digital-content systems. When it comes to filling senior leadership positions, these people, and other talented contemporaries, provide public radio's national organizations with a pool of highly qualified candidates to draw from. Industry-wide efforts to groom such people for greater responsibilities will continue to be very important.[32]

AUDIENCES, OLD AND NEW

An ongoing matter of debate in public radio is whether NPR needs to do anything about the fact that its audience is aging. About two-thirds of the people who listen during the average quarter-hour period of programming fall, roughly speaking, into the baby boom generation—those people born from 1946 through 1964. Though the network's audience has a median age of about forty-nine, with a fair number of twenty-five- to thirty-four-year-olds, the oldest of NPR's devoted boomers are, on average, fast approaching the age of sixty. There are two schools of thought about the way that NPR should address the graying of its audience—or, more precisely, the fear that its present-day programming may not hold much appeal for future listeners. One group of experts, including public radio's leading audience research-ers, argues that no drastic changes should be made; after all, the youngest boomers will probably still be listening in thirty years. If we subscribe to this viewpoint, NPR's primary task, for now, is to hold onto its present-day core audience, while freshening up the sound of its signature programs whenever possible. Some of the moves made by Jay Kernis and his programming team, especially the changes at *Morning Edition* and *All Things Considered*, provide evidence that this strategy has been taken seriously.[33]

The second way for NPR to ensure a healthy level of listening in the future is to improve the quality of programming it offers during periods of the day, and week, that are now comparatively unpopular. This includes a search for shows that will better captivate audiences during the midday hours, Monday through Friday. Research shows that people who tune in to *Morning Edition* often listen to radio during the middle of the day; how-ever, they generally turn away from *public* radio and return later in the af-ternoon, when *All Things Considered* comes on. Some people want to hear music while focusing on their jobs, and many apparently get their fix from commercial stations. Another problem in recent years has been the uneven appeal of NPR's midday news and information programs, including *Talk of the Nation*. The network has tried to remedy this situation by distributing, and even creating new shows. In early 2001, it began national distribution of *The Connection*, produced by WBUR-FM in Boston. Hosted by former CBC newsman Dick Gordon, it is billed as an energetic, edgy program that "links curious, engaged listeners to street-smart conversations." *Day to Day*, produced at NPR's new West Coast facility, debuted two years later. Some station managers are not holding their breaths while NPR tries to find a new midday hit. KCRW-FM in Santa Monica, for example, has taken one of its programs into national distribution with PRI. *To the Point*, hosted by former journalist Warren Olney, blends interviews, roundtable discussions, and commentary, utilizing, in the words of his staff, "one of the richest rolodexes in broadcasting." *Odyssey*, from Chicago Public Radio (also distributed by PRI), is a program about ideas that purposely moves beyond the topical repertoire of breaking news. Host Gretchen Helfrich "explores topics ranging from religion to risk; pacifism to post-national identity; and memory to Microsoft" and offers listeners a chance to interact with her guests toward the end of each hour. Perhaps these programs, or others now under development, will give some stations the lift they need in the middle of the day.[34]

Weekends, especially Saturday afternoons, are also a soft spot in the public radio schedule. NPR and PRI distribute a slate of Saturday morning shows that hold significant appeal for people who listen Monday through Friday: *Weekend Edition Saturday*, *Car Talk*, and *Michael Feldman's Whad'Ya Know*. Holding on to this audience throughout the day has been a difficult task, however, since early afternoon broadcasts from the Metropolitan Opera, demanded in many locations by small but extremely vocal groups of listeners, tend to alienate almost everyone else. People do come back, in large numbers, for Saturday evening broadcasts of *A Prairie Home Companion*; yet many station managers wish they had never gone away in the first place. NPR now offers two programs that could help local stations solve at least part of this problem. The first program, *Wait, Wait . . . Don't Tell Me!*, is an hour-long quiz show that lets audience members match wits with celebrities such as Roy Blount Jr., Paula Poundstone and P. J. O'Rourke. The second, *Says You!*, is another celebrity panel show produced by Boston's WGBH-FM. The *New York Times* describes this program of riddles, anagrams, and other puzzles as "hyperliterate, but not smug," and *Time* magazine claims that it "restores some intellectual equilibrium to the airwaves."[35]

Minnesota Public Radio and two sister organizations, *Marketplace* and Southern California Public Radio, have taken another path toward boosting weekend audiences by developing *Weekend America*. Its producers, led by former NPR newsman Jim Russell, say they have created a "radio companion" for listeners and a "tool kit" that will enable stations to "build their own strengthened, customized, branded local weekends." *WA*, which debuted October 9, 2004, contains segments that deal with news, culture, and "people talking to people," among many other things. In theory, stations can run it as a full program, a national show with local breaks, a "backbone" program whose elements can be preempted by local segments, or a series of excerpts dropped into a broadcast that is primarily local. If *Weekend America* takes off, it could be a boon for listeners and station managers alike.[36]

MIGRATING TO NEW AUDIO PLATFORMS

The terrestrial radio service we have known for generations will continue to be the primary means of delivering public radio programs for the next decade, if not longer. Nearly 225 million Americans listen to radio each week; that compares with a few million page visits per month to npr.org and a somewhat smaller number of subscribers to satellite radio. Given these figures, one can expect public broadcasters to focus first on capturing a bigger share of the traditional radio audience than they currently attract.

Some observers have been quick to dismiss the possible impact of streaming audio on present-day radio stations; because of this, the industry is not yet prepared for the day when most listeners will be willing to receive content through their computers. Right now, the main impediment to Web radio's greater success is the frustration many people have with slow, unreliable dial-up connections, and with the sometimes prohibitive cost of broadband service. Research has shown that as DSL and other broadband connections penetrate into more households and businesses, Web users become more likely to listen to audio files online. More people will appreciate the chance to hear their favorite programs asynchronously—time shifting their content in the same manner that cable and satellite TV viewers do with the digital recorders and hard drives that comprise the TiVo technology. The continued rollout of wireless broadband or "wi-fi" devices for both car and home will also whet the appetite of public radio listeners who want to experiment with streaming audio or downloadable versions of their favorite programs.[37]

As mentioned earlier, Kevin Klose and his management team see a bright future for satellite radio. Sirius, the company that carries two NPR channels, had about 260,000 subscribers at the end of 2003, a far cry from the two million people it will need to break even. But the growth rate for subscribers to domestic satellite radio increased rapidly over the course of the year, and Sirius had 400,000 people signed up by May of the following year (it now has more than 700,000 subscribers). The company expects to break even sometime in 2005, and progress toward that goal may come a bit faster now that Sirius has made its audio channels available to Dish Network satellite TV subscribers. The potential market for automotive installations of satellite radio receivers is also quite promising, given the huge number of registered vehicles in the United States. By tapping just 10 percent of this market, content providers such as Sirius and XM could reel in 20 million listeners or, roughly speaking, the same number of people who listened to NPR programs each week during the spring of 2003. Aside from its more traditional shows, the network may use satellite radio to incubate programs that are not yet viable for release on terrestrial stations. A stronger presence on this content platform may play an important role in NPR's future success, as XM has now created a channel called XM Public Radio through distribution deals with PRI, American Public Media, and other producers. XM's president and CEO, Hugh Panero, has expressed interest in carrying NPR programs, as well, when the network's exclusive deal with Sirius expires in 2007.[38]

Finally, NPR has covered its bases by investing in new forms of terrestrial radio. After a long, painful birthing process of more than a decade, digital-audio broadcasting, or HD radio, is ready to roll. Analogous to the development of digital television, HD radio will "allow listeners to enjoy CD-quality sound on FM and FM sound quality on AM radio." In early 2004, NPR announced that its Tomorrow (HD) Radio project had undergone successful field tests in four cities. Local stations that switch to this technology can broadcast two simultaneous program streams on the same frequency that could previously carry only one signal.[39] Mike Starling, NPR's vice president for engineering and operations, says HD radio will become a key part of the network's future.

> Having the ability to broadcast multiple channels using existing spectrum means that nonprofit radio stations can do more with what they already have, and [this] lessens the pressure to compete for scarce and expensive new frequencies. And listeners could be the biggest winners, with even more public radio and services at their fingertips.[40]

Public radio stations in Idaho, New Hampshire, and Oklahoma were among the first to adopt HD radio technology. Specially equipped receivers are now available for purchase, with up to a dozen electronics firms planning to enter the business.[41]

The first likely consequence of all these developments is that land-based stations will serve as "megaphones" for the newer technologies; that is, people who find public radio attractive will be able to listen to a wider selection of both mainstream and specialized content by switching to Web radio, satellite radio, or some other platform. As the cost of hooking up with these services comes down, the new technologies will approach coequal status with today's public radio system. Though all of these delivery systems are promising, it will take some time for them to blossom. The amount of money and human capital they would need in order to succeed will not be forthcoming until sizeable audiences, big enough to generate both pledge and underwriting income, are identified and reliably measured. Until that time, public radio's space in the world of new media will be used for recycling programs that already exist, testing new programs, and—as we shall see—offering listeners greater access to textual data and other specialized forms of content.[42]

MAINTAINING A HEALTHY BANK ACCOUNT WHILE STAYING TRUE TO MISSION

Despite Joan Kroc's large bequest, NPR and its member stations will continue to rely on funds from other private sources, including corporations that see great value in reaching well-educated (and well-heeled) listeners. Underwriting credits and pledge-week specials have been familiar fixtures on public radio and TV for many years, yet broadcasters and academics who want to preserve the noncommercial nature of the medium continue to monitor them closely. The most animated discussions have focused on PBS, whose televised pledge programs have sometimes crossed the line between the softer, image-based messages of underwriting and the kind of selling that is often seen on commercial TV. In recent years, critics have questioned the public TV system's collective wisdom in airing programs such as *How to Live Forever* by nutritionist Gary Null and the wrinkle-cure specials hosted by Yale dermatologist Nicholas Perricone. When PBS president Pat Mitchell complained about the frequent airing and promotional content of such programs, she was roundly criticized by development specialists at many local stations—people who wish to have every possible tool at their disposal when it comes to bringing in pledge dollars.[43]

Audience researcher Dave Giovannoni claims that if people watched the "infomercials" on PBS and the Home Shopping Network side-by-side, they would be hard pressed to tell the difference. Giovannoni is thankful that the underwriting messages heard on public radio seldom approach this level of salesmanship. He is concerned, however, that rising pressure for additional income is fueling an "incipient willingness . . . to adopt practices that erode [the industry's] core values and our listeners' trust." Public radio listeners want their news delivered in a manner that is comprehensive, socially aware, and cognizant of the potential ties between themselves and people in other parts of the world. Classical music lovers turn to public radio because of high quality performances, hosts who know the music (but keep their commentaries brief), and the aura of timeless inspiration that carries them away from the stresses of everyday life. Thus, even the perception of commercialism on public radio would offend many listeners.[44]

So far as public broadcasting is concerned, the Federal Communications Commission has long forbidden promotional "calls to action" regarding specific products, as well as comparative product descriptions, price information, and inducements to make a purchase. Imagine the shock that many broadcasters felt in early 2003 when NPR accepted a national underwriting spot that told listeners to ask their doctors about "Nexium, the purple pill, at purple pill dot com." Underwriting specialists across the country fired off angry e-mail messages when this blurb hit the airwaves, since their stations are contractually bound to broadcast all of the underwriting credits embedded in national programming—whether the copy is legal or not. Others were perturbed by a spot that urged listeners to "learn more about software for the agile business at Microsoft dot com," and another that reminded listeners to contact one of the companies that sponsors *A Prairie Home Companion*, whose employees "always love to hear from you . . . at 1-800-LAND'S END." Dave Giovannoni warns that if audiences feel the content they hear on public radio is somehow tied to the marketing plans of commercial sponsors, it will not take long to compromise the high level of trust the industry has built up over more than thirty years. He says the Corporation for Public Broadcasting can help preserve this trust by supporting high quality programs, maintaining the industry's core values, and ensuring the independence and integrity of public radio content. In the meantime, it is encouraging to know that each time a questionable underwriting message is proposed, development specialists from local stations—people imbued with the industry's public service values—will call it into question and, if possible, find a suitable alternative.[45]

A PERSONAL PUBLIC RADIO ODYSSEY

Earlier, I mentioned that the process of studying National Public Radio has been part of a wider personal journey for me. After several years of work in commercial radio news, I was eager to learn whether long-form journalism was still possible; whether some stations or networks still valued reporting that digs well beneath the headlines and helps people to become better citizens. Reading and writing about the history of NPR has taught me that there are hundreds of stations around the country whose journalists work precisely in this manner and whose efforts are genuinely appreciated. By examining public radio's roots in the university culture of the 1960s and 1970s, I have been able to locate myself among the ranks of the baby boomers who became part of the network's core audience. It has been helpful to look at the collective history of this group in political, economic, and social terms. Indeed, this multilayered history—of which I can present only a small portion—goes a long way toward explaining why NPR evolved in the particular way it did and why the people who work in public radio have formed such a tight bond with those who listen.

Before making a final analysis of NPR, I wish to resurrect, and then properly bury, a few ill-fitting theories about the role this network plays in American society. One widely circulated myth about NPR is that its journalists, and the tone if its news programs, are largely and irrevocably tied to the political Left. In Washington, conservative politicians have often described the network as a welfare program for liberals, one whose government support should be curtailed or ended altogether. This brand of criticism is often colorful and vehement.[46] It ranges from the notion that NPR is little more than a patronage mill for loyal Democrats, to the claim that *Morning Edition* and *All Things Considered* "amplify the voices of the militant feminists, the homosexual activists, the most radical elements of the civil rights and environmental movements and the trendy-left's intellectual and cultural elites."[47]

Some of the central figures at NPR during its first five years of existence take issue with the claim that its news coverage ever had, on balance, a left-of-center political tone. Certain stories have surely embodied an ideological slant that conservatives would find displeasing. But over time, NPR's coverage of politics, the economy, and other topics has drawn upon ideas from both the Right and Left—a sort of carefully balanced polemic, if you will. The swift repulsion of attacks on public broadcasting's government funds in the 1980s and 1990s showed, more than anything else, that so-called country club Republicans constitute a loyal part of the bipartisan coalition that wishes to maintain federal support. Even Newt Gingrich, who once tried to abolish public broadcasting, admits that he now supports NPR as both a fan and contributor. "Either it is a lot less on the Left," he says, "or I have mellowed."[48]

Another criticism, from the opposite side of the political spectrum, holds that NPR has wrongly abandoned an initial vision of serving "underserved" segments of the American populace, as defined by ethnicity, class, or sexual orientation. Much of this criticism comes from people who bemoan the fact that NPR did not develop along the same lines as Pacifica Radio, the radical, listener-supported network formed by a group of San Francisco Bay Area pacifists in the 1940s. Pacifica's founders were true innovators in terms of challenging the commercialized tone of mainstream news and information programs. But most of NPR's founding figures, including the author of its original mission statement, Bill Siemering, say their vision for public radio did not include the aura of social radicalism that Pacifica has always maintained.

> Even though NPR was born amidst a tumultuous political climate, I never thought of it as "alternative" such as Pacifica. Beginning at 5:00 ET, I wanted *ATC* to be the first and best electronic record of the day's events. . . . [NPR's] mission grew out of the shortcomings in the commercial sector as much as from a vision of new possibilities for creative uses for radio. . . . *We were radicals for radio* and more inclusive journalism, not for any political agenda [emphasis added].[49]

Many of NPR's leftist critics assume that public radio should promote the interests of society's disenfranchised groups, thereby helping them to gain a wider voice. Noble as this may seem, its logic fails on a number of counts. First, radio has become a *narrowcast* medium in which individual stations thrive by "superserving" discrete segments of the overall audience; it had to do this in order to survive the onslaught of television in the 1950s. If Pacifica is committed to serving disenfranchised groups, there is no logical compulsion for National Public Radio to do the same (NPR airs many stories and programs *about* these groups, phrased in a manner that speaks to the sensibilities of its core listeners). If NPR stations offered something for everyone in their daily schedules, their overall appeal for current listeners would drop markedly—the failure of the "checkerboard" programming strategies that were once common in commercial radio (and are still common in community radio) proves this point amply. Finally, there is no reliable evidence that disenfranchised Americans who do not like NPR have somehow become "underserved" or have stopped listening to radio altogether.[50]

While formulating my dissertation topic at the University of Wisconsin—a place, like many other universities, that is inhabited by lots of well-meaning liberals—I sensed that committed intellectuals on the Left felt NPR had become too timid, a place where journalists were no longer willing to see the world through progressive-colored glasses. Possessed of the best liberal intentions, I became a critic of the same stripe. At first, I thought I could use Bill Siemering's mission statement as a yardstick for measuring the network's performance, with respect to the federal government's historical charge that

American broadcasters should serve the "public interest, convenience, and necessity." This was a noble idea, but it simply did not work. Siemering's ideas are truly inspirational, but very few people who have worked at NPR over the years ever thought they could be implemented in a literal sense. Next, I toyed with the concept of *gentrification* and wrote that NPR, since the time of its discovery by American elites, had "changed from a boisterous row house of creative, sound intensive journalism into an elegant audio townhome" that was "too intellectually pricey for ordinary people." While momentarily impressed by my own words, I soon learned that this idea did not hold much water either. If we argue that something has become gentrified, we must prove that the neighborhood (or radio network) in question was downtrodden to begin with and that its inhabitants (or listeners) were "driven from their homes" by people of higher cultural or socioeconomic status. Since public radio had always been the province of America's most educated and discerning people, I was forced to put this line of reasoning out of its misery.[51]

Finally, I attempted to analyze a programming aesthetic that many others have wrestled with as well—a sense that public radio had caught a bad case of "yuppie angst." The most notable examples of this malady could be found on *A Prairie Home Companion* where, each Saturday evening, Garrison Keillor salves the emotional wounds of modern-day city dwellers who long to recapture the innocent wonders of their childhood. Since this is impossible (the good old days were, after all, seldom as good as we remember), these people do the next best thing by turning on the radio, or even traveling to St. Paul to hear Keillor tell stories about the mythical Lake Wobegon. With respect to NPR, I also became fascinated by the commentaries I heard on *All Things Considered* during the drive home from work, extended monologues by listeners who seemed to inhabit the same psychological neighborhood that Keillor's radio persona does. In one episode, a psychiatrist recalled how deeply troubled she became, years ago, when the mother of one of her childhood friends caught her in a fib. All these years later, we learn that the memory of this fabrication (one of many, unfortunately) has helped this woman to therapeutically reconstruct *the ideal father*: the sort of man that she, of course, never knew. Confused? How about this one: A woman lies awake at night, listening to the howls of mating coyotes in the distance, and is somehow reminded by these love-struck canids that menopause has now ended her childbearing days. As this observation tickled the membranes of the stereo speakers and worked its way into my ears, my brain froze in a momentary fit of incredulity, nearly causing the car to veer off the road and over a steep hillside.[52]

Trying desperately to validate a new, cutting-edge form of cultural critique, I shared these observations with my wife and with some trusted friends in the public radio industry. Their responses came as a total shock: in the eyes of my friends and loved ones, I, too, was an upscale baby boomer who longed for a sense of childlike innocence, feared the natural process of aging, and expressed these emotions through a unique and (hopefully) endearing set of personal quirks. Soon, I found myself in front of the computer taking an electronic version of VALS, the psychographic segmentation test that audience researchers have used to pinpoint the values and lifestyles of the people who listen to public radio most—a group that industry insiders know as "Actualizer-Fulfilleds." The primary, or Actualizer traits of this group include a take-charge attitude, an active lifestyle, and a sense of receptiveness to new ideas and technologies. The secondary, or Fulfilled traits include maturity, a need for personal reflection, and an affinity for order, knowledge, and responsibility.[53] Much to my horror, I realized that *I was an Actualizer-Fulfilled*, the very same kind of Volvo-driving, latte-sipping person I had begun to write about in condescending fashion. In short, *I was busted*; without even knowing it, I had taken on many of the characteristics that were common to NPR's core listeners.

Some Final Thoughts . . . and Humble Suggestions

Some people have criticized NPR News because it is made by people like me and for people like me. Former board member and *All Things Considered* producer Jack Mitchell once used the term "objective non-involvement" to describe the aesthetic feel of the news and information programs that are created through this symbiotic relationship.

> Which means lots of rational, relatively objective, fair and balanced inquiry and argument . . . all somewhat abstract and distant from reality, all engaged in by a very comfortable and moderately privileged group of people whose personal interests make them generally support the [political and economic] status quo, while they may see the need for change intellectually. Public radio and the broader academic world are liberal or progressive in their thinking, but are not radical. [The people who live in this world] are not about to jeopardize their own comfortable situations by fostering fundamental change.[54]

Some of these qualities are irksome to critics on the Left because they are not entirely compatible with the practice of social change. Media critic

Norman Solomon has complained that NPR's news and information content is "ideologically balanced between the views of 'the Gingriches and the Clintons.'" (In terms of political outlook, the network's listeners *are* almost evenly split between liberal, conservative, and middle-of-the-road positions.) Implicit in his statement is the fear that a clubby, Washington-centric brand of journalism will ignore stories that might offend politicians, board members, station managers, or people who contribute to public radio. NPR clearly does not approach stories from the fierce, radical viewpoint of Pacifica's Amy Goodman, but this should not be taken as evidence that it simply offers bland programs to an audience of political milquetoasts. People who make this sort of blanket indictment may have missed a long series of news reports that seriously questioned the veracity of U.S. intelligence prior to the latest war in Iraq. They also may have missed the large volume of political stories in which various experts criticized the policies of George W. Bush, or the investigative gems that Peter Overby has filed as the network's power, money and influence correspondent.[55]

The rational, fair, and balanced inquiry that is heard on NPR News is a function of the educational attainment of the network's journalists and listeners and the value systems these people have developed through higher education. Research demonstrates that possession of a college degree is the single best predictor of whether a person will listen to public radio. It should come as no surprise, then, that nearly 60 percent of NPR listeners have at least a bachelor's degree; in addition, these people are nearly four times more likely to have graduate degrees than the average American. Statistically speaking, the educational achievement of NPR listeners *causes* them to have many of the other characteristics that Jack Mitchell has described. Twenty-seven percent of all audience members hold professional jobs, compared to about 10 percent of adults in the general population; 16 percent describe their jobs as executive, administrative, or managerial. Household income for this group is substantial. About 17 percent of NPR families bring home between $75,000 and $100,000 per year, and nearly 13 percent make $150,000 or more. Image is certainly important to these Actualizer-Fulfilleds, but apparently not as a symbol of status or power. Rather, their possessions and recreational activities reflect "a cultivated taste for the finer things in life." NPR listeners are more likely than average to partake in just about any kind of leisure activity including exercise, sports, dining out, and attending live musical and theatrical performances. Nearly 70 percent purchased books over the year that culminated in NPR's 2003 audience survey. These people are also much more likely than average to read prestige publications such as the *Atlantic Monthly*, the *New Yorker*, the *New York Times*, *Architectural Digest*, and *Smithsonian*.[56]

In examining these traits, we must avoid the temptation to think that NPR listeners have somehow become "better than" or "unsympathetic toward" people from other socioeconomic groups. To the contrary, people who listen to the network's programs are distinctive for their high levels of political activity and community involvement. Sixty-five percent have voted in an election, compared to 48 percent of the overall adult population. They are about twice as likely as other people to take an active role in a local civic issue, work for a political party or candidate, write a letter to the editor, write or visit an elected official, address a public meeting, or take part in an environmental group or class. NPR listeners are also more likely than average to belong to unions, fraternal orders, church boards, charitable groups, and local government bodies.[57] Given these measures of civic and political involvement, it seems that NPR's most vociferous critics are not upset that the network (and its listeners) are biased in one way or another but rather that its news programs do not always tell them the things they want to hear. NPR, in the most basic terms, is a network founded by well-educated baby boomers and targeted toward listeners with similar demographic and psychographic profiles. It is not an example of audio welfare for liberals, nor is it some unfortunate mutation of the radical network that many on the Left had once mistaken it for. To borrow a favorite saying from Molly Ivins, the people who produce the network's signature programs have simply been "dancin' with the ones what brung 'em" for more than thirty years now.

One source of proof about NPR's positive impact on communities, and on the nation as a whole, is the volume of phone calls, letters, and email messages that listeners typically send to their favorite stations.[58] The tragedies of September 11, 2001, prompted an outpouring of appreciative comments, for example.

> My very sincere appreciation for the responsible coverage you are giving to this disaster. Restraint and compassion are both evident and go far in establishing a thoughtful response among all of us who feel so bewildered by such terrible acts of violence.

> I was so relieved when you resumed programming music after Tuesday's disaster. Good music has an enormous healing effect, yet I could maintain a contact with the news world with the hourly updates and appropriate interruptions when needful. Thank you for being there.

> I have always loved your station—intelligent, sensitive, humorous—but in the past few weeks it has been SUPERB. At a time when nothing makes sense, your station does.

Apart from disasters and other breaking news, listeners deeply appreciate the civilized voice that public radio beams into their homes, cars, and places of business.

> I consider myself to have received a college education from public radio. . . . You guys are wonderful. I began listening in the early [19]40s, and am so happy you've kept it going all these years!

> Last Monday on *Morning Edition* there was a piece using letters from [listeners] who had received generous gestures. My husband and I were so touched that we were both in tears. They said they had received more letters than they could share. Wouldn't it be great to share one every morning, to give us a little relief from all the bad news?

> Thank you for your wonderful programming. I have been a somewhat obsessive listener for many years. Last week I was home, ill, for two days . . . I had to FORCE myself to turn off the radio to get some rest. Every hour was super!

How can NPR continue to provide the best service possible for its current audience? Should the network court audiences that are younger and more demographically diverse, as the age of new media continues to unfold? If so, how? And what are the implications of these strategic questions for the continued use of our public airwaves in service of a well-informed citizenry and a healthy democracy? With these questions in mind, I offer three broad imperatives that NPR management might keep in mind when crafting a vision for the future.

THE NATURE OF NPR'S CONTENT, AUDIO AND OTHERWISE, SHOULD CHANGE IN ACCORDANCE WITH NEW MODELS OF CITIZENSHIP, MEDIA USE, AND DEMOCRACY

In pondering the changes that audience members will face over the next several years, Laura Walker, president and CEO of WNYC Radio in New York, writes about a prototypical listener named "Gene."

> It's Sunday afternoon. Gene . . . sits down with his Palm XXV, viewing an electronic menu of audio programs for the coming week. He decides that he'd like to hear the 7–8 a.m. hour of *Morning Edition* Monday through Thursday and *The World*'s music selections on Friday. . . . Given the volatility of the markets, he decides that hearing *Marketplace*,

which he normally doesn't listen to, is important this week. . . . [He also] selects the "illustrated" Webcast of the Orpheus Chamber Orchestra, featuring play-by-play by Peter Schickele and concert audio from several perspectives.[59]

For many of public radio older listeners, Gene's wish list would suggest a certain psychosis—a megalomaniacal belief that somehow, through one time-and-space-bound device, a person could coax all of this content to jump through cyberspace for playback at the precise hour of his or her choosing. But Walker and other farsighted public radio managers know that this scenario is no joke, that Gene will soon be able to use his Web browser, cell phone, MP3 player, and other devices to take control of his own media experience.

> He chooses the programs he is loyal to, arranges them in a way that allows him to listen to as much or as little as he desires, requests the audio in a no-fuss way from a provider, pays for it in some transparent fashion. . . . He no longer cares when something is scheduled to play on the radio; he only cares that he can find programs he likes or finds useful in a way that is most convenient.[60]

The manner in which Gene's local radio station responds to these new habits will be the deciding factor in whether he remains a loyal patron, or not.

The emerging picture of an avalanche of content available through a dizzying variety of digital platforms is undoubtedly troublesome for some public radio managers who, like PBS executives during the heyday of cable, once thought that no new technology could supplant their hold on audience members—and the underwriting revenue they made possible. In the near term, listeners may also become concerned that the digital revolution will add to the already vexing problem of information overload. Successful navigation of this terrain will depend on public radio's willingness to ask listeners what they really want from new media (especially in the news and information realm) and to create services that honor newly emerging patterns of citizenship.

Kevin Klose speaks freely, and at great length, of his desire that NPR maintain, even improve its current level of service to the American democracy by "assisting citizens in the act of citizenship." Minnesota Public Radio's Bill Kling also supports this position, speaking fondly of the typical in-depth political story from NPR News that compels people to phone, fax, and e-mail their congressmen in apoplectic fits. The ideal of the *informed citizen* that these statements imply has long been ingrained in the folklore of American politics, and of public radio as well. Media sociologist Michael Schudson says the idea that each voting citizen should be informed about parties, people, and issues, for the purpose of making rational choices in all relevant public matters, has been a staple of our national mythology from the 1880s to the present day. In the earliest years of this period, the great democratic reformers—the Mugwumps and Progressives—transformed the act of voting "from a social and public duty to a private right, from a social obligation to [one's political party] to a civic obligation or abstract loyalty, enforceable only by private conscience." Generally speaking, *informed citizens* were the first group of Americans for whom a fair amount of literacy, civic and otherwise, was considered to be a prerequisite for voting. This brand of citizenship has inspired much rhetorical admiration; however, its deployment in the real world had unforeseen consequences: voter turnout levels, often around 70 percent in the late nineteenth century, began to sag through the 1920s, when they dropped below 50 percent.[61]

In his book *The Good Citizen*, Schudson explains this seeming incongruity—of people who are supposedly much better informed, yet tend to shy away from the polls—with an analogy to the modern-day family camping trip.

It is fun to go camping and to be able to take care of one's every need for a few days in the mountains. But in everyday life most people are glad to turn on the stove rather than rub two sticks together and to buy a packaged chicken at the supermarket rather than trap a rabbit in the woods. We rely on the farms, milk processors, and government inspectors to see that milk is pasteurized, we do not do it ourselves; we trust in the metropolitan water supply to purify water, not our own chemicals. Why, then, in public life, do we expect people to be political backpackers?[62]

NPR, PRI, Minnesota Public Radio, and their affiliate stations offer plenty of supplies to America's "political backpackers" in the form of in-depth news magazines, documentaries, political forums, and other programs that delve far beneath the surface of any topic one cares to mention. This laudable service constitutes the best system of journalism in America, indeed, one of the finest in the world. But given all the recent concerns about political apathy in this country—at a time when our polity can scarcely afford it—one can legitimately wonder how much is too much when it comes to the delivery in-depth news and information.

How can NPR provide listeners with the basic informational tools necessary for civic competence, while minimizing the chance that they will become mired in a state of information overload? How can audience members learn exactly where to go for the specific information they need to cast an intelligent vote, or the perfect piece of music that would allow them to escape the stresses of the day? How can all of this happen in ways that transcend, when necessary, public radio's long-standing formulas for success—in particular, the content, cadence, and format of *Morning Edition* and *All Things Considered*? To sum it all up, how can NPR's content better reflect, in the words of Ira Glass, "the qualities that make people want to listen, that make people loyal to public radio, that make people pledge?" I suggest the network can best accomplish this by making a slow, steady change from its traditional role of service to the omnicompetent, informed citizen to a role that better serves people who Michael Schudson refers to as "monitorial citizens."[63]

America's public radio audience will always contain people who are insatiable news junkies. Any strategic plan for the industry's future would have to honor these people and, in fact, offer niche channels designed specifically for them. But Schudson contends that today's citizens—including public radio listeners, in my view—do not have to consume news programs with constant voracity in order to fulfill some ideal democratic function. Monitorial citizens can sample the information landscape for precisely the things they need.

> Picture parents watching small children at the community pool. They are not gathering information; they are keeping an eye on the scene. They look inactive, but they are poised for action if action is required. The monitorial citizen is not an absentee citizen but watchful, even while he or she is doing something else.[64]

Critics may find this brand of citizenship to be something less than proactive. Yet in our rights-based society—whose citizens can make their voices heard at the ballot box and in the courthouse—a monitorial strategy helps ensure that people can receive and act upon the key bits of information, on the most important issues, through the pathways that work best for them. This new model of citizenship is preferable, in my view, to the political life of the informed citizen, who gobbles up mountains of superficial data—yet often fails to make good use of it.[65]

NPR and Minnesota Public Radio have already migrated much of their content to the Internet—an ideal medium, perhaps, for those who prefer to monitor the news environment judiciously, lest they overindulge. Listeners often hear that "for more on the story," they can go to the Web site of their favorite network or station. While this is a positive development, NPR and other public broadcasters can use the Internet to enhance the listening experience in at least three more ways. First, they should offer audience members better access to *enabling information*—specific details about stories in the news that will help people take further action, if they so choose. This information might include contact numbers or addresses for government officials, expert sources or citizen groups, or the times and places of important public events. In most cases, the information would not be used to incite or mobilize people toward particular outcomes but rather to help them follow up on the information they hear on public radio—perhaps because of a preexisting disposition to act. Enabling information can also be used to steer people toward positive outcomes in issues of public health and safety. PRI's Stephen Salyer offers the example of a public radio story about Lyme disease that promotes Web-based content about diagnosis and treatment options.[66]

In examining this concept, let us briefly consider two Internet operations that are maintained, in full or in part, by public broadcasters. Npr.org, the Web site for National Public Radio, has a very busy home page that connects to a large volume of digitized content. This page has links for submitting story ideas or contacting NPR's ombudsman, and others that take the viewer to digital program streams, audio archives, and discussion groups. Aside from the first two links, however, one can find no easy pathways to information about actions he or she might take regarding a particular story. A second-level "News" page offers pathways to in-depth coverage of several top stories, but none of them actually leads to enabling information, as defined above. The only way a listener can get to this sort of content is by navigating expertly through multiple layers of Web pages. Take political coverage, for example. Surfers can find their way to an expanded menu of political items by clicking an obvious button located at the top-left portion of NPR's home page. The second-level "Politics and Society" page has links to a wealth of in-depth coverage, commentaries, and poll results, but there are no pathways to genuine *enabling* information. In the early fall of 2004, a second-level "Politics" page contained a rather inconspicuous link to "more" information about candidates. A third-level page featured excellent links to interviews and transcripts, analyses of each candidate's favorite "buzzwords," and the candidates' own Web sites. These *fourth-level* pages were the first ones in which the viewer encountered legitimate enabling information—material that suggested ways of becoming more involved, financially or otherwise, in a given candidate's campaign. Political Web surfers who desired this sort of information had to travel a more circuitous route to find it in the weeks leading up to the national election. Specifically, a second-level "News" page—not the "Politics and Society" page—contained an item titled "Contesting the Issues." A link from this item led to the Web sites of the Bush and Kerry campaigns, though it is arguable they were harder for interested viewers to find.

Another Web site offers a better model for helping citizens find their way to information that is both useful and actionable. "We the People: Wisconsin," billed as the nation's oldest civic-journalism project, is a partnership between Wisconsin Public Radio and Television, a local newspaper and commercial TV station, and a public relations firm. The right side of its home page (www.wtpeople.com) features five highly visible "program areas," with most of them containing obvious links to a "Resources" page. In the "Civics" program area, for example, the link to additional resources lands the surfer on a secondary page that describes eleven relevant agencies and provides links to each of their Web sites. There, one can find enabling information about civic education initiatives or, at the very least, a comprehensive overview of the things each agency does. Program areas on the "We the People: Wisconsin" home page also contain links to program descriptions, relevant articles and editorials, political candidate profiles, and other useful background information. Though NPR's third-level "Politics" page contains much more information than the corresponding pages of the "We the People" site, the editors and Web specialists who manage it might take note of the latter site's overall design, including its comparatively easier pathways to enabling information. The network could make significant strides in this area if, for example, it formed closer partnerships with political Web sites such as "By the People: Election 2004" and "Project Vote Smart." The former site (www.pbs.org/elections), sponsored by PBS, provides content from a wide variety of sources on American politics, including easy-to-use features that help individuals learn about races in their own states. "Project Vote Smart" (www.vote-smart.org) offers quick links to similar data, as well as information on voter registration, polling places, absentee ballots, and the public statements of U.S. Senators and governors. Another possible approach for NPR would be to promote a politically balanced collection of online "tool kits," such as the AFL-CIO's "Working Families Toolkit" and the NRA's "Institute for Legislative Action Center."[67]

Many public broadcasters are also rethinking the ways in which they serve their communities—in fact, refining their very definitions of the term "community." When analog radio was the only game in town, the communities it served were primarily geographic, including only those people who lived in the places covered by a station's broadcast signal. With the development of NPR's satellite interconnection system and, more recently, a collection of new digital-media outlets, audience members have a greater opportunity to form *communities of interest* that transcend geographic boundaries. In general, public broadcasters are off to a good start in their efforts to foster such communities. NPR runs about one hundred online discussion groups based on individual items in the news; it also offers comprehensive multimedia coverage of important stories, such as the continuing Arab-Israeli conflict. In the future, NPR might take note of community-building efforts in other parts of the public radio system. For example, Wisconsin Public Radio has joined several other organizations in operating "Portal Wisconsin" (www.portalwisconsin.org), a site that helps catalyze participation in cultural activities with an events calendar, online galleries, course listings, and moderated chats. Minnesota Public Radio has also developed several interesting initiatives. "Talking Volumes" provides an in-depth look at particular authors and books, with the goal of getting listeners all across the state to work through the same book, at the same time. Another interesting project included a series of reports and call-in shows that sought to identify the common goals and challenges of struggling farmers, as well as African Americans from a depressed neighborhood in North Minneapolis.[68]

Finally, public radio organizations should create more space for user-generated content. With all due respect to James Earl Jones, the phrase "if you build it, they will come" may no longer apply to the world of public media. "If they help build it, they will stay"[69] is a phrase that may better describe a successful strategy for keeping listeners happy. Joe Richman's Radio Diaries and David Isay's StoryCorps are two projects that could serve as templates for expanding the capability of listeners to share their own stories with a wider audience. Richman is a former public radio reporter who, since 1996, has been helping teenagers (and the occasional adult) use microphones and recorders to document their own lives. His "diarists" typically record more than thirty hours of raw tape over the course of a year, and help to edit that tape into fifteen-to-thirty-minute documentaries for rebroadcast on *All Things Considered*. StoryCorps is modeled after an oral history project conducted in the 1930s by the federal Works Progress Administration. Isay and his associates will use mobile studios and StoryBooths across the country in which a person can interview a friend, relative, or anyone else for the purpose of uncovering that person's life story. The resulting forty-minute recording is reproduced for the interviewer on CD, archived at the Library of Congress, and, with permission, made available for broadcast on WNYC Radio in New York. In the future, NPR might borrow the techniques used by StoryCorps and Radio Diaries to get even more people taking about their political, economic, and social views.[70]

In summary, NPR and other public radio organizations will need to become content aggregators and organizers—crossmedia portals through which citizens can take better control of their own media experiences. Maintaining the strength of today's successful programs, developing other content for public radio's core audience, and expanding the number of venues through which these services are offered will be critically important. In terms of terrestrial radio, the producers of *Marketplace* and *Weekend America* seem to be paying more attention than anyone else to the task of producing content that monitorial citizens will appreciate. Their approach to public radio may also give local program directors a good model for retooling their sagging midday schedules.

NPR SHOULD FOCUS ON ITS CORE AUDIENCE, INSTEAD OF AUDIENCES THAT ARE MERELY "DIFFERENT"

When considering the ways in which NPR might target its news and information programming in the future, it is important to first acknowledge the extraordinary success the network has already realized in terms of service to college-educated Americans. Nearly 60 percent of the network's listeners have at least a bachelor's degree, and the audience for its news programs resembles, in other demographic terms, the college-educated population of the United States. As NPR helps current listeners to become even better informed, it will naturally face the question of whether it also should do more to attract people who have generally not listened in the past. This is an interesting question since members of two such groups, Hispanics and African Americans, are now joining the public radio audience at a faster rate than people from any other ethnic groups. The Corporation for Public Broadcasting has thrown its support behind minority-focused projects in radio and new media, including African American– and Native American–owned radio stations, a satellite network for Native American programs, and Radio Bilingue, a nonprofit network controlled and managed by Latinos. Nobody would question the good intentions behind these projects or their importance to the local communities they serve. On a national scale, however, the effectiveness of programs that are targeted specifically to nonwhite audiences is a matter of debate. In the year 2000, more than 20 percent of the people who listened to NPR member stations were nonwhite or Spanish-speaking; however, programs and formats targeted specifically to these groups accounted for less than 3 percent of all public radio listening. Most nonwhite Americans who listen to NPR tune in for programs such as *Morn-*

ing Edition and *All Things Considered*—whose appeal to college-educated listeners transcends any cultural differences.[71]

The network's plans for serving people from different demographic groups, as defined by ethnicity and age, have unfolded most rapidly at its new production center, NPR West. *The Tavis Smiley Show*, the first major program produced in Los Angeles, premiered in January 2002. It is the product of a series of discussions between network executives and managers from African American public radio stations, who, among other things, had expressed a desire for more news and information programming. In particular, they wanted a new morning-drive-time program since many African American listeners were switching to commercial radio programs, such as ABC's *Tom Joyner Morning Show*. Soon after NPR approved the concept for a new program, Tavis Smiley, who had previously hosted a show for Black Entertainment Television, became available as a possible host. His new one-hour radio program was designed to blend hard news, interviews, and feature stories in a way that appealed to African Americans and, hopefully, to other listeners who sought fresh perspectives. Network executives originally thought it would air on weekday mornings, opposite one segment of *Morning Edition*.[72]

When NPR unveiled *The Tavis Smiley Show*, it created a barrage of program-related publicity that is perhaps unheard of since the debut of *Morning Edition* in 1979. Its press releases promoted exclusive interviews with the likes of Bill and Hillary Clinton, Condoleeza Rice, Kofi Annan, Bill Gates, Maya Angelou, and Oprah Winfrey. This program seemed to be the favorite venue for prominent African Americans to announce new developments in their lives. Most notably, Cornell West used *Tavis* to announce his controversial decision to leave Harvard University, and J. C. Watts appeared on the program just one hour after announcing his departure from Congress (both men became regular commentators). Apart from its focus on news and notables, the program regularly tackled issues of health and fitness, motivation and empowerment, and racial balance and harmony.[73]

On the surface, one might conclude that *Tavis* was an ideal fit for NPR's socially conscious audience. That said, the program aired on only 8 percent of NPR's member stations and attracts only 4 percent of the people who listen to the network's programs each week. Audience growth for *Tavis* leveled off considerably after the fall of 2002, which marked the end of its initial growth spurt. Only six stations used the program in morning drive time, as initially intended, while more than 80 percent of the stations that carried it did so during the midday and evening hours, when fewer people were listening. Despite claims to the contrary by NPR management, then, many of the network's current listeners have been less than eager to embrace a black Bob Edwards. In addition, many African American listeners never warmed up to a host who, by his own admission, had to cultivate "an authentically black, but not too black" on-air style.[74] Smiley left the show in late 2004.

How could the good intentions that underpinned the launch of *The Tavis Smiley Show* lead to such disappointing results? First of all, it bears emphasizing that the program was well hosted and produced, with interesting guests and compelling topics. The central problem with *Tavis* is that it was not being (and, perhaps, could not be) offered to listeners within an appropriate programming context. To maximize this program's chances for success, NPR would first need to create an alternative network with programs that appeal primarily to African American and, perhaps, Hispanic audiences. It would also need to hire and train more African American and Hispanic broadcasters who could, with all due respect to the current news team, craft this sort of programming in a manner that is both credible and authentic. Unfortunately, the NPR board, dominated as it is by station managers, would almost certainly reject any proposal for an alternative network; after all, why would these people tamper with an existing program service that works just fine for millions of present-day listeners? Even if member stations would agree to such an arrangement, the task of creating one or more new networks would be prohibitively expensive. In the words of one observer, NPR would need bequests from "many, many Joan Krocs" before even thinking about such a project.[75]

Day to Day, a midday news magazine, was the second new program to be launched from NPR West. If this program took off, it would provide a bonus for station managers who have been looking for ways to retain the many listeners who leave public radio sometime between *Morning Edition* and *All Things Considered*. *Day to Day* is built upon the premise that the audience gets much of the hard news it wants from the network's popular morning program; its purpose, then, is to explore "the ideas, beliefs, and behaviors" that underlie major stories in the news. The individual segments of this program are shorter than those on *ME* and *ATC*, since few people can listen to lengthy news stories during the work day. NPR also sought, and got, an agreement from Microsoft's *Slate* magazine to collaborate on the show, with *Slate* reporters becoming part of host Alex Chadwick's regular group of "radio buddies."[76]

NPR had originally hoped that some of *Slate*'s "younger, hipper audience" would find *Day to Day* attractive. But three weeks before the program's debut in July 2003, producer J. J. Sutherland said that its primary target audience would be "the standard NPR listener." Sutherland and his bosses may well be on the right track. To repeat a point I have made several times, a college education—and the mature set of values that comes with it—is the primary variable that predicts whether a person will listen to public radio. At last check, members of Generation X (those people born between 1965 and 1980) were going to college *and entering the public radio audience* at a faster rate than their baby boom counterparts did when they were younger. "Whenever people get around to going to college," says audience researcher Dave Giovannoni, "they'll learn about NPR as well." *Day to Day*'s producers are wise to target the program to the standard NPR listener instead of other listeners who are distinctive in terms of their age. In the fall of 2003, the first period for which Arbitron compiled ratings for *Day to Day*, this program's audience was significantly larger than that of *The Tavis Smiley Show*, which had, at that point, seen two years' worth of ratings reports.[77]

The startup of NPR West is clearly one of the most important initiatives the network has ever undertaken. This new production center offers NPR a perfect opportunity to counter the long-standing criticism that its programming focuses disproportionately on Washington, D.C., and the East Coast. Happily, the $225 million gift that Joan Kroc bestowed has accelerated a new round of strategic planning at NPR. The size of this gift will certainly help the network stay healthy and competitive for decades to come, but its top managers should continue to exercise great care when pondering what to do with the interest this money will accrue. Creating programs for new and diverse audiences is truly a noble goal, but NPR may not always be well suited for the job. A programming strategy that appeals to the network's traditional audience of well-educated citizens would transcend the differences that NPR might create if it designs specialized programming for people from other demographic groups.[78]

IN ALL THAT IT DOES, NPR SHOULD *SPARKLE*

A stiff, pedantic style of presentation was one of the hallmarks of the old educational broadcasting system, which prized book and newspaper content over that which was produced explicitly for radio and TV. People who get their information from printed sources typically develop more sophisticated stores of knowledge than their friends who partake only in broadcast programming; yet broadcasters who are content to simply read from print-style scripts can alienate listeners who expect more warmth and empathy from the human voice. The founders of our modern public broadcasting system wanted to create programs with depth and intelligence and to produce them in a style that was both conversational and compelling. Unfortunately, public television and radio have not always lived up to this promise. For example, critics have periodically complained, over the years, that NPR's newsmagazines are geared toward the "intellectualoid" or "raised pinky" crowds, or that the interviews heard on those same programs "don't crackle or excite the way they once did." In some ways, these comments still hit the mark today. Former NPR intern Brian Montopoli writes about the self-re-flexive nature of NPR, whose journalists seem to be keenly aware of the way the network is *supposed* to sound—like a "knowledgeable, but vaguely condescending college professor." By way of comparison, he says the news and information programs distributed by Public Radio International, both now and in the past, sound like "a bull session with particularly astute friends." One can understand this comment best by listening to *Marketplace*, where David Brown, Kai Ryssdal, and Tess Viegland employ a "cooler," more relaxed style that helps them explain complicated economic subjects in a thoroughly engaging manner.[79]

When thinking about "the NPR Sound of the Future," I concur with Ira Glass, the producer and host of *This American Life*, who calls for a sincere effort to help the industry's producers and reporters hone their craft. All too often, says Glass, today's noncommercial stations and networks produce formulaic stories that have no strong characters, emotional moments, or sense of humor. Listeners, after all, enjoy stories that convey "the sense that the reporter or host is our smart and interesting surrogate, pointing us to interesting and amusing ideas, to people and perspectives we've never heard of before."[80] Glass warns that public radio can ill afford to stagnate, to allow new stories to be told in the tired, old narrative style that audiences have grown accustomed to over the past thirty years. His comments seem quite appropriate these days, when the percentage of public radio donors who renew their pledges has been slipping and when Bob Edwards leads an all-star cast of public radio performers whose programs are now featured on XM Satellite Radio.[81]

The public radio industry has recognized the need for better training in all aspects of the business; still, there is much room for improvement, especially in terms of reporting, editing, and newsroom management. For example, more than one NPR staff member has been exasperated, over the years, by the degree to which the top stories on any given day have been culled from the front pages of prestige newspapers, especially the *New York Times*. The practice of "story selection by proxy" can ensure a program's relevance, to some extent, but it can also blind editors and reporters to the prospect of running other stories that may merit top billing. To be fair, this problem may be tied to the relatively small size of NPR's news staff, which, in the spring of 2004, was smaller than that of the *Baltimore Sun*. Top management wants to staff NPR "like a premier news organization," and it will use part of the interest income from the Joan Kroc bequest to expand its efforts in national, international, and investigative reporting.[82]

On another front, NPR has expended much effort, in recent years, to bring the writing and vocal skills of its young journalists up to the standards that one might expect of a network news operation. The network has also given dozens of interns the chance to produce a Web-only newsmagazine called *Intern Edition* and to partake in other training activities as part of its Next Generation radio initiative. But some of its veteran newscasters and reporters have yet to master the basics of broadcast newswriting and delivery. Some people may actually prefer newscasts in which the announcer seems to be reading a newspaper over the air—with past-tense leads and long dependent clauses—or in which sound bites are used simply for the sake of novelty, without adding any additional context or meaning to the story. But in most cases, this undisciplined sort of presentation interferes with the ability of listeners to comprehend the words they hear. Fortunately, NPR will use another portion of the Kroc bequest to invest in the further training of its journalists, in workshops for station-based reporters and in fellowships that will help groom young people for jobs in the industry. Every journalist would benefit from training that suggests new ways to develop story concepts, to interview and write better, and to inject more humor, emotion, and surprising moments into his or her work. To its credit, NPR continues to freshen-up the sound of *Morning Edition* and *All Things Considered*. New voices like the ones on *Marketplace* (and, perhaps, *Weekend America*) will also help ensure that the industry's audience continues to grow, even in the face of stiff competition from satellite radio, Internet radio, downloadable audio, and other new technologies.[83]

Writing about National Public Radio from the standpoint of a benevolent critic has been an odd thing for me to do over the last ten years. This is especially the case since I, like Kevin Klose and others at NPR, have an abiding love for radio and the possibilities it holds for entertaining and captivating us and for making our country a better place to live. In 1989, when I left commercial radio to "find a better way," I had only a vague idea that NPR would hold so much promise for engaging the highest sensibilities of its audience—through in-depth news coverage that is just not available anywhere else and through cultural programs that touch us, make us laugh, and show us the ways in which our fellow human beings push the boundaries of creativity. I have criticized some aspects of NPR's operations, to be sure—not in a whining or gratuitous manner but rather from the standpoint of a journalist and scholar who has taken the time to learn what others think about the network (including dozens of people who have worked there). Some people will chafe at my comments but others, I trust, will receive them in the spirit I intend. A person who cares about the well-being of any enterprise must give an honest account of the things he sees, without regret. I hope the insights I have gained, and the suggestions I have made, will somehow be useful to the many people who have helped me along the way.

It is true that the U.S. public radio system literally had to invent itself, since its origins lie in a pile of money from the federal government, not in any widespread sense of need among the stations that constituted the old educational radio system. The industry would undoubtedly have made more progress in its first thirty years if not for a combination of funding problems, unseasoned leadership, turf battles, and federal lawmakers who thought the ever-dwindling amount of money they provided should give them far more influence over the system than they have ever actually enjoyed. It is a tribute to the people who work in this industry that they have addressed many of these difficulties in a satisfactory manner. The proof of the pudding is the more than 20 million Americans who listen to NPR programs each and every week, and more than 27 million who listen to public radio in toto. Some say this audience will double over the next ten years: hence the need for today's leaders to take special care of the resources they have been given. Public radio cannot offer something for everyone; indeed, the vast majority of Americans do not listen at all. Still, its practitioners have a responsibility to expose as many people as they can to the kind of radio that, in the words of their most eloquent champion, celebrates the human experience, regards the differences among men with respect and joy, and encourages among our citizens a sense of active, constructive participation.

NOTES

1. A LYCEUM OF THE AIRWAVES

1. William Kling, interview by author, tape recording, transcript, St. Paul, Minn., 26 July 1995, 23, in Michael McCauley NPR Oral History Collection, National Public Broadcasting Archives, Hornbake Library, University of Maryland, College Park (hereafter cited as NPR OHC).

2. Kevin Klose, interview by author, tape recording, transcript, Washington, D.C., 7 June 2000, NPR OHC.

3. Throughout the book, I will use the term "baby boom" to refer to the large cohort of Americans who were born in the post–World War II era, from 1946 through 1964.

4. *Thirtysomething* aired on ABC from 1987 through 1991. For an excellent analysis of the cultural dynamics this program portrayed, see Robin Andersen, *Consumer Culture and TV Programming* (Boulder, Colo.: Westview, 1995), 118–45.

5. William Chafe, *The Unfinished Journey: America Since World War II*, 2d ed. (New York: Oxford University Press, 1991), 431.

6. Accuracy In Media, "No Tears for National Public Radio," *AIM Report* (July-A 1983): 1. For other conservative critiques of NPR, and of public radio in general, see David Horowitz and Laurence Jarvik, eds., *Public Broadcasting and the Public Trust* (Los Angeles: Second Thought Books, 1995), esp. 173–213; Fred Barnes, "All Things Distorted: The Trouble with NPR," *New Republic* 27 October 1986, 17–19; Benjamin Hart, "Ventriloquist Journalism at National Public Radio," *Policy Review* (Spring 1984): 75–78;

and Joseph P. Duggan, "Some Things Considered: Does 'Public Radio'—Financed by the Taxpayers—Represent the Citizenry's Views?" *The Alternative: An American Spectator* (March 1977): 13–15. For examples of liberal critique, see Ralph Engelman, *Public Radio and Television in America: A Political History* (Thousand Oaks, Calif.: Sage, 1995), 83–132; Sam Husseini, "The Broken Promise of Public Radio, *The Humanist* (September/October 1994): 29; Charlotte Ryan, "A Study of National Public Radio," *EXTRA!* (April/May 1993): 18–21, 26; Nicols Fox, "NPR Grows Up," *Washington Journalism Review* (September 1991): 30–36; Bruce Porter, "Has Success Spoiled NPR? Becoming Part of the Establishment Can Have Its Drawbacks," *Columbia Journalism Review* (September/October 1990): 26–32; Marc Fisher, "The Soul of a News Machine," *Washington Post Magazine*, 22 October 1989, 16–23, 37–42; and Laurence Zuckerman, "Has Success Spoiled NPR?" *Mother Jones* (June/July 1987): 32–39, 44–45.

7. Carnegie Commission on Educational Television, *Public Television: A Program for Action* (New York: Bantam, 1967), 13. Ironically, the first Carnegie Commission was concerned solely with designing a more uplifting variety of *television*. Chapter 2 contains details about the radio advocates who fought for their place in The Public Broadcasting Act of 1967.

8. For a detailed description of some of NPR's most memorable programs, see Mary Collins, *National Public Radio: The Cast of Characters* (Washington, D.C.: Seven Locks Press, 1993).

9. McKinsey&Company, "Public Service Broadcasters Around the World: A McKinsey Report for the BBC," January 1999, 29; Jerold M. Starr, "Public Television in the Digital Age: Town Hall or Cyber Mall?" in *Public Broadcasting and the Public Interest*, ed. Michael P. McCauley, Eric E. Peterson, B. Lee Artz, and DeeDee Halleck (Armonk, N.Y.: M. E. Sharpe, 2003), 247; "About the BBC: BBC Channels," BBC Web site, http://www.bbc.co.uk/info/channels; Tom Thomas, Station Resource Group, e-mail message to author, 24 February 2004; and Andrew Crisell, review of *Public Broadcasting and the Public Interest*, ed. Michael P. McCauley, Eric E. Peterson, B. Lee Artz, and DeeDee Halleck, *European Journal of Communication* 18, no. 4 (December 2003): 550.

10. Thomas, e-mail, 24 February 2004.

11. See Douglas J. Bennet, "Bennet Reviews His First Year as NPR Head," *Public Broadcasting Report*, 16 November 1984, 4–6; Jack Mitchell, e-mail message to author, 26 April 2001; Christopher H. Sterling and John M. Kittross, *Stay Tuned: A Concise History of American Broadcasting*, 2d ed. (Belmont, Calif.: Wadsworth, 1990), 563–66; Jeff Rosenberg, interview by author, tape recording, transcript, Washington, D.C., 14 August 1995, NPR OHC.

12. Rosenberg, interview, NPR OHC.

2. THE VERY FIRST BRUSH STROKES

1. Erik Barnouw, *A Tower in Babel* (New York: Oxford University Press, 1966), 4; Harold E. Hill, *The National Association of Educational Broadcasters: A History* (Urbana, Ill.: National Association of Educational Broadcasters, 1954), 9; Harold D. Lasswell, "Educational Broadcasters as Social Scientists," *Quarterly of Film, Radio, and Television* 7 (1952): 157–62.

2. C.M. Jansky Jr., "The Beginnings of Radio Broadcasting," transcript of remarks presented at the WHA Family Dinner at the University of Wisconsin, 24 November 1958, Pamphlet Collection, State Historical Society of Wisconsin; University of Wisconsin Extension, "The University of Wisconsin Extension Telecommunications Center," promotional pamphlet, 1972, 4; Barnouw, *A Tower in Babel*, 61; Robert J. Blakely, *To Serve the Public Interest: Educational Broadcasting in the United States* (Syracuse, N.Y.: Syracuse University Press, 1979), 5; Werner J. Severin, "Commercial vs. Non-Commercial Radio During Broadcasting's Early Years," *Journal of Broadcasting* 22, no. 4 (1978): 492–93; John Witherspoon and Roselle Kovitz, *A History of Public Broadcasting*, with an update by Robert K. Avery and Alan G. Stavitsky (1987; Washington, D.C.: Current, 2000), 6, 58.

3. Witherspoon and Kovitz, *A History*, 6.

4. Ibid., 59.

5. Barnouw, *A Tower in Babel*, 122.

6. Blakely, *To Serve*, 54–55; Severin, "Commercial vs. Non-Commercial," 496–502; Christopher H. Sterling and John M. Kittross, *Stay Tuned: A Concise History of American Broadcasting*, 2d ed. (Belmont, Calif.: Wadsworth, 1990), 110–11.

7. *Radio Act of 1912*, Public Law 264, 62nd Congress, 13 August 1912; see Frank J. Kahn, ed., *Documents of American Broadcasting*, 4th ed. (Englewood Cliffs, N.J.: Prentice-Hall, 1984), 14–22; Susan J. Douglas, *Inventing American Broadcasting, 1899–1922* (Baltimore, Md.: Johns Hopkins University Press, 1987), 234–39; Blakely, *To Serve*, 42–45.

8. *Radio Act of 1927*, Public Law 632, 69th Congress, 2nd sess., 23 February 1927, in Kahn, *Documents*, 40–56; U.S. Federal Radio Commission, "FRC Interpretation of the Public Interest: Statement Made by the Commission on August 23, 1928, Relative to Public Interest, Convenience, or Necessity," in Kahn, *Documents*, 57–62; James C. Foust, *Big Voices of the Air: The Battle Over Clear Channel Radio* (Ames: Iowa State University Press, 2000), 3; Robert W. McChesney, *Telecommunications, Mass Media, and Democracy: The Battle for the Control of U.S. Broadcasting, 1928–1935* (New York: Oxford University Press, 1993), 24–25, 28, 267–68.

9. McChesney, *Telecommunications*, 244; Witherspoon and Kovitz, *A History*, 10; Blakely, *To Serve*, 69–73, 79; George H. Gibson, *Public Broadcasting: The Role of the Federal Government, 1912–76* (New York: Praeger, 1977), 33–39; Hill, *The National Association of Educational Broadcasters*, 22–23; Leslie F. Smith, John W. Wright II, and David H. Ostroff, *Perspectives on Radio and Television: Telecommunication in the United States*, 4th ed. (Mahwah, N.J.: Lawrence Erlbaum, 1998), 62.

10. Hill, *National Association of Educational Broadcasters*, 20; Sterling and Kittross, *Stay Tuned*, 159; Blakely *To Serve*, 9–12, 102–06; Witherspoon and Kovitz, *A History*, 11–13.

11. James Michael Haney, "A History of the Merger of National Public Radio and the Association of Public Radio Stations" (Ph.D. diss., University of Iowa, 1981), 26–27; Blakely, *To Serve*, 127–28; Donald R. Quayle, interview by author, tape recording, transcript, Bethesda, Md., 14 August 1995, Michael McCauley NPR Oral History Collection, National Public Broadcasting Archives, Hornbake Library, University of Maryland, College Park (hereafter cited as NPR OHC).

NETRC later changed its name to NET, a reflection of the Ford Foundation's decision to focus on educational television. Some readers will remember NET as a precursor network, of sorts, to PBS.

12. Quayle, interview, NPR OHC.

13. Sterling and Kittross, *Stay Tuned*, 388; John E. Burke, *An Historical-Analytical Study of the Legislative and Political Origins of the Public Broadcasting Act of 1967* (New York: Arno Press, 1979), 56, 83–94; Blakely, *To Serve*, 143–44; Robert M. Pepper, "The Formation of the Public Broadcasting Service" (Ph.D. diss., University of Wisconsin–Madison, 1975), 34.

14. Witherspoon and Kovitz *A History*, 14; Mark Gelfand, "Ralph Lowell—Brief Life of a 'Grand Bostonian': 1890–1978," *Harvard Magazine* Web site, May–June 1997, http://www.harvard-magazine.com/issues/mj97/vita.html.

15. Blakely, *To Serve*, 168; Pepper, "The Formation of the Public Broadcasting Service," 50; News Release, Carnegie Corporation of New York, 10 November 1965, Carnegie Commission on Educational Television Papers, 1963–1967, State Historical Society of Wisconsin, Madison, Wis. (hereafter cited as CC MSS), B6, F2.

16. Adapted from the report of the Carnegie Commission on Educational Television, *Public Television: A Program for Action* (New York: Bantam, 1967), 4–9.

17. Joseph Cahalan, "Congress, Mass Communications, and Public Policy—the Public Broadcasting Act of 1967" (Ph.D. diss., New York University, 1971), 111, 172, 224–28; U.S. Senate Committee on Commerce, 90th Cong., 1st sess., *The Public Television Act of 1967: Hearings Before the Subcommittee on Communications of the Committee on Commerce* (Washington, D.C.: Government Printing Office, 1967), 455–60, 465–79, 484–85, 489–93; "An Alternate ETV Plan From NAB," *Broadcasting*, 10 April 1967, 85.

18. Cahalan, "Congress, Mass Communications, and Public Policy," 111.

19. Ibid., 112–113; Burke, *An Historical-Analytical Study*, 145–51, 155.

20. Cahalan, "Congress, Mass Communications, and Public Policy," 321–25; U.S. Senate, *Report on the Public Broadcasting Act of 1967*, 90th Cong., 1st sess., 11 May 1967, S. Rept. 222 (Washington, D.C.: Government Printing Office, 1967); U.S. Congress, *House of Representatives Report on the Public Broadcasting Act of 1967*, 90th Cong., 1st sess., 21 August 1967, H. Rept. 572 (Washington: Government Printing Office, 1967); U.S. Congress, *House of Representatives Conference Report on the Public Broadcasting Act of 1967*, 90th Cong., 1st sess., 18 October 1967, H. Rept. 794 (Washington: Government Printing Office, 1967).

21. Jerrold Sandler, interview with Burt Harrison, 24 October 1978, Silver Springs Md., tape recording, transcript, Public Radio Oral History Project, Burt Harrison Papers, National Public Broadcasting Archives, College Park, Md.

22. Ibid.

23. Blakely, *To Serve*, 149.

24. Herman W. Land Associates, "The Hidden Medium: A Status Report on Educational Radio in the United States," prepared for National Educational Radio (New York, 1967), iv, I-1.

25. Herman Land, telephone interview by author, tape recording, transcript, 3 November 1995, NPR OHC; Sandler, interview.

26. Sandler, interview.

27. Ibid.

28. Corporation for Public Broadcasting. "From Wasteland to Oasis: A Quarter Century of Sterling Programming," CPB 1991 Annual Report (Washington, D.C.: Corpora-

tion for Public Broadcasting, 1991), 5; Hartford N. Gunn Jr., "A Model for A National Public Radio System," WHA Radio and Television Papers, University of Wisconsin, Madison, Wis. (cited hereafter as WHA MSS), 2, General Correspondence, B7, F6.

29. Samuel Holt, interview by author, tape recording, transcript, Washington, D.C., 23 August 1995, NPR OHC; Samuel Holt, *The Public Radio Study* (New York: Corporation for Public Broadcasting, 1969), 96–124.

30. Haney, "A History of the Merger of National Public Radio," 52–57; capsule biography of Albert Hulsen, "Curriculum Vitae," *NAEB Newsletter* 34, no. 7 (August 1969): 3; Albert Hulsen, telephone interview by author, tape recording, transcript, 2 August 1995, NPR OHC; "Corporation for Public Broadcasting; Grants and Awards, July 1, 1968 to June 30, 1969," and "Summary of Corporation for Public Broadcasting Authorizations and Appropriations, Fiscal Years 1969–1997"—both documents provided by Sarah Sloan, NPR Budget Director, 5 April 1996; Cahalan, "Congress, Mass Communications, and Public Policy," 101–2.

31. "Hulsen Announces Details For National Public Radio," *NAEB Newsletter* 34, no. 11 (Convention Issue 1969): 13; Haney, "A History of the Merger of National Public Radio," 58; Joseph Brady Kirkish, "A Descriptive History of America's First National Public Radio Network: National Public Radio, 1970 to 1974" (Ph.D. diss., University of Michigan, 1980), 15, 19–20; Elizabeth Young, Minutes, NPR Board Meeting, Milwaukee, Wis., 19 December 1969, 4, National Public Broadcasting Archives, University of Maryland, College Park, Md. (cited hereafter as NPBA MSS), Elizabeth Young Papers, F10; Young, Minutes, NPR Board Meeting, San Diego, California, 20–22 January, 1970, NPBA MSS, Elizabeth Young Papers, F10.

32. William H. Siemering, "National Public Radio Purposes," NPBA MSS, Elizabeth Young Papers, B1, F11, 1.

33. Young, Minutes, NPR Board meeting, San Diego, NPBA MSS.

34. Jack Mitchell, interview by author, tape recording, transcript, Madison, Wisconsin, 28 April 1995 (hereafter cited as Mitchell-1), NPR OHC; Karl Schmidt, interview by author, tape recording, transcript, Madison, Wisconsin, 11 July 1995, NPR OHC; William Kling, interview by author, tape recording, transcript, St. Paul, Minnesota, 26 July 1995, NPR OHC.

35. Haney "A History of the Merger of National Public Radio," 69; Richard Estell to John Witherspoon, 26 March 1970, NPBA MSS, Elizabeth Young Papers, F7; Lee Frischknecht, telephone interview by author, tape recording, transcript, 4 August 1995, NPR OHC; John Witherspoon, telephone interview by author, tape recording, transcript (unedited), 1 August 1995, NPR OHC. Quayle, interview, NPR OHC; Mitchell-1, NPR OHC; Donald Quayle, telephone conversation with author, 7 December 1995; Richard Estell to John Witherspoon, 23 April 1970, NPBA MSS, Elizabeth Young Papers, F7.

36. Bob Mott, interview with Burt Harrison, tape recording, transcript, San Diego, Calif., 24 July 1978, 20, Public Radio Oral History Project, Burt Harrison Papers, National Public Broadcasting Archives, College Park, Md.; "Biography of Donald Quayle," Archives of the Corporation for Public Broadcasting, Donald R. Quayle Files, National Public Broadcasting Archives Web site, http://www.lib.umd.edu/NPBA/papers/quayle.html5; Kling, NPR OHC; Donald Quayle, telephone conversation, 7 December 1995;

Quayle, NPR OHC; Elizabeth Young, telephone interview by author, tape recording, transcript (unedited), 22 September 1995, NPR OHC; Mitchell-1, NPR OHC.

37. Mitchell-1, NPR OHC; Schmidt, NPR OHC; William Siemering, interview by author, tape recording, transcript, Philadelphia, Penn., 8 August 1995, NPR OHC.

38. Schmidt, NPR OHC; Mitchell-1, NPR OHC.

39. Hulsen, NPR OHC.

40. Mitchell-1, NPR OHC; Young, NPR OHC (unedited).

41. Cleve Mathews, telephone interview by author, tape recording, transcript, 30 June 1995, NPR OHC.

42. Jeff Rosenberg, interview by author, tape recording, transcript, Washington, D.C., 14 August, 1995, NPR OHC.

43. Mary Collins, *National Public Radio: The Cast of Characters* (Washington, D.C.: Seven Locks Press, 1993), 18, 26; Susan Stamberg, interview by author, tape recording, transcript, Washington, D.C., 16 August 1995, NPR OHC (unedited); Linda Wertheimer, interview by author, tape recording, transcript, Washington, D.C., 18 August 1995, NPR OHC (unedited); Siemering, NPR OHC.

44. Mitchell-1, NPR OHC.

45. Siemering, NPR OHC.

46. Ibid.; Kirkish, "A Descriptive History of America's First National Public Radio Network," 74.

47. Rosenberg, NPR OHC.

48. Siemering, NPR OHC.

49. Lee Frischknecht, interview by Burt Harrison, tape recording, transcript, Washington, D.C., 2 November 1978, Public Radio Oral History Project, Burt Harrison Papers; Quayle, NPR OHC; William Siemering, telephone conversation with author, 26 May 2004.

50. Telephone conversations with Siemering and Cleve Mathews, 12 March 1996; Kirkish "A Descriptive History of America's First National Public Radio Network," 84–89.

51. Collins, *National Public Radio*, 25; Haney dissertation, 82; Schmidt, quoted in Kirkish, "A Descriptive History of America's First National Public Radio Network," 92; Rosenberg, NPR OHC.

52. "Natl. Public Radio Making With Lotsa Cross-U.S. Live Feeds From Capital," *Variety*, 6 October 1971, 38; "Summary of Corporation for Public Broadcasting Authorizations" and "Corporation for Public Broadcasting; Fiscal Year 1971," both documents provided by Sarah Sloan, NPR Budget Director, 5 April 1996; Kirkish "A Descriptive History of America's First National Public Radio Network," 38–45, 87–92; "Nat'l Public Radio's $3 mil CPB Grant," *Variety*, 6 October 1971, 47; Tom Warnock, "An Early Look at *All Things Considered*," *Educational Broadcasting Review* 5, no. 3 (June 1971): 61–62.

53. Rosenberg, NPR OHC.

54. Susan Stamberg to Cleve Mathews, 15 May 1971, quoted in Kirkish, A Descriptive History of America's First National Public Radio Network," 98–101.

55. Stamberg, NPR OHC (unedited).

56. Young, NPR OHC.

57. Schmidt, NPR OHC.

58. Mitchell-1, NPR OHC.

59. Deborah Emanatian, telephone interview by author, tape recording, transcript, 13 October 1995, NPR OHC; Rosenberg, NPR OHC; Siemering, NPR OHC.

60. Quayle, NPR OHC; Mitchell-1, NPR OHC; Kirkish, "A Descriptive History of America's First National Public Radio Network," 103–5.

61. Siemering, NPR OHC.

62. Ibid., 15; Rosenberg, NPR OHC.

63. Quayle, NPR OHC; Biography of Donald Quayle, Archives of the Corporation for Public Broadcasting; Stamberg, NPR OHC (unedited); Mitchell-1, NPR OHC.

64. Siemering, NPR OHC; Pew Fellowships in the Arts: 1997 Panelists, Pew Fellowship for the Arts Web site, http://www.pewarts.org/papantext.html.

65. Mitchell-1, NPR OHC.

66. Kling, NPR OHC.

67. Rosenberg, NPR OHC.

68. Quayle, NPR OHC.

69. Les Brown, *Keeping Your Eye on Television* (New York: Pilgrim Press, 1979), 32–35; Brown, *Television: The Business Behind the Box* (New York: Harcourt Brace Jovanovich, 1971), 323–24; James L. Baughman, *Television's Guardians: The FCC and the Politics of Programming, 1958–1967* (Knoxville: University of Tennessee Press, 1985), 160–65.

70. For a general treatment of Nixon's dislike for public broadcasting, see David M. Stone, *Nixon and the Politics of Public Television* (New York: Garland, 1985). For details about Antonin Scalia's involvement in public broadcasting policy, see Stone, 69, and NAEB, "Nixon Administration Public Broadcasting Papers: Summary of 1971," available from Public Broadcasting PolicyBase Web site, http://www.current.org/pbpb/nixon/nixon71. html. For a brief, focused treatment of the circumstances surrounding the 1972 veto, see Michael P. McCauley, "From the Margins to the Mainstream: The History of National Public Radio" (Ph.D. diss., University of Wisconsin–Madison, 1997), 123–33.

71. Witherspoon and Kovitz, *A History*, 78–81; Ralph Engelman, *Public Radio and Television in America: A Political History* (Thousand Oaks, Calif.: Sage, 1995), 188–189; Dan Odenwald, "Knocking God's Party: Moyers, PBS hear from Angry Conservatives," *Current*, 2 December 2002, 18; Steve Behrens, "How Reform Can Minimize Politics in Presidential Appointments," *Current*, 8 September 1997, available from http://www.current.org/cpb/cpb716a.html; "CPB Board: Eight Appointees and One Vacancy," *Current*, 19 January 2004, 21; David Stewart, "The Emperor's Old Clothes: It's Time to Retailor CPB," *Current*, 8 September 1997, available from http://www.current.org/cpb/cpb716s.html; and Marc Gunther, "At NPR, All Things Reconsidered," *New York Times*, 13 August 1995; "Public Ranks Pubcasting High in Value per Dollar," *Current*, 19 June 1995, available from http://www.current.org/mo511p.html.

72. Kirkish, "A Descriptive History of America's First National Public Radio Network," 140–54.

3. THE PRICE OF FAME

1. Lee Frischknecht, telephone interview by author, 4 August 1995, tape recording, transcript, Michael McCauley NPR Oral History Collection, National Public Broadcasting Archives, Hornbake Library, University of Maryland, College Park (hereafter cited

as NPR OHC); Jeff Rosenberg, interview by author, 14 August 1995, tape recording, transcript, Washington, D.C., NPR OHC; Deborah Emanation, telephone interview by author, 13 October 1995, tape recording, transcript, NPR OHC; James Russell to Lee Frischknecht, 19 March 1976, National Public Broadcasting Archives, University of Maryland, College Park, Md. (cited hereafter as NPBA MSS), Lee Frischknecht Papers, B3, F1; Albert Hulsen, telephone interview by author, 2 August 1995, tape recording, transcript, NPR OHC.

2. Joseph Gwathmey, telephone interview by author, 3 August 1995, tape recording, transcript, NPR OHC; "Public Radio Sees Brighter Days," *Broadcasting*, 18 March 1974, 48; Corporation for Public Broadcasting, "1973 Annual Report" (Washington: CPB, 1973), 19; Kenneth John Garry, "The History of National Public Radio: 1974–1977" (Ph.D. diss., Southern Illinois University at Carbondale, 1982), 44–45; Joseph Brady Kirkish, "A Descriptive History of America's First National Public Radio Network: National Public Radio, 1970 to 1974" (Ph.D. diss., University of Michigan, 1980), 163; Linda Wertheimer, interview by author, 18 August 1995, tape recording, transcript (unedited), Washington, D.C., NPR OHC; "NPR Salary Schedule," NPBA MSS, NPR Board Minutes, 16–17 November 1974; Frischknecht, NPR OHC.

3. Garry, "The History of National Public Radio," 136–137; "Natl. Public Radio Streamlines; Info and Program Revamp," *Variety*, 12 February 1975, 68; Robert Zelnick, interview by author, 11 August 1995, tape recording, transcript (unedited), Great Falls, Va., NPR OHC; Jack Mitchell, interview by author, tape recording, transcript, Madison, Wis., 19 September 1995 (hereafter cited as Mitchell-2), NPR OHC; James Russell, telephone interview by author, 3 August 1995, tape recording, transcript, NPR OHC.

4. Mitchell-2, NPR OHC.

5. Frischknecht to Quayle, 5 November 1973; Henry Loomis to Hartford Gunn, 7 October 1974; Frischknecht to NPR Board, 13 September 1974; Gunn to Loomis, 19 September 1974; Michael Hobbs to Ralph Rogers, Memorandum on "Radio-TV Split" Decision, 11 October 1974; and Ron Bornstein to Scott Miller and Michael Hobbs, 3 April 1975—all contained in NPBA MSS, Lee Frischknecht Papers, B1, F5; and Mitchell-2, NPR OHC.

6. Emanation, NPR OHC. Steve Symonds, telephone interview by author, tape recording, transcript (unedited), 24 September 1995, NPR OHC; Gwathmey, NPR OHC; Russell, NPR OHC.

7. Susan Stamberg, interview by author, tape recording, transcript (unedited), Washington, D.C., 16 August 1995, NPR OHC.

8. Symonds (unedited), NPR OHC.

9. Emanation, NPR OHC; Minutes, NPR Board of Directors Executive Committee Meeting, April, 1976, 14–15, NPBA MSS, NPR Board Minutes; Frischknecht, NPR OHC; "National Public Radio: An Assessment of Internal Communication/Organization and Actions Required to Move Toward Fulfillment of the Mission," NPBA MSS, Lee Frischknecht Papers, B2, F8.

10. Zelnick (unedited), NPR OHC.

11. For more on this volatile situation, see the documents contained in NPBA MSS, Lee Frischknecht Papers, B3, F1.

12. Mitchell-2, NPR OHC; Emanation, NPR OHC.

13. Jack Mitchell, e-mail message to author, 21 March, 2001; Mitchell, Stamberg, and Zel-nick to Frischknecht, undated; Mitchell to Frischknecht, Memorandum of concern, re: Frischknecht's plan to reorganize, 23 April 1976; Mitchell to Presley Holmes, 29 April 1976; "NPR Programming Division Restructured," NPR press release, 6 May 1976—all contained in NPBA MSS, Lee Frischknecht Papers, B3, F1. See also Mitchell-2, NPR OHC. Another source claims that Bob Zelnick was fired; see Russell, NPR OHC.

14. Mitchell-2, NPR OHC.

15. Patricia W. Francisco, "The Life and Times of MPR," *Minnesota Monthly* 21, no. 1 (January 1987): 50–51.

16. Karl Schmidt, interview by author, tape recording, transcript, Washington D.C., 11 July 1995, NPR OHC; "Two Decades at a Glance," *Minnesota Monthly* 21, no. 1 (January 1987): 58; Francisco, "The Life and Times," 52.

17. Jack Mitchell, interview by author, 28 April 1995, tape recording, transcript, Madison, Wis. (hereafter cited as Mitchell-1), NPR OHC; William Kling, interview by author, tape recording, transcript, St. Paul, Minn., 26 July 1995, NPR OHC.

18. "Public-Radio Audience: Lean but Loyal," *Broadcasting*, 8 May 1972, 41, 44; "Two Decades," 59.

19. "Two Decades," 59.

20. Kling, NPR OHC.

21. James Michael Haney, "A History of the Merger of National Public Radio and the Association of Public Radio Stations" (Ph.D. diss., University of Iowa, 1981), 110–11; Ronald Bornstein, interview by author, tape recording, transcript, Madison, Wis., 3 July 1995, NPR OHC.

22. Kling, NPR OHC; Joe Welling, telephone interview by author, tape recording, transcript (unedited), 10 July 1995, NPR OHC; Haney, "A History of the Merger of National Public Radio and the Association of Public Radio Stations," 120–24, 206–10; Susan Harmon, telephone interview by author, tape recording, transcript, NPR OHC; Samuel Holt, "Organizational Options for Public Radio," NPBA MSS, Lee Frischknecht Papers, B2, F2; "Propose a Merger of Pub Radio Orgs," *Variety*, 17 March 1976, 56; "Public Radio Ponders Switch to One National Organization," *Broadcasting*, 22 March 1976, 81.

Details of the request to remove Frischknecht and his top aides come from an off-the-record statement by one of the author's interview sources, a person who played a central role in the NPR-APRS negotiations. Evidence that the leaders of APRS were thinking about this sort of action may be found in Harmon, NPR OHC; and Mitchell-2, NPR OHC. Details about the takeover of NPR may be found in Frischknecht, NPR OHC; Bornstein, NPR OHC; and Gwathmey, NPR OHC.

23. Minutes, NPR Board of Directors Meeting, New Orleans, La., 4 May 1977, NPBA MSS; NPR Board of Directors, Board Minutes, Resolution for Merger of APRS into NPR," 4 March 1977, NPBA MSS; "Natl. Public Radio Merges With APRS," *Variety*, 11 May 1977, 462; Robert K. Avery and Robert Pepper, "The Politics of Public Broadcasting at the National Level, 1973–1978," CC2 MSS, B25, F1, 62–65; Edward Elson, telephone interview by author, tape recording, transcript, 2 November 1995, NPR OHC.

24. Elson, NPR OHC, 7.

25. Frank Mankiewicz, interview by author, tape recording, transcript, Washington, D.C., 14 August 1995, NPR OHC.

26. Kling, NPR OHC; Hulsen, NPR OHC; Elson, NPR OHC.

27. Mankiewicz, NPR OHC.

28. Neal Conan, interview by author, tape recording, transcript, Washington, D.C., 15 August 1995, NPR OHC; Siegel, NPR OHC; Stamberg (unedited), NPR OHC; Wertheimer (unedited), NPR OHC.

29. Conan, NPR OHC.

30. Russell, NPR OHC.

31. Russell, NPR OHC.

32. "Radio is Pro Tem in the Senate for Canal Debates," *Broadcasting*, 13 February 1978, 27–28; Suzanne Perry, "All Things Considered, She's Glad She's in Radio," *Minneapolis Star*, 10 February 1979, National Public Radio: Sample Press Clippings, 1979; "Public Radio Perks Up," *Newsweek*, 12 March 1979, 84.

33. NPR, NPR Annual Report, FY 1981 (Washington, D.C.: National Public Radio.), 2; Mankiewicz, NPR OHC; William Tucker, "Public Radio Comes to Market," *Fortune*, 18 October 1982, 205; Kling, NPR OHC; Scott Simon, interview by author, tape recording, transcript, Washington, D.C., 23 August 1995, NPR OHC; Sanford Ungar, interview by author, tape recording, transcript (unedited), Washington, D.C., 16 August, 1995, NPR OHC.

34. Siegel, NPR OHC.

35. Robert Goldfarb, e-mail message to author, 28 July 2002; Robert Goldfarb, telephone conversation with author, 30 July 2002; Kling, NPR OHC; Susan Harmon, telephone interview by author, tape recording, transcript, 20 September 1995, NPR OHC; Schmidt, NPR OHC; William Buzenberg, interview by author, tape recording, transcript, St. Paul, Minn., 28 May 1998, NPR OHC.

36. Francisco, "The Life and Times," 52–56; "What's Up at Lake Wobegon?" *Time*, 9 November 1981, 95; George P. Wilson, "Laid-Back Variety Hit Emerging," *Current*, 11 August 1980, 3; "Two Decades at a Glance," 59–60.

37. Tucker, "Public Radio Comes to Market," 205; George Bailey and Tom Church, "Public Radio and the Ratings," *Public Telecommunications Review* (November/December 1979): 47; "Two Decades," 59; Corporation for Public Broadcasting, *A Report to the People: Twenty Years of Your National Commitment to Public Broadcaasting, 1967–1987* (Washington, D.C.: Corporation for Public Broadcasting, 1987), 4–5; Jack Mitchell, e-mail message to author, 26 April 2001; Kling, NPR OHC.

38. Kling, NPR OHC.

39. Ibid., 16.

40. "Two Decades," 59.

41. Siegel, NPR OHC; Frischknecht, NPR OHC, 7; Joseph McLellan and Michael Kernan, "National Public Radio's Voice at the Top: Frank Mankiewicz Says He's There 'to Raise Less Corn and More Hell,'" *Washington Post*, 26 February 1979; Jack Mitchell, personal correspondence with author.

42. Barbara Cochran, interview by author, tape recording, transcript, Washington, D.C., 15 August 1995, NPR OHC. See also Jim Russell to Sam Holt and Joe Gwathmey, Memorandum regarding the "Morning Program," NPBA MSS, NPR Executive Of-

fice, Frank Mankiewicz Files, B4, F9; and L. Carol Christopher, "The King of Coffee Talk," *Quill*, December 1999.

43. "All the News Fit to Hear," *Time*, 27 August 1979, 70; Christopher, "The King"; Jay Kernis, telephone interview by author, tape recording, transcript, 8 September 2003, NPR OHC.

44. Kernis, NPR OHC; Mary Collins, *National Public Radio: The Cast of Characters* (Washington, D.C.: Seven Locks Press, 1993), 43, 45; Christopher, "The King;" Kernis, NPR OHC; and Frank Ahrens, "Healthy, Wealthy, Wise: NPR's Early Riser Celebrates Its Twentieth," *Washington Post*, 14 May 1999.

45. Kernis, NPR OHC; Ahrens, "Healthy, Wealthy;" Kernis, e-mail messages to author, 15 June 2004 and 24 June 2004; Stamberg, NPR OHC; Cochran, NPR OHC; Conan, NPR OHC; and "Morning Numbers," *Broadcasting*, 10 November 1980, 60. See also "'Morning Edition' Hits the Airwaves," *Broadcasting*, 12 November 1979, 80–81; and Irvin Molotsky, "Public Radio Tried 'Morning Edition,'" *New York Times*, 25 November 1979, National Public Radio: Sample Press Clippings, 1979; Frank Mankiewicz, Memorandum to NPR Station Managers, "Occasional Monthly Report No. 3," 12 November 1979; Mankiewicz to NPR Board, "Weekly Report No. 20," 16 November 1979; and Mankiewicz to Board, "Weekly Report No. 21," 3 December 1979—all in NPBA MSS, NPR Executive Office, Thomas Warnock Files, "Frank's Weekly Reports."

46. Simon, NPR OHC.

47. Jack Mitchell, interview by author, tape recording, transcript, Madison, Wis., 25 September 1995, NPR OHC (hereafter cited as Mitchell-3); "What's Up at Lake Wobegon?" 9; Eric Scigliano, "Prairie Fire: Garrison Keillor and the Radio Robber Barons," *The Seattle Weekly*, 8 September 1982; Don Clark, "New Public Radio Network Spurs Dispute," *St. Paul Sunday Pioneer Press*, 26 September 1982; and Joe Saltzman, "Radio Wars," *Performing Arts Magazine*, November 1982—all from NPBA MSS, NPR Executive Office, Frank Mankiewicz Files, B3, F5.

48. Mankiewicz, NPR OHC.

49. Clark, "New Public Radio Network"; Mankiewicz, NPR OHC; David Colker, "The New Competition in Non-commercial Radio," *Los Angeles Herald Examiner*, 13 September 1982; Wallace Smith to Frank Mankiewicz, 31 December 1980, NPBA MSS, NPR Executive Office, Frank Mankiewicz Files, B2, F11; Smith to Sam Holt, 5 January 1981, NPBA MSS, NPR Executive Office, Frank Mankiewicz Files, B2, F17; Smith to Mankiewicz, 11 March 1982 and Mankiewicz to Smith, 8 April 1982 (undelivered)— both from NPBA MSS, NPR Executive Office, Frank Mankiewicz Files, B2, F13.

50. Kling, NPR OHC.

51. Ibid.

52. Ibid.

53. Public Radio International no longer distributes *A Prairie Home Companion*. This change, effective 1 July 2004, is a result of Minnesota Public Radio's decision to coordinate all of its national production and distribution efforts in-house. See Mike Janssen, "MPR To Rep Its Own Shows, Mainstays of PRI Catalog," *Current*, 23 February 2004, 1, 10; and Nicole Garrison-Sprenger, "MPR to Drop PRI for Program Distribution," *The Minneapolis–St. Paul Business Journal*, 9 February 2004, available from http://www.bizjournals.com/twincities/stories/2004/02/09/daily27.html.

54. James Brown, "Five NPR Stations Form New Group," *Los Angeles Times*, 14 March 1982, NPBA MSS, NPR Executive Office, Frank Mankiewicz Files, B2, F13; Brooke Gladstone, "APRA: 'Willing to Exist in a Market,'" *Current*, 30 April 1982, 1.
55. Mitchell-3, NPR OHC; Mankiewicz, NPR OHC; Joe Saltzman, "Radio Wars," 25; Rosenberg, NPR OHC.
56. Mankiewicz to NPR Board, "Weekly Report No. 38," NPBA MSS, NPR Executive Office, Tom Warnock Files, Frank's Weekly Reports [to Board]; "Budget Cuts Spell Demise of NPR, Claims Mankiewicz," *Broadcasting*, 30 March 1981, 29; "Recision 83: What Happened?" *Current*, 15 June 1981, 1; "Want Cable Radio? How Much? NPR Asks," *Current*, 29 June 1981, 1; "NPR Going Private for Public Radio," *Broadcasting*, 16 November 1981, 31–32; Brooke Gladstone, "Emergency at NPR: This Is Not a Test," *In These Times*, 4 May–10 May 1983, 9; Mankiewicz to U.S. Rep. Anthony Toby Moffett, 10 February 1981, NPBA MSS, NPR Executive Office, Frank Mankiewicz Files, B1, F22; and Robert Goldfarb, telephone interview by author, tape recording, transcript, 12 September 1995, NPR OHC.
57. "Recision 83," 1; Mitchell-3, NPR OHC; Kling, NPR OHC; "Want Cable Radio?" 1; "NPR Going Private," 31–32; Gladstone, "Emergency," 9; Neil Henry and Lucy Howard, "Going Private in Public," *Newsweek*, 7 December 1981, 105–6; "A Sound Investment?" *Forbes*, 15 February 1982, 158, 160; "'We Mean to Survive': NPR Talking Tough, Moving Fast," *Current*, 30 April 1982, 1, 3.
58. "GAO Auditors Report on NPR," *Current*, 14 February 1984, 4; Henry and Howard, "Going Private," 105–6; "A Sound Investment?" 158, 160; "'We Mean to Survive," 1, 3; Brooke Gladstone, "APRA" 1, 5; "Vertical Service Gets Nod, but Reserved SCAs Don't" (NPR Board Report), *Current*, 20 August 1982, 5; Irvin Molotsky, "What Went Wrong at National Public Radio?" *New York Times*, 12 June 1983, 27.
59. National Public Radio, "New Ventures," NPR Annual Report 1982, 24–25; Frederick D. Wolf (General Accounting Office), Statement Before the House Subcommittee on Oversight and Investigations, 10 February 1984, 2–9, NPBA MSS, NPR Oversight and Investigation Files, B2, Folder: "Congressional Investigation [4]"; Richard A. Shaffer, "Public Broadcasting Sees New Technology Producing Revenue," *Wall Street Journal*, 23 June 1982, NPBA MSS, NPR Executive Office, Frank Mankiewicz Files, B3, F16; Jack Mitchell, personal correspondence with author; "GAO Auditors Report," 4.
60. "'We Mean to Survive'," 1, 3; Brooke Gladstone, "No Villains, Just Miscast Characters in Budget Saga," *Current*, 9 August 1983, 1, 8.
61. Minutes, NPR Board Meeting, 22 February 1982, Irving, Tex., NPBA MSS, NPR Board of Directors, Board Minutes; National Public Radio, 1982 Annual Report, 1.
62. Stamberg (unedited), NPR OHC.
63. Rosenberg, NPR OHC.
64. Michael J. Weiss, "What Happened to NPR?" *Washingtonian*, June 1983, NPBA MSS, NPR Oversight and Investigation Files, B1, Folder: "NPR Budget Cuts 1983 [2]"; Siegel, NPR OHC; Phil McCombs and Jacqueline Trescott, "NPR: Camelot in Crisis," *Washington Post*, 15 August 1983.
65. Siegel, NPR OHC.
66. "NPR Network Ratings Summary, 1977–1996, Arbitron Nationwide Report, Persons 12+," supplied by David Giovannoni, Audience Research Analysis; "NPR Numbers,"

Broadcasting, 14 March 1983, 62, 66; Minutes, Special session of NPR Board, 7 December 1982, NPBA MSS, NPR Board of Directors, Board Minutes; "NPR Ventures OK'd," *Current,* 28 January 1983; Minutes, NPR Board Meeting, 14 January 1983, NPBA MSS, NPR Board of Directors, Board Minutes; Minutes, NPR Board Special Executive Session, 11 March 1983, NPR Board of Directors, Board Minutes; Minutes, NPR Board Special Open Session, 11 March 1983, NPBA MSS, NPR Board of Directors, Board Minutes; "NPR Pays for '82 Optimism with '83 Cuts," *Current,* 11 March 1983, 1–2; Jason DeParle, "I.O.U.s at NPR: All Things Considered—Except One," *New Republic,* 30 May 1983, 17–18.

67. Jack Mitchell, personal correspondence with author; Sara Solovitch, "NPR's Crisis Quarter," *Washington Journalism Review,* June 1983, NPBA MSS, NPR Oversight and Investigation Files, B1, Folder: "NPR Budget Cuts 1983 [2]"; Brooke Gladstone, "Retrenchment: 'First Phase of Reality,'" *Current,* 25 March 1983, 1–2; Minutes, NPR Board Special Executive Session, 13 April 1983, NPBA MSS, NPR Board of Directors, Board Minutes; Minutes, Executive Session, NPR Board, 17 April 1983, NPBA MSS, NPR Board of Directors, Board Minutes; "What Happened to Mankiewicz?" *Broadcasting,* 25 April 1983, 28; DeParle, "I.O.U.s at NPR," 17–18; "National Public Radio's Mankiewicz to Resign As Operating Chief," *Wall Street Journal,* 20 April 1983; and Lee Margulies, "Public Radio Chief to Step Aside Soon," *Los Angeles Times,* 20 April 1983—both from NPBA MSS, NPR Oversight and Investigation Files, B1, Folder: "1983 Budget Cuts [1]."

68. Brooke Gladstone, "Fade Out For Mankiewicz," *Current,* 19 April 1983, 1; Minutes, Executive Session, NPR Board, 20 April 1983, NPBA MSS, NPR Board of Directors, Board Minutes; "No Bailout 'til Dust Clears in NPR Probes," *Current,* 3 May 1983, 1, 3; Symonds, NPR OHC.

69. Bornstein, NPR OHC, 11.

70. "No Bailout 'til Dust Clears in NPR Probes," 1, 3; Brooke Gladstone, "Bornstein Drops the Other Shoe," *Current,* 24 May 1983, 1, 6; Coopers and Lybrand to NPR Board and NPR Ventures Board, Report on Consolidated Financial Statements, 13 June 1983, NPBA MSS, NPR Oversight and Investigation, Box 1, Folders: "Audit" (4f); "NPR Failed to Make Tax Withholding, Social Security, and Unemployment Payments," *Communications Daily,* 14 June 1983; Martha M. Hamilton and Jacqueline Trescott, "NPR Said to Use Withheld Taxes for Daily Operations," *Washington Post,* 15 June 1983; and "National Public Radio Audit Shows Network Owes $850,000 Taxes," *Wall Street Journal,* 16 June 1983—all from NPBA MSS, NPR Oversight and Investigation Riles, B1, Folder: "NPR Budget Cuts 1983 [2]."

71. "Withheld Taxes Part of NPR Debt; Finance Aide Quits," *Current,* 21 June 1983, 1, 5; Irvin Molotsky, "Public Radio Chairman Resigns in Fiscal Crisis," *New York Times,* 22 June 1983; "NPR Gets the Bad News," *Broadcasting,* 20 June 1983, 78–79; "NPR's Bad News Gets Worse," *Broadcasting,* 27 June 1983, 36–37; Jack Mitchell, personal correspondence with author; "Public Radio Board Trims '84 Budget 30 Percent," *New York Times,* 17 September 1983; Gladstone, "Bornstein Drops," 1; Minutes, NPR Board Executive Session, 20 April 1983, NPBA MSS, NPR Board of Directors, Board Minutes; "Going and Gone from NPR," *Current,* 7 June 1983, 2; Minutes, NPR Board, Executive Session, Washington, D.C., 21 June 1983, NPBA MSS, NPR Oversight and

Investigation Files, B1, Folder: "O&I Board [3]"; "Uneasy NPR Board Edges Out Chairman Jones: Board Alert for Sign of Approval from CPB Brass," *Current*, 21 June 1983, 1–2; "Mankiewicz Joins Blue Chip PR Firm," *Current*, 21 June 1983, 2; Dennis Wharton, "NPR Slept While Money Burned; Auditors Hit Slipshod Operation," *Variety*, 22 June 1983, 56; Eric Zorn, "At Its Peak, NPR Falls Through the Bottom Line," *Chicago Tribune*, 1 August 1983, personal files of James L. Baughman.

72. Simon, NPR OHC.

73. Bornstein to NPR Board, Memorandum, "Status Report for the Week of May 9, 1983," NPBA MSS, NPR Oversight and Investigation Files, B1, Folder: "O&I Board [1]"; Jacqueline Trescott, "NPR Predicts $9.1 Million Deficit," *Washington Post*, 23 June 1983; "Arts Programming, News Hit by Cuts in NPR Budget," *Broadcasting*, 30 May 1983, 50; Brooke Gladstone, "Even More Distress Signals from NPR," *In These Times*, 29 June–12 July 1983, 7; "The News Turns Worse at National Public Radio," *BusinessWeek*, 4 July 1983, 41–42.

74. "$9.1 Million Loan Proposed for NPR," *New York Times*, 28 June 1983.

75. Mullally, NPR OHC.

76. Brooke Gladstone, "Lenders Friendly as Auditors Probe," *Current*, 7 June 1983, 1, 8; Douglas Bennet to NPR Board, Memorandum, "Status Report on the Debt Retirement Situation," 28 November 1983, NPBA MSS, NPR Board of Directors, Board Books, 8 December 1983.

77. Mullally, NPR OHC.

78. "Last-minute Salvation for NPR," *Broadcasting*, 1 August 1983, 21; Sally Bedell Smith, "Loan Is Approved for Public Radio," *New York Times*, 29 July 1983.

79. Brooke Gladstone, "Mixed Signals from New Pact," *In These Times*, 10 August–23 August 1983, 6, 11; Bornstein, conversation with author (following NPR OHC interview), Madison, Wis., 3 July 1995; Irvin Molotsky, "Public Radio Stations Backing Network Aid Plan," *New York Times*, 30 June 1983; "Public Radio Mounts Effort to Raise $1.8 Million by July 29," *New York Times*, 16 July 1983, 48; Sally Bedell Smith, "Loan is Approved"; Jacqueline Trescott, "Loan Gives NPR 'Breathing Room,'" *Washington Post*, 4 August 1983; "NPR Plucked From Brink by 'Creative' Compromise," *Current*, 9 August 1983, 5; Mullally, NPR OHC.

80. Jack Mitchell to NPR Staff, Memorandum, "NPR's Drive To Survive," 15 July 1983, NPBA MSS, NPR Oversight and Investigation Files, B1, Folder: "NPR Budget Cuts 1983 [3]"; Jacqueline Trescott, "NPR Looks to the Future," *Washington Post*, 30 July 1983; Trescott, "Loan Gives NPR 'Breathing Room'"; "Loan Is Set for Public Radio," *New York Times*, 4 August 1983; "Drive to Survive" (statistical summary), NPBA MSS, NPR Board of Directors, Board Books, 28 October 1983. "Debt Peaks at $7.5 Mil. (NPR Board Report), *Current*, 27 September 1983, 3; Douglas Bennet to NPR Board, Memorandum, "Status Report on the Debt Retirement Situation," NPBA MSS, NPR Board Books, 8 December 1983; Frederick D. Wolf (General Accounting Office), Statement Before the House Subcommittee on Oversight and Investigations, 10 February 1984, 18, NPBA MSS, NPR Oversight and Investigation Files, B2, Folder: "Congressional Investigation [4]"; "Bailout Burden May Be Cut 2/3," *Current*, 13 Sept. 1983, 1; "Public Radio Board Trims '84 Budget 30 percent," *New York Times*, 17 September 1983.

81. Mullally, NPR OHC.
82. Jacqueline Trescott, "NPR Names New Head: Bennet Brings Political Skills to Network Job," *Washington Post*, 29 October 1983; Irvin Molotsky, "Ex-Aid Director Heads Public Radio," *New York Times*, 29 October 1983.
83. "GAO Auditors Report on NPR," *Current*, 14 February 1984, 4–5.
84. "GAO Auditors Report," 4–5; "Board OK's NPR-Plus; Dean Boal Coordinator," *Current*, 10 December 1982, 4; "NPR Plus Lives, But No Longer 'Round the Clock,'" *Current*, 13 September 1983, 1.
85. Ronald Bornstein, "Report and Recommendations of Ronald C. Bornstein, Acting President, National Public Radio to NPR Board of Directors," Washington, D.C., 31 October 1983, NPBA MSS, NPR Oversight and Investigation Files, B2, Folder: "Oversight Hearing Testimony [1]," 6.
86. Goldfarb, NPR OHC.
87. Ibid.
88. Brooke Gladstone, "No Villains," 1, 8; Richard Kolm, telephone interview by author, tape recording, transcript, 31 August 1995, NPR OHC; Siegel, NPR OHC; Mitchell-3, NPR OHC; Bornstein, NPR OHC; Goldfarb, NPR OHC.
89. Ronald Kramer to Frank Mankiewicz, cover letter and draft document titled, "Plain Talk About American Public Radio," 10 February 1983, NPBA MSS, NPR Executive Office, Frank Mankiewicz Files, B2, F16; Brooke Gladstone, "Aftermath: We Shot the Wrong Man," *Current*, 20 August 1982, 1, 6–7; "Myron Jones Elected to Chair NPR Board," *Current*, 12 November 1982, 2; Bornstein, NPR OHC; "GAO Auditors Report," 5.
90. Bornstein, NPR OHC; Thomas Kigin, interview by author, tape recording, transcript, St. Paul, Minn., 28 May 1998, NPR OHC; Delano Lewis, interview by author, tape recording, transcript, Washington, D.C., 15 August 1995, NPR OHC; Mitchell-3, NPR OHC; "... But Will the Boy in Mankiewicz Win Out?" *Current*, 14 January 1983; "Mankiewicz Officially Leaves NPR Presidency," *Broadcasting*, 16 May 1983, 78; Weiss, "What Happened," NPBA MSS, NPR Oversight and Investigation Files, B1, Folder: "NPR Budget Cuts 1983 [2]"; Conan, NPR OHC; "Man, oh Mankiewicz," *Broadcasting*, 13 August 1979, 7; Rosenberg, NPR OHC; David Giovannoni, telephone interview by author, tape recording, transcript, 30 August 1995, NPR OHC.
91. "American Public Radio Extending Its Network," *New York Times*, 10 August 1983; Francisco, "The Life and Times," 56; Buzenberg, NPR OHC; Robert Goldfarb, telephone conversation with author, 30 July, 2002; Kigin, NPR OHC; and "Making a Day in the Life of NPR Possible," National Public Radio 1993 Annual Report, 21.

4. PHOENIX RISING

1. Irvin Molotsky, "Ex-Aid Director Heads Public Radio," *New York Times*, 29 October 1983; Douglas J. Bennet biography, Wesleyan University Web site, http://www.wesleyan.edu/home/DJB_Bio.htm; Jacqueline Trescott, "NPR Names New Head," *Washington Post*, 29 October 1983; Robert Goldfarb, telephone interview by author, tape recording, transcript, 12 September 1995, Michael McCauley NPR Oral History Collection, National Public Broadcasting Archives, Hornbake Library, University of

Maryland, College Park, Md. (hereafter cited as NPR OHC). Phil McCombs and Jacqueline Trescott, "NPR: Camelot in Crisis," *Washington Post*, 15 August 1983; Elizabeth Alexander, "Tight Rein on NPR," *Washington Post*, 1 July 1983.

2. Tom Thomas, telephone interview by author, tape recording, transcript, 23 September 2003, NPR OHC.

3. Ibid.

4. Douglas J. Bennet, "Bennet Reviews His First Year as NPR Head," *Public Broadcasting Report*, 16 November 1984, 4–6; Brooke Gladstone, "Even More Distress Signals from NPR," *In These Times*, 29 June–12 July 1983, 7; Michael J. Weiss, "What Happened to NPR?" *Washingtonian*, June 1983, National Public Broadcasting Archives, University of Maryland, College Park, Md. (cited hereafter as NPBA MSS), NPR 94–74, B1, NPR Budget Cuts 1983–NPR Finances/Budget Cuts [2]; Robert Siegel, interview by author, tape recording, transcript, Washington, D.C., 21 August 1995, NPR OHC; " 'Save NPR' Pitch Catches Bornstein, et al. by Surprise," *Variety*, 29 June 1983, 35.

5. "Briefing Paper on National Public Radio," United States General Accounting Office, 14 March 1985, 7–8, NPBA MSS, NPR Oversight and Investigation Files, B1, Oversight and Investigations; Elizabeth T. Robinson, "No Action on NPR Debt Now Planned," *Current*, 27 March 1984, 3; "$6 million Is Pledged to Public Radio Stations," *New York Times*, 1 May 1985.

6. Jacqueline Trescott, "CPB Votes Funds for NPR News Shows," *Washington Post*, 16 March 1985; Jeff Rosenberg, e-mail message to author, 8 March 2001; Penny Pagano, "New Weekend Life for 'All Things Considered,'" *Los Angeles Times*, 22 July 1985; Jacqueline Trescott, "Radio: NPR Gets Grant for News Show," *Washington Post*, 26 July 1985; telephone conversation with Jeff Rosenberg, 30 October 2003; Administration Profile: H. Wayne Huizenga, Miami Dolphins Web site, http://www.miamidolphins.com/contacts/administration/admin_huizenga_w.asp.

7. Robert Siegel, interview by author, tape recording, transcript, Washington, D.C., 21 August 1995, NPR OHC.

8. Ibid.

9. Ibid.

10. Jay Kernis, telephone interview with author, tape recording, transcript, 8 September 2003, NPR OHC; "NPR Launches 'Weekend Edition' Over Some Complaints from Some Members," *Broadcasting*, 4 November 1985, 45.

11. Kernis, NPR OHC.

12. "NPR Board Report," *Current*, 14 February 1984, 3; Kathryn Buxton, "Wicket Lives; Celebrity Croquet, Mallets for NPR," *Washington Post*, 16 April 1984; Jack Mitchell, e-mail message to author, 7 April 2000; David M. Stone, *Nixon and the Politics of Public Television* (New York: Garland, 1985), xiv, 85, 88–89; News Summary, 23 September 1971, 18, Nixon Presidential Materials, National Archives and Records Administration, College Park, Md. (hereafter cited as Nixon MSS), the President's Office Files, Daily News Summaries Annotated by the President, 1969–1973, B33; Charles Colson, memo to H. R. Haldeman, 9 July 1971, in *Richard Nixon's Secret Files*, ed. Bruce Oudes (New York: Harper and Row, 1989), 290; Thomas, NPR OHC; William Kling, interview with author, tape recording, transcript, St. Paul, Minn., 26 July 1995, NPR OHC.

13. Thomas, NPR OHC; Kling, NPR OHC; Curtis Wenzel, "APR: Rivalry or Diversity?" *In These Times*, 4–10 May 1983, 9; Brooke Gladstone, "Mixed Signals From New Pact," *In These Times*, 10–23 August 1983, 6; Elizabeth T. Robinson, "NPR Restructuring Panel Formed to Guide Debate," *Current*, 22 November 1983, 3; Robinson, "Restructuring Vote Pushed to Week After PRC," *Current*, 20 December 1983, 1, 6.

14. Thomas, NPR OHC.

15. Statement of Donald P. Mullally, Chairman, NPR Board of Directors, 6 February 1985, NPBA MSS, NPR 97–83, B2, Archival Clips from NPR, Clips: NPR five-year business plan; Jack Mitchell, e-mail message to author, 26 April 2001; Frieda Werden, "Station Resource Group Recommends Revisions of NPR Business Plan," *Current*, 30 April–14 May 1985, 1, NPBA MSS, NPR 97–83, B2, Archival Clips from NPR, Clips: NPR five-year business plan; Dennis McDougal, "Public Radio Mainstays Survive Latest Crisis," *Los Angeles Times*, 25 May 1985; Jack Mitchell, e-mail message to author, 24 October 2003.

16. "Funding, Unbundling Top Public Radio Conference," *Broadcasting*, 4 May 1987, 37; "Bennet Assesses State of Public Radio," *Broadcasting*, 11 May 1987, 72; Stephen L. Salyer, "Monopoly to Marketplace—Competition Comes to Public Radio," *Media Studies Journal* 7, no. 3 (Summer 1993): 180; "NPR Sees Bigger Dues in 1989," *Broadcasting*, 14 December 1987, 52; Jack Mitchell, e-mail messages to author on 7 April 2000, 26 April 2001, and 24 October 2003.

17. Jack Mitchell, e-mail message to author, 7 April 2000; Thomas, NPR OHC, 17; Mike Janssen, "Public Radio Hails Rick Madden for Life's Work," *Current*, 25 February 2002, 1, 13; Steve Behrens, "Award Honors Not Only a Leader, but Also a Philosophy of Service," *Current*, 28 May, 2001, 1, 22; Stephen Singer, "Slings and Arrows: Richard H. Madden, *No Good Deed Goes Unpunished*," *Current*, 17 December 1990, 18.

18. "PRI Announces Changes in Network Program Lineup for 2005," press release, Public Radio International Web site, http://www.pri.org/PublicSite/press/index.html; Salyer, "Monopoly to Marketplace," 178, 180–82; PRI Programs, Public Radio International Web site, http://www.pri.org/PublicSite/inside/index.html.
    PRI's agreement to distribute *Marketplace* and *Marketplace Morning Report* will end on July 1, 2005. Though PRI helped create these programs, they are now owned by Minnesota Public Radio. MPR decided to end most of its distribution agreements with PRI in February 2004 so it could coordinate the production and distribution of its programs in-house. See Nicole Garrison-Sprenger, "MPR to Drop PRI for Program Distribution," *The Minneapolis-St. Paul Business Journal*, 9 February 2004, http://www.bizjournals.com/twincities/stories/2004/02/09/daily27.html.

19. "APR, NPR Convene Back-to-Back," *Broadcasting*, 21 April 1986, 105; NPR, NPR Annual Report, FY 1988 (Washington, D.C.: NPR, 1989), 31; Eleanor Blau, "National Public Radio Gets by with Help from Its Friends," *New York Times*, 27 February 1989.

20. Station Resource Group, "Public Radio Income 80–98," is a spreadsheet compiled by the Station Resource Group, based on data from the Corporation for Public Broadcasting. All figures taken from this document and cited in this chapter have been adjusted for inflation (CPI-U) to reflect the value of the dollar in 1998.

21. David Giovannoni, "A Long View of Public Radio's National Audience Growth: Availability and Accessibility Revisited, Part 1: 1970 to 1983" (Washington, D.C.:

Corporation for Public Broadcasting, February 1992), Audience Research Analysis, ARAnet Publications page, http://www.aranet.com, 1–3; Thomas, NPR OHC, 21, 24; Giovannoni, "A Long View of Public Radio's National Audience Growth: Availability and Accessibility Revisited, Part 2: 1993 to Today" (Washington, D.C.: Corporation for Public Broadcasting, March 1992), Audience Research Analysis, ARAnet Publications Page, http://www.aranet.com, 5–8; Audience Building Task Force Report, July 1986, NPBA MSS, NPR 97–88, B1, Audience Studies [1986–1988, n.d.].

22. The AQH audience is defined as the number of people listening to a station or network for at least five minutes within a given quarter-hour segment. To obtain an "average" figure, AQH is measured across a particular programming daypart (e.g., Monday through Friday, 6 A.M. to 10 A.M.). Radio managers regard AQH as the best measure of programming effectiveness, since it allows direct comparison with programs that run on other stations at the same time. For more details, see "Components of Average Quarter-Hour Audience," a research paper available on the ARA Web site, http://www.aranet.com.

23. Jack Mitchell, e-mail message to author, 4 April 2000.

24. Alan G. Stavitsky, "Listening for Listeners: Educational Radio and Audience Research," *Journalism History* 19, no. 1 (Spring 1993): 11–18; Stavitsky, "Guys in Suits with Charts: Audience Research in U.S. Public Radio," *Journal of Broadcasting and Electronic Media* 39, no. 2 (Spring 1995): 177–81.

25. David Giovannoni, telephone interview by author, tape recording, transcript, 30 August 1995 (hereafter cited as Giovannoni-1); "New Research System Provides Program Specific Audience Estimates for Public Radio," News Briefs, CPB Office of Communication Research, 18 May 1981, NPBA MSS, NPR Executive Office, Frank Mankiewicz Files, B5, F22; Holt to Station Managers/Program Managers, Memorandum, "Audience Research—PRAP Programming Information," NPBA MSS, Samuel C. O. Holt Papers, B18, F7.

26. Thomas, NPR OHC.

27. Ibid.

28. Stavitsky, "Guys in Suits," 184–85; and three electronic documents available on the ARA Web site (http://www.aranet.com): David Giovannoni, "The Cheap 90. Public Radio Listeners: Supporters and Non-Supporters—an Examination of the Causes Influencing the Decision of Public Radio's Listeners to Support or Not Support Public Radio"; Corporation for Public Broadcasting, "Audience 88 Newsletters"; and Thomas J. Thomas and Theresa R. Clifford, "Audience 88: Issues and Implications."

29. David Giovannoni to Public Radio Stations, memo about Program Affinity, Audience Response, and Program Economics, provided to author by Giovannoni; Leslie Peters, ed., *Audience 98: Public Service, Public Support* (Washington, D.C.: Audience Research Analysis and Corporation for Public Broadcasting), available from the ARA Web site, http://www.aranet.com/library/pdf/doc-0100.pdf.

30. Giovannoni, "A Long View, Part 1," 1–2; Station Resource Group, "Public Radio Income 80–98"; Corporation for Public Broadcasting, "Recipients of the Edward R. Murrow Award," CPB Web site, http://www.cpb.org/about/awards/murrow/murrowlist.html.

31. NPR News Milestones, NPBA MSS, NPR—Communications Division 97–88, B1; Frank Ahrens, "Boyz Under the Hood: 'Car Talk' Hosts Mix Advice and Idle Chatter

in High-Octane Show," *Washington Post*, 21 August 1999; "The History of Car Talk," Car Talk Web site, http://cartalk.com/content/about/history/; NPR, Terry Gross Biography, NPR Web site, http://www.npr.org/about/people/bios/tgross.html; NPR, "About Fresh Air," http://freshair.npr.org/about_fa.jhtml.

32. "Morning Report: TV and Video," *Los Angeles Times*, 23 May 1988; John Carmody, "The TV Column," Washington Post, 24 June 1992; John Carmody, "Hockenberry Leaves NPR for ABC," *Washington Post*, 22 July 1992; Sharon Bernstein, "NPR: A Pool for Network Fishing," *Los Angeles Times*, 11 August 1992; John Carmody, untitled article, *Washington Post*, 28 August 1992; Scott Simon, interview with author, tape recording, transcript, Washington, D.C., 23 August 1995, NPR OHC; "Cokie Roberts, Senior News Analyst," NPR Web site, http://www.npr.org/about/people/bios/croberts.html; ABC News, Cokie Roberts biography, ABC News Web site, http://abcnews.go.com/sections/ThisWeek/ThisWeek/roberts_cokie_bio.html.

33. Linda Wertheimer, interview with author, tape recording, transcript (unedited), Washington, D.C., 18 August 1995, NPR OHC.

34. Kernis, NPR OHC.

35. Marc Fisher, "The Soul of a News Machine," *Washington Post Magazine*, 22 October 1989, 23, 37; Kernis, NPR OHC, 38.

36. Bob Dart, "Hill Story Puts Face to NPR Voice: Nina Totenberg Becomes the News," *Atlanta Journal-Constitution*, 21 October 1991; Guy Gugliotta, "Two Face Questions on News Leaks in Thomas Case," *Washington Post*, 17 January 1992; "Public Radio Pulls Plug on Programs by Cop Killer," *Chicago Tribune*, 17 May 1994; Mary Collins, *National Public Radio: The Cast of Characters* (Washington, D.C.: Seven Locks Press, 1993), 104.

37. Conan, NPR OHC.

38. Collins, *National Public Radio*, 101–2.

39. NPR, biographical sketches of Poggioli, Gradstein, Shuster, and Garrels, NPR Online, http://www.npr.org/about/people/bios; Howard Rosenberg, "Caught in the Middle," *Los Angeles Times*, 23 February 2003; Steve Carney, "Television and Radio: Around the Dial: She's Back from Iraq, Well Clothed," *Los Angeles Times*, 24 October 2003.

40. "Succession Watch: Radio Excellence," *Los Angeles Times*, 10 March 1993; Station Resource Group, "Public Radio Income 80–98"; National Public Radio, NPR Annual Report, FY 1992 (Washington, D.C.: NPR, 1993), 2; "Its an SDX Hat Trick for National Public Radio: Three Journalism Awards in One Year," *The Quill*, July 1992; Douglas Bennet, telephone interview with author, tape recording, transcript, 31 July 1995, NPR OHC; Douglas J. Bennet biography, Wesleyan University Web site, http://www.wesleyan.edu/home/DJB_Bio.htm.

41. Carl Matthusen to Authorized Station Representatives and NPR Staff, memo "Re: NPR Presidential Search," NPBA MSS, NPR—Communications 97–88, B1; Thomas, NPR OHC; Delano E. Lewis, President and Chief Executive Officer, NPR News Release, NPBA MSS, NPR—Communications 97–88, B1; Donna Petrozzello, "Getting Radio Onto the Superhighway," *Broadcasting and Cable*, 6 June 1994, NPBA MSS, NPR—Communications 97–88, B1, 1.

42. Timothy J. McNulty, "Don't Touch That Dial: National Public Radio Hopes New Boss Can Fine-tune a Well-Oiled Machine," *Chicago Tribune*, 25 March 1994, NPBA

MSS, NPR—Communications 97–88, B1; Delano Lewis, interview with author, tape recording, transcript, 15 August 1995, Washington, D.C., NPR OHC.

43. Lewis, NPR OHC.

44. McNulty, "Don't Touch That Dial"; Blair S. Walker, "His Mission: Recharge Public Radio," *USA Today*, 8 September 1993, NPBA MSS, NPR—Communications 97–88, B1; Karen De Witt, "New Chief Wants to Widen NPR's Financial Base," *New York Times*, 28 March 1994.

45. "NPR Programming Attacked by Conservatives," *Broadcasting*, 24 June 1985, 59; Charlotte Ryan, "A Study of National Public Radio," *EXTRA!* (April/May 1993): 18–21; Michael P. McCauley, "From the Margins to the Mainstream: The History of National Public Radio" (Ph.D. diss., University of Wisconsin–Madison, 1997), 340–45; "No Tears for National Public Radio," Accuracy In Media, *AIM Report*, (July-A 1983), 1; "National Public Radio Out of Tune," *AIM Report* (May-A 1985), 1; Bob Dart, "GOP Firm in PBS Aid Debate: Democrats Say Cuts Jeopardize Popular Shows," *Wisconsin State Journal*, 20 January 1995; Gugliotta, "Two Face Questions"; Editorial, "The Wrong Way to Plug a Leak," *Chicago Tribune*, 15 February 1992.

46. Ralph Engelman, *Public Radio and Television in America: A Poltical History* (Thousand Oaks, Calif.: Sage, 1996), 298; Karen Everhart Bedford, "Porter Panel Eyes Take-Backs for '96–97, then Pressler Proposal Takes the Stage," *Current*, 16 January 1995, 1; Jerry Gray, "House Committee Discusses Public Broadcasting Budget: The Issue Is Said to Be Money, Not Merit," *New York Times*, 20 January 1995; Dart, "Hill Story." See McCauley, "From the Margins to the Mainstream," 296, for details about the response of NPR's National Affairs office to the Republican funding threat.

47. Marc Gunther, "At NPR, All Things Reconsidered," *New York Times*, 13 August 1995.

48. Lewis, NPR OHC, 7.

49. Bill Buzenberg, interview with author, tape recording, transcript, St. Paul, Minn., 28 May 1998, NPR OHC; "Minnesota Public Radio Organizational Structure," MPR Web site, http://access.minnesota.publicradio.org/aboutMPR/docs/structure.htm; and Jacqueline Conciatore, "Minnesota Net Endows Itself with Sale of Mail-order Firm," *Current*, 6 April 1998, available at http://www.current.org/mo/mo806k.html.

50. Robert K. Avery and Alan G. Stavitsky, *A History of Public Broadcasting*, chapter updates appended to the original publication by John Witherspoon and Roselle Kovitz (Washington, D.C.: Current, 2000), 78–79; Jacqueline Conciatore, "Delano Lewis Will Retire from Running NPR," *Current*, 6, April, 1998, available at http://www.current.org/rad/rad806l.html; Nicholas Nash, "Double, Double Toil and Trouble," consultant's draft paper for NPR's Audience Building Task Force, 18 June 1986, 6, NPBA MSS, NPR 97–88, B1, Audience Studies [1986–1988, n.d.].

51. Jacqueline Conciatore, "His Contributions to NPR News Department 'Can't Be Measured,' Colleagues Attest," *Current*, 3 February 1997, 1, 14; Buzenberg, NPR OHC; "Buzenberg, Sutton Step Down at NPR," *Current*, 20 January 1997, 4; Jack Mitchell, e-mail message to author, 13 March 2001; Jacqueline Conciatore, "Worries About Diversity, Independence Surface with Resignation of News Chief," *Current*, 3 February 1997, 1, 11–12.

52. Jacqueline Conciatore, "To Succeed Lewis, NPR Board Seeks 'Partner' for Stations," *Current*, 12 October 1998, 21; Conciatore, "No 'Low-hanging Fruit' in Sight to Solve

NPR's Revenue Problem, Interview with Del Lewis, *Current*, 17 November 1997, available from http://www.current.org/rad/rad721d.html; Station Resource Group, "Public Radio Income 80–98"; Thomas J. Thomas and Theresa R. Clifford, "Audience 88: Issues and Implications," 8.

53. Sidney Brown Obituary, NPBA MSS, NPR 97–83, B3, NPR People Clips; Conciatore, "Worries," 11, Conciatore, "No 'Low-hanging Fruit'"; Conciatore, "Delano Lewis Will Retire from Running NPR," *Current*, 6 April 1998, available from http://www.current. org/rad/rad806l.html; Ambassador Delano E. Lewis, U.S. Department of State, Web site of U.S. Embassies and Consulates, http://usembassy.state.gov/pretoria/wwwham5.html.

54. NPR, Sid Brown, Chief Financial Officer at NPR, Died Today, *All Things Considered*, transcript, 15 November 1994, Segment 12, NPBA MSS, NPR 97–83, B3, NPR People Clips; Conciatore, "To Succeed Lewis."

5. A CIVILIZED VOICE IN A NEW MEDIA ENVIRONMENT

1. Jacqueline Conciatore, "To Succeed Lewis, NPR Board Seeks 'Partner' for Stations," *Current*, 12 October 1998, 21; Felicity Barringer, "National Public Radio Network Names New Chief Executive," *New York Times*, 12 November 1998; Frank Ahrens, "NPR Names New President," *Washington Post*, 12 November 1998; Christopher Stern, "National Public Radio Taps Klose Prez, CEO," *Daily Variety*, 12 November 1998; Elizabeth A. Rathbun, "Klose to Head NPR," *Broadcasting and Cable*, 16 November 1998—all available in NPBA MSS, NPR—Communications 2000–52, B1, F11.

2. Jack Mitchell, e-mail message to author, 26 April 2001; Barringer, "National Public Radio"; Conciatore, "To Succeed Lewis," 21.

3. Kevin Klose, interview by author, tape recording, transcript, Washington, D.C., 7 June 2000 (hereafter cited as Klose-1), Michael McCauley NPR Oral History Collection, National Public Broadcasting Archives, Hornbake Library, University of Maryland, College Park, Md. (hereafter cited as NPR OHC); Joe Pollack, "NPR President Has St. Louis Press Connections," *St. Louis Journalism Review* 30, no. 227 (June 2000), available from http://www.stljr.org/archives/june2000.htm.

4. Laurence Zuckerman, "Has Success Spoiled NPR?" *Mother Jones*, June/July 1987, 32–39, 44–45; Marc Fisher, "The Soul of a News Machine," *Washington Post Magazine*, 22 October 1989, 16–23, 37–42; Bruce Porter, "Has Success Spoiled NPR? Becoming Part of the Establishment Can Have Its Drawbacks," *Columbia Journalism Review* (September/October 1990): 26–32.

5. Brian Montopoli, "All Things Considerate: How NPR Makes Tavis Smiley Sound Like Linda Wertheimer," *Washington Monthly* (January/February 2003).

6. Mike Janssen, "Davis Comes in, Dvorkin Moves Over at NPR," *Current*, 24 January 2000, 1, 6; Steve Behrens, "PRPD Notes from Memphis: Tinkering and Promotion Prescribed for Newsmags," *Current*, 4 October 1999, 10; "SCPR Names Bill Davis New CEO," Minnesota Public Radio Press Release, 18 December 2000, MPR Web site, available from http://access.minnesota.publicradio.org/press_releases/releases/20001219_scprceo.html.

7. Mike Janssen and Steve Behrens, "'Good Parent' Jay Kernis Will Return to NPR," *Current*, 12 March 2001, 11; Jay Kernis, telephone interview by author, tape recording, transcript, 7–8 September 2003, NPR OHC.

8. Kernis, NPR OHC.

9. Ibid.

10. Lori Robertson, "Quicker *and* Deeper?" *American Journalism Review* (June/July 2004), available from http://www.ajr.org/Article.asp?id=3700.

11. Mike Janssen, "NPR Goes All Out with Live Coverage," *Current*, 24 September 2001, 1, 12. *Morning Edition*'s coverage on September 11, and in the days that followed, can be heard via streaming audio by clicking the appropriate links at the following Web page: http://www.npr.org/rundowns/calendar/monthly_calendar.php?month=9&year=2001&prgId=3.

12. Those interested in hearing 9/11 coverage on *All Things Considered* and *Weekend Edition* can find those audio files by going to NPR.org and clicking the appropriate program link on the left side of the network's home page. Each program's home page contains a link on the right side titled "previous shows." By clicking this link and going to the appropriate year and month, one can find a day-by-day archive of relevant broadcasts.

13. "Search for Winners," the Peabody Awards Web site, http://www.peabody.uga.edu/archives. Search by "organization." Look for "NPR." Year: "2001."

14. Robertson, "Quicker *and* Deeper?"; Mike Janssen, "NPR: Co-host Needed to Improve Coverage," *Current*, 12 April 2004, 19.

15. Teresa Wiltz, "NPR's Wertheimer Leaves Anchor Post," *Washington Post*, 11 December 2001; Mike Janssen et. al., "People in Public Telecommunications: Production and Programming," *Current*, 24 February 2003, 8; Mike Janssen, "Fresh Talent Gives All Things Considered License to Experiment," *Current*, 2 December 2002, 1, 13; "NPR's Bob Edwards Leaving Morning Edition Host Chair to Take on New Assignments as NPR Senior Correspondent," NPR Press Release, 23 March 2004, http://www.npr.org/about/press/040323.bobedwards.html; Fred Barbash, "NPR Replaces 'Morning Edition' Host," *Washington Post*, 23 March 2004; Janssen, "Morning Minus Bob: Announcement Shocks, Explanations Befuddle," *Current*, 12 April 2004, 1, 16; Janssen, "NPR: Co-host Needed," 1, 19; XM Satellite Radio, "Acclaimed Public Radio Newsman Bob Edwards Joins XM Satellite Radio to Host Morning Show Exclusively on XM," XM Satellite Radio Press Release, 29 July 2004, available at http://www.xmradio.com/newsroom/screen/pr_2004_07-29.html.

16. Mike Janssen, "Kernis Sends NPR's Arts Fare to Drawing Board," *Current*, 25 February 2002, 1; Paul Farhi, "NPR Cultural Programming Put to Triage," *Washington Post*, 27 February 2002; Philip Kennicott, "At NPR, A Sudden Shift in Culture: Network Announces Staff Cuts, 'Refocusing' of Arts Programming," *Washington Post*, 12 April 2002; "NPR Announces Partnership with CPRN Music Service," NPR Press Release, 5 May 2003, http://www.npr.org/about/press/030505.cprn.html.

In an email message on 19 March 2004, David Giovannoni confirmed that *Performance Today* is tops among discrete classical music programs. Taken together, however, the classical music programs produced by local public radio stations account for a much larger fraction of overall listening. PRI's round-the-clock service, Classical 24, also generates about three times more listening than *Performance Today*.

17. Robert Goldfarb, telephone conversation with author, 7 September 2003; Mike Janssen, "NPR Lands Most Listeners Ever: News Shows Drive Gains at Network, Sta-

tions," *Current,* 25 March 2002, 1; AudiGraphics, "Listening to All NPR Programming: Weekly Cume Audience," National AudiGraphics Consultation Guides, based on audience research data from Arbitron, Inc, 9 October 2003.

18. Terence A. Shimp, *Advertising Promotion: Supplemental Aspects of Integrated Marketing Communications* (Fort Worth, Tex.: The Dryden Press, 2000), 23; Naomi Klein, Remarks made in the keynote address at the international conference of the Union for Democratic Communications, Ottawa, Ont., Canada, 18 May 2001.

19. Jerry M. Landay, "An Eloquent Campaign Wrap-up From a Virtual News Division," *Current,* 4 December 2000, 14; Karen Everhart Bedford, "'Frontline' and NPR Share Info for Reports on Russia, Drugs," *Current,* 22 May 2000, A8.

20. NPR, "NPR Worldwide," NPR Web site, http://www.npr.org/worldwide; NPR, "NPR Names M. J. Bear as Vice President, NPR Online," NPR Press Release, 28 January 2000, http://www.npr.org/about/press/000128.mjbear.html; Douglas Heingartner, "Now Hear This, Quickly," *New York Times,* 2 October 2003; Steve Behrens, "Jog with Wertheimer for $49.95 a Year," *Current,* 31 July 2000, A10; Sky Radio, "Now Airing on Delta Airlines: Sky Business," Sky Radio Web site, http://www.skyradionet.com/delta.cfm; Nick Wingfield, "RealNetworks to Deliver News, Sports, Video on Mobile Phones," *Wall Street Journal,* 5 May 2003; John Markoff, "2 Will Announce an Audio-on-Demand Service for Cellphones," *New York Times,* 11 August 2003.

21. Jacqueline Conciatore, "NPR, PRI Make Satellite Deals with CD Radio," *Current,* 21 June 1999, 1; NPR, "Margaret Low Smith Named Vice President for NPR2, NPR's New Satellite Radio Unit," NPR Press Release, 17 October, 2000, http://www.npr.org/about/press/001017.npr2.html; "NPR Loses Host for Little-heard Sirius Morning Newsmag," *Current,* 12 March 2001, 4; Mike Janssen, "NPR Plans Midday Show With Idled Sirius Staffers," *Current,* 28 May 2001, 16; Alex Markels, "100 Channels, but Where Are the Subscribers?" *New York Times,* 3 November 2002; "From Space to Car, Satellite Radio Is Making Waves World Over," *Asia Intelligence Wire,* 30 November 2003, Hoover's Online, http://www.hoovers.com/free, search terms: Sirius Satellite Radio, News.

22. Stephen Holden, "Critic's Notebook: High-Tech Quirkiness Restores Radio's Magic," *New York Times,* 26 December 2003; David Pogue, "Satellite Radio Extends Its Orbit," *New York Times,* 18 December 2003; Brad Stone, "Greetings, Earthlings: Satellite Radio for Cars Is Taking Off and Adding New Features—Now Broadcasters Are Starting to Fight Back," *Newsweek,* 26 January 2004, 55; NPR, "NPR Now," NPR Web site, http://www.npr.org/programs/nprnow/index.html; NPR, "NPR Talk," NPR Web site, http://www.npr.org/programs/nprtalk/index.html; PRI, "PRI Cultural Programming Premieres on XM Public Radio," PRI Press Release, 1 September 2004, http://www.pri.org/PublicSite/press/recent/pri_premiere_xm.cfm; Minnesota Public Radio, "American Public Media to Supply Programming to New XM Satellite Radio Channel," Minnesota Public Radio Press Release, 29 July 2004, http://access.minnesota.publicradio.org/press_releases/releases/20040729_xm.php; PRI, "PRI's Public Radio Channel: Connecting the World to Your Life," PRI Web site, http://www.pri.org/PublicSite/listeners/sirius_schedule.html; Conciatore, "NPR, PRI"; "CEOs Optimistic About 2004 Outlook," *Satellite News,* 8 March 2004, Hoovers Online, http://www.hoovers.com/free, search terms: Sirius Satellite Radio, News; and "NPR Leaders Seek to Soothe Satellite Radio Worries," *Current,* 20 September 2004, A4.

23. NPR, "NPR News Wins 2003 Dupont Award," NPR Press Release, http://www.npr.org/about/press/031217.dupont.html, December 2003; NPR, "Baghdad Reaction," Bob Edwards, conversation with Anne Garrels, available through *Morning Edition*'s audio archives, 20 March 2003, http://www.npr.org/rundowns/rundown.php?prgId=3&prgDate=20-Mar-2003; NPR, "Dozens Dead in Attack on Baghdad Market," Robert Siegel, conversation with Anne Garrels, available through the *All Things Considered* audio archives, 28 March 2003, http://www.npr.org/rundowns/rundown.php?prgId=2&prgDate=28-Mar-2003; NPR, "NPR News Wins 2002 Overseas Press Club Award for Series on Mideast Conflict," NPR Press Release, http://www.npr.org/about/press/030428.overseas.html.

24. NPR, "The Expansion of NPR News," NPR Web site, http://www.npr.org/about/news.html; Klose-1, NPR OHC.

25. Klose-1, NPR OHC.

26. NPR, "NPR Expands Westward Coverage, Presence Enhanced with New Production Center," NPR Press Release, 16 April 2002, http://www.npr.org/about/press/020416.nprwest.html; NPR, "NPR Establishes Major Production Center in California: NPR West Opens November 2, Expanding Network's Presence and Reach," NPR Press Release, 16 October 2002, http://www.npr.org/about/press/021016.nprwest.html.

27. NPR, "Statement of Activities," in NPR Annual Report, FY 2002, 35. Data on member stations and audience size come from reports cited earlier in the book.

28. Station Resource Group, "Listener Support and Underwriting: Revenue, Costs, and Net Return to Operations," May 2004, http://www.srg.org/funding/02revenueupdate.pdf; Dan Odenwald, "Cash-strapped States Trim Pubcasting Funds," *Current*, 8 April 2002, 1; Odenwald, "Layoffs Proliferate as Stations Near July 1," *Current*, 24 June 2002, A3; and Odenwald, "Key Measure of Public Radio Fundraising Suffers 12 percent Decline," *Current*, 5 August 2002, 3.

29. Daren Fonda, "National Prosperous Radio," *Time*, 24 March 2003; NPR, "NPR Receives $14 Million from MacArthur Foundation: $4 Million for Endowment Support, $10 Million for News/Public Affairs Programming," NPR Press Release, 13 January 2003, http://www.npr.org/about/press/030113.macarthur.html; Reilly Capps and Paul Farhi, "Magnanimity and McMuffins: NPR's Arch-Angel," *Washington Post*, 7 November 2003; NPR, "NPR to Invest Additional $15 Million in NPR News," NPR Press Release, 16 June 2004, http://www.npr.org/about/press/040616.kroc.html; and Mike Janssen, "Kroc Gift Lets NPR Expand News, Lower Fees," *Current*, 24 May 2004, 1, 10.

30. William Kling, interview by author, tape recording, transcript, St. Paul, Minn., 26 July 1995, NPR OHC.

31. "Bennet Reviews His First Year as NPR Head," *Public Broadcasting Report*, 16 November 1984, 4–6; Jack Mitchell, e-mail message to author, 26 April 2001; Tom Thomas, telephone conversation with author, 9 January 2004.

32. PRI, "About Laura Walker," in "PRI Envisions 2005," PRI Web site, http://www.pri.org/infosite/networknews/pri_envision.pdf, 26 May 2000, 7; NPR, "Mark Handley: President, New Hampshire Public Radio," NPR Board of Directors Bios, http://www.npr.org/about/people/bios/mhandley.html; WEAA-FM, "Who Is WEAA," WEAA-

FM Web site, http://www.weaa.org/about/who_is_weaa.php; KUT-FM, "KUT GM Named 'General Manager of the Year' at National Conference," KUT-FM Press Release, 17 July 2003, http://www.kut.org/site/PageServer?pagename=7_17_03.

33. NPR, "NPR Stations and NPR Programming: Average Quarter Hour Listening, Monday–Sunday, 6a–12m," based on Arbitron Spring Nationwide data, NPR Audience and Corporate Research, Spring 2003; AudiGraphics, "Qualities of All NPR Programming's Listening," National AudiGraphics Consultation Guides, based on audience data from Arbitron, Inc., Spring 2003; Leslie Peters, telephone conversation with author, 16 January 2004.

34. Mike Janssen, "Networks Offer National Talkers to Help Fix Sagging Middays," *Current*, 2 October 2000, 1; WBUR.org, "About the Show," *The Connection* Web site, http://www.theconnection.org/about; NPR, "About the Show," *Day to Day* Web site, http://www.npr.org/programs/day/about.html; *To The Point*, Web site, http://www.moretothepoint.com; Chicago Public Radio "About Odyssey," Chicago Public Radio Website, http://www.chicagopublicradio.org/programs/odyssey/odyssey_about.asp; Raoul Mowatt, "Intellectual 'Odyssey,'" *Chicago Tribune*, 16 June 2004.

35. Jacqueline Conciatore, "With All Ears on Changes in Weekend Programming, Producers Tune Up New Saturday Shows," *Current*, 16 September 1996; Mike Janssen, "New Programs Brighten Radio's Weekend Mood," *Current*, 13 January 2003; NPR, "Wait, Wait ... Don't Tell Me!" Web Site, http://www.npr.org/programs/wait-wait/about.html; "Says You" Web sites, http://www.wgbh.org/schedules/program-info?program_id=30608 and http://www.wgbh.org/radio/saysyou.

36. Public Radio Weekend, Web site, http://www.publicradioweekend.org; Janssen, "New Programs"; American Public Media, "*Public Radio Weekend* Changes Name to *Weekend America*," press release, 1 September 2004, http://www.americanpublicmedia.us/press/pr_090104.html; Minnesota Public Radio, "Major New Public Radio Program, *Weekend America*, Makes Its Debut, Saturday, Oct. 9," press release, 4 October 2004, http://access.minnesota.publicradio.org/press_releases/releases/20041004_weekendamerica.php.

37. Tom Thomas, telephone interview by author, tape recording, transcript, 23 September 2003, NPR OHC; Jacobs Media, "Competitive Scan," prepared for the Corporation for Public Broadcasting, January 2001, 36–40; "Satellite and Wireless Services Gain Traction," *Satellite News*, 20 January 2004, Hoover's Online, http://www.hoovers.com/free, search terms: Sirius Satellite Radio: News.

38. Klose-1, NPR OHC; Stone, "Greetings, Earthlings," 55; Jimmy Schaeffler, "Satellite Radio Growth Beats Expectations," *Satellite News*, 15 December 2003, Hoovers Online, http://www.hoovers.com/free, search terms: Sirius Satellite Radio: News; "Innovations Boost Satellite Radio," *Satellite News*, 20 January 2004, Hoovers Online, http://www.hoovers.com/free. Search terms: Sirius Satellite Radio, News; Sirius Satellite Radio, "Sirius Satellite Radio Reaches 400,000 Subscribers," Sirius News Release, 11 May 2004, http://www.siriusradio.com/servlet/ContentServer?pagename=Sirius/CachedPage&c=PresReleAsset&cid=1083868828228; Sirius Satellite Radio, "Sirius Satellite Radio Passes 700,000 Subscriber Mark," Sirius News Release, 19 October 2004, http://www.siriusradio.com/servlet/ContentServer?pagename=Sirius/CachedPage&c=PresReleAsset&cid=1097008928642; Sirius Satellite Radio, "Sirius Satellite Radio

Now Offered to Millions of Dish Network Homes," Sirius News Release, 20 May 2004, http://www.siriusradio.com/servlet/ContentServer?pagename=Sirius/CachedP age&c=PresReleAsset&cid=1084991108412; XM Satellite Radio, "XM Public Radio," http://www.xmradio.com/programming/channel_page.jsp?ch=133; Lynette Clemetson, "All Things Considered, NPR's Growing Clout Alarms Member Stations," *New York Times*, 30 August 2004.

39. NPR, "Tomorrow Radio Project Announces Stellar Test Results, Declares Victory in Multi-Channel HD Radio Research," NPR Press Release, 9 January 2004, http://www.npr.org/about/press/040109.tomorrowradio.html.

40. Ibid.

41. Boise State Radio, "Idaho's First Digital Radio Station Is on the Air, Boise State Radio News Release, 19 Ocotber 2004, http://radio.boisestate.edu/stations/DigitalRadio.asp; Public Radio Tulsa, "About Us: History," Public Radio Tulsa Web site, http://www.kwgs.org/about.html; Leslie Stimson, "Commercial HD Radios Debut at CES," *RW Online*, 2 January 2004, http://www.rwonline.com/reference-room/iboc/02_rw_ces_preview.shtml.

42. Tom Thomas, telephone conversation with author, 9 January 2004.

43. Karen Everhart Bedford, "Gary Null Special Sparks Debate on Pledge Program Standards," *Current*, 25 January 1999, 1, 16; Karen Everhart, "After Interviews Criticizing Station Practices: She'll Shush About Pledge, Mitchell Says," *Current*, 4 November 2002, 1, 17.

44. Giovannoni-2, NPR OHC; Leslie Peters and David Giovannoni, "Principled Pragmatism," a report to the Corporation for Public Broadcasting, Audience Research Analysis, June 2003, 2; Thomas, NPR OHC.

45. Dan Odenwald, "Hot Over Heartburn Credit: Sounds Illegal to Some," *Current*, 7 April 2003, 1, 5; Giovannoni-2, NPR OHC.

46. Laurence Jarvik, interview by author, tape recording, transcript, 11 August 1995, NPR OHC.

47. Accuracy In Media, "National Public Radio Out of Tune," AIM Report (May-A 1985), 1.

48. William Siemering, e-mail message to Tom Thomas, 16 December 1999, copy of message provided to author by Siemeirng; Donald Quayle, interview by author, tape recording, transcript, Bethesda, Md., 14 August 1995, NPR OHC; James Russell, telephone interview by author, tape recording, transcript, 3 August 1995, NPR OHC; Fonda, "National Prosperous Radio."

49. Siemering to Thomas, 16 December 1999.

50. David Giovannoni, "The Critical Distinctions Between Public and Commercial Radio" (Washington, D.C.: National Public Radio, June 1980), Audience Research Analysis, ARAnet Publications Page, http://www.aranet.com, 4; Tom Thomas and Terry Clifford, "Audience 88: Making Choices: Strategies and Targets," Audience 88 Newsletter, no. 5, Audience Research Analysis, ARAnet Publications page, http://www.aranet.com/library/pdf/doc-0019.pdf, 2–3; Giovannoni, "A Long View of Public Radio's National Audience Growth: Availability and Accessibility Revisited, Part 1: 1970 to 1983" (Washington, D.C.: Corporation for Public Broadcasting, February 1992), Audience Research Analysis, ARAnet Publications page, http://www.aranet.

com. See also David Giovannoni, telephone interview by author, tape recording, transcript, 30 August 1995 (Giovannoni-1), NPR OHC.

51. See Michael P. McCauley, "From the Margins to the Mainstream: The History of National Public Radio" (Ph.D. diss., University of Wisconsin–Madison, 1997), esp. chap. 8.

52. Elissa Ely, "Lying and Meatloaf," January 2001, and Carol Wasserman, "Coyotes Roar," March 2001—both pieces were commentaries that aired on *All Things Considered*. Streaming audio presentations are available at http://www.npr.org/programs/atc/commentaries.

53. SRI Consulting Business Intelligence, "Welcome to VALS," SRI Web site, http://www.sric-bi.com/VALS. Please note that SRI now refers to Actualizer-Fulfilleds as "Innovators and Thinkers"—see SRI Consulting Business Intelligence, "The VALS Segments," SRI Web site, http://www.sric-bi.com/VALS/types.shtml.

54. Jack Mitchell, written correspondence to author, 25 July 1996.

55. Norman Solomon, telephone interview by author, tape recording, transcript, 21 September 1995, NPR OHC; Tom McCourt, *Conflicting Communication Interests in America: The Case of National Public Radio* (Westport, Conn.: Praeger, 1999), esp., 132–41.

56. Frank Tavares and David Giovannoni, "You Get Who You Play For," in *Audience 98: Public Service, Public Support*, ed. Leslie Peters (Washington, D.C., 1999), 33, available through ARAnet Publications, Audience Research Analysis, http://www.aranet.com/library/pdf/doc-0100.pdf; NPR, *Profile 2004: Demographics, Lifestyle Preferences, Consumption Patterns*, NPR Audience and Corporate Research, compiled with data from the Mediamark Research Doublebase 2003/Spring 2003/Fall 2003 MRI studies; SRI Consulting Business Intelligence "Innovators (formerly Actualizers)," SRI Web site, http://www.sric-bi.com/VALS/innovators.shtml.

57. NPR, *Profile 2004*.

58. Copies of the listener comments that appear below were supplied by Rhonda Morin of Maine Public Radio and Bonniejean Hutchison of Wisconsin Public Radio. All names, dates, and other identifying information have been removed to protect the privacy of these listeners.

59. Laura Walker, "The Sound of 2005," in "PRI Envisions 2005," PRI Web site, http://www.pri.org/infosite/networknews/pri_envision.pdf, 26 May 2000, 8.

60. Ibid.

61. Kevin Klose, telephone interview by author, tape recording, transcript, 10 September 2003 (Klose-2), NPR OHC; Kling, NPR OHC; Michael Schudson, *Good Citizens and Bad History: Today's Political Ideals in Historical Perspective*, monograph reproduction of keynote address from "The Transformation of Civic Life: A Conference on Michael Schudson's *The Good Citizen*," 12 November 1999, College of Mass Communication, Middle Tennessee State University, 7–12.

62. Michael Schudson, *The Good Citizen: A History of American Civic Life* (New York: Martin Kessler Books/Free Press, 1998), 310–11.

63. Ira Glass, "The Producer of the Future," in "PRI Envisions 2005," PRI Web site, http://www.pri.org/infosite/networknews/pri_envision.pdf, 26 May 2000, 18; Schudson, *The Good Citizen*, 310.

64. Ibid.,, 311.

65. Schudson, *Good Citizens and Bad History*, 12, 22.

66. Marshel D. Rossow and Sharon Dunwoody, "Inclusion of 'Useful' Detail in Newspaper Coverage of a High-Level Nuclear Waste Siting Controversy," *Journalism Quarterly* 68, nos. 1–2 (1991), 88–94; Stephen Salyer, "Realizing Radio's Power to Transform Lives," a speech the PRI President and CEO presented to public radio development and marketing staff, July 2001, available on the page "From PRI's President," PRI Web site, http://www.pri.org/PublicSite/public/index.html.

67. AFL-CIO, Working Families Toolkit, http://www.aflcio.com/issuespolitics/toolkit; National Rifle Association, Institute for Legislative Action, "Legislative Action Center," http://capwiz.com/nra/state/main/?state=NY&view=media. Land-based public radio stations have taken part in other innovative political communication projects in recent years. See, for example, Public Radio Collaboration, "Whose Democracy Is It?" http://www.whosedemocracy.org; and PRI, "Capitol Hill Bureau From PRI," Inside PRI: PRI Programs, PRI Web site, http://www.pri.org/PublicSite/inside/index.html.

68. Alan G. Stavitsky, "The Changing Conception of Localism in U.S. Public Radio," *Journal of Broadcasting and Electronic Media* 38, no. 1 (Winter 1994): 19–33; NPR, "NPR Discussions," NPR Web page, http://www.npr.org/yourturn/index.html; NPR, "NPR's Mideast Coverage," NPR Web site, http://www.npr.org/news/specials/mideast; Bill Buzenberg, "Seven Ideas for Becoming More Indispensable Locally (It's About Adding Value)," in "Increasing Your Community Value: Becoming Indispensable Locally," 2001, Public Radio International Web Site, http://www.pri.org/PublicSite/public/pdf/community_value.pdf, 8, 11.

69. Lawrence Wilkinson, "The Audience(s) of the Future," in "PRI Envisions 2005," PRI Web site, 26 May 2000, 16, http://www.pri.org/infosite/networknews/pri_envision.pdf.

70. Radio Diaries, "About Radio Diaries," Radio Diaries Web site, http://www.radio-diaries.org/aboutus.html; StoryCorps, "About StoryCorps," StoryCorps Web site, http://www.storycorps.net/about; Mike Janssen, "StoryCorps to Hit the Road, Collecting Intimate Tales," *Current*, 6 September 2004, 1.

71. David Giovannoni, e-mail message to author, 23 March 2004; Corporation for Public Broadcasting, "Public Broadcasting's Services to Minorities and Diverse Audiences: A Report to the 107th Congress and the American People Pursuant to Pub. L. 100–626," December 2002, http://www.cpb.org/pdfs/minority/2002/02_minority_rpt.pdf, 13–15; NPR, *Profile 2001: Demographics, Lifestyle Preferences, Consumption Patterns*, NPR Audience and Corporate Research, compiled with data from the Mediamark Research Fall 2000 MRI Study, July 2001, 4; Audience Research Analysis, "Discrete Programs and Formats," 2001–0429 Listening to Public Radio, based on Arbitron audience research data, provided to author, via e-mail, by David Giovannoni.

72. Mike Janssen, "Stations, NPR Inventing Black-themed Newsmag," *Current*, 28 May 2001, 14; Stephanie Briggs et. al., "People in Public Telecommunications: NPR Wins Tavis Smiley for Black Morning Show," *Current*, 11 June 2001, B21; Mike Janssen, "Tavis: Created for Blacks, but All Are Welcome," *Current*, 24 June 2002, 1, 16; NPR, "NPR and African American Public Radio Stations Announce Agreement with Tavis

Smiley to Develop New Morning Show," NPR Press Release, 31 May 2001, http://www.npr.org/about/press/010531.tavissmiley.html.

73. NPR, NPR Press Releases, http://www.npr.org/about/press; Janssen, "Tavis," 16.

74. AudiGraphics, "Listening to All NPR Programming," "Listening To The Tavis Smiley Show," and "Station Clearance of the Tavis Smiley Show"—all from National AudiGraphics Consultation Guides, based on audience data from Arbitron, Inc., Spring 2002–Fall 2003; "The Tavis Smiley Show on NPR," station listing, http://www.tavistalks.com/TTcom/nprStation.html; Montopoli, "All Things Considerate;" Janssen, "Tavis," 1.

75. Giovannoni, e-mail, 23 March 2004; Leslie Peters, telephone conversation with author, 16 January 2004; Jack Mitchell, e-mail messages to author, 29 December 2003 and 5 January 2004.

76. Steve Carney, "NPR Finds New Home for Its West Coast Push," *Los Angeles Times*, 16 April 2002; Carney, "Around the Dial: Seeing the Light of 'Day' "; "NPR Launches a Culver-City-based Features-Style Magazine Aimed at Younger Listeners," *Los Angeles Times*, 25 July 2003; Mike Janssen, "NPR's *Day to Day* debuts to High Expectations," *Current*, 4 August 2003, 1, 17.

77. Carney, "Around the Dial," Carney, "NPR Finds," Transom.org, "J. J. Sutherland's Topic," http://talk.transom.org/WebX?128@142.HueUau6ojMC.0@.eeaf812; Leslie Peters, ed., *Audience 98: Public Service, Public Support* (Washington, D.C.: Audience Research Analysis and Corporation for Public Broadcasting, 1999), 40, available from the ARA Web site, http://www.aranet.com/library/pdf/doc-0100.pdf; Peters, telephone conversation, 16 January 2004; Giovannoni, e-mail, 23 March 2004; AudiGraphics, "Listening to *Day to Day*" and "Qualities of *Day to Day*'s listening"—both from National AudiGraphics Consultation Guides, based on audience data from Arbitron, Inc., Fall 2003.

78. Peters, ed., *Audience 98*, 33–34, 40.

79. Joseph P. Duggan, "Some Things Considered: Does 'Public Radio'—Financed by the Taxpayers—Represent the Citizenry's Voice?" *The Alternative: An American Spectator* 10, no. 6 (March 1977): 15; Montopoli, "All Things Considerate."

When Montopoli's article was published, PRI was the sole national distributor of *Marketplace, Marketplace Morning Report*, and other Minnesota Public Radio programs. MPR ended most of these agreements in July 2004, and will take over distribution of the *Marketplace* programs in July 2005. These changes are part of MPR's decision to coordinate all of its national production and distribution efforts in-house. See Nicole Garrison-Sprenger, "MPR to Drop PRI for Program Distribution," *The Minneapolis-St. Paul Business Journal*, 9 February 2004, http://www.bizjournals.com/twincities/stories/2004/02/09/daily27.html.

80. Ira Glass, "The Producer of the Future," 19.

81. Ibid.; Jeremy Enger, "Renewal Rate Clouds Public Radio's Horizon," *Current*, 23 August 2004, 1.

82. Sanford Ungar, interview by author, tape recording, transcript (unedited), Washington, D.C., 16 August 1995, NPR OHC; Mike Janssen, "Kroc Gift Lets NPR Expand News, Lower Fees," *Current*, 24 May 2004, 1.

83. NPR, "NPR to Invest Additional $15 Million in NPR News," NPR Press Release, 16 June 2004, http://www.npr.org/about/press/040616.kroc.html; NPR, "We're Recording: NPR Hands the Mic to the Next Generation," NPR Press Release, 12 July 2004, http://www.npr.org/about/press/040712.intern.html; Janssen, "Kroc Gift," 1, 10; Janssen, "Coalition Arises to Coordinate Training in Public Radio System," *Current*, 15 January 2001, 10; Livingston Associates, "Training Programs," Livingston Associates Web site, http://www.livingstonassociates.net/services/training.html; Public Radio News Directors Incorporated, "Training: PRNDI NewsWorks," PRNDI Web site, http://www.prndi.org/training.php; Glass, "The Producer," 20.

SELECTED BIBLIOGRAPHY

ARTICLES, BOOKS, BOOK CHAPTERS, DISSERTATIONS, AND REPORTS

Accuracy In Media. "Conservatives Don't Exist." *AIM Report* (April-A 1988).
——. "National Public Radio Out of Tune." *AIM Report* (May-A 1985).
——. "No Tears for National Public Radio." *AIM Report* (July-A 1983).
AFL-CIO. Working Families Toolkit. http://www.aflcio.com/issuespolitics/toolkit.
Andersen, Robin. *Consumer Culture and TV Programming*. Boulder, Colo.: Westview, 1995.
Audience Research Analysis. "Components of Average Quarter-Hour Audience." ARAnet
    Publications page. http://www.aranet.com/library/pdf/doc-0007.pdf.
——. "Discrete Programs and Formats." 2001–0429 Listening to Public Radio. Based on
    Arbitron audience research data. Provided to author, via e-mail, by David Giovan-
    noni, 2001.
——. "NPR Network Ratings Summary, 1977–1996: Arbitron Nationwide Persons 12+."
    1996.
AudiGraphics. "Listening to All NPR Programming: Weekly Cume Audience." National
    AudiGraphics Consultation Guides. Based on audience research data from Arbitron,
    Inc. 9 October 2003.
——. "Listening to *Day to Day*." National AudiGraphics Consultation Guides. Based on
    audience data from Arbitron, Inc. Fall 2003.
——. "Listening to *The Tavis Smiley Show*." National AudiGraphics Consultation Guides.
    Based on audience data from Arbitron, Inc. Spring 2002–Fall 2003.

———. "Qualities of All NPR Programming's Listening." National AudiGraphics Consultation Guides. Based on audience data from Arbitron, Inc. Spring 2003.

———. "Qualities of *Day to Day*'s Listening." National AudiGraphics Consultation Guides. Based on audience data from Arbitron, Inc. Fall 2003.

———. "Station Clearance of *The Tavis Smiley Show*." National AudiGraphics Consultation Guides. Based on audience data from Arbitron, Inc. Spring 2002–Fall 2003.

Aufderheide, Patricia. "After the Fairness Doctrine: Controversial Broadcast Programming and the Public Interest." *Journal of Communication* 40, no. 3 (1990): 47–72.

———. "Will Public Broadcasting Survive?" *The Progressive* (March 1995): 19–21.

Bailey, George. "Mega Trends: The Public Radio Tracking Study. Special Report." Greenbush, Wis.: Walrus Research December 2003. ARAnet Publications page. http://www.aranet.com/library/pdf/doc-0110.pdf.

———. "The Public Radio Tracking Study: Trend Report, Winter–Fall 1999." Greenbush, Wis.: Walrus Research, August 2000. Audience Research Analysis. ARAnet Publications page. http://www.aranet.com/library/pdf/doc-0103.pdf.

Bailey, George, and Tom Church. "Public Radio and the Ratings." *Public Telecommunications Review* 7 (November/December 1979): 47–49.

Barnes, Fred. "All Things Distorted: The Trouble with NPR." *New Republic*, 27 October 1986, 17–19.

Barnouw, Erik. *A Tower in Babel.* New York: Oxford University Press, 1966.

Baughman, James L. *Television's Guardians: The FCC and the Politics of Programming, 1958–1967.* Knoxville: University of Tennessee Press, 1985.

Bennet, Douglas J. "Bennet Reviews His First Year as NPR Head." *Public Broadcasting Report*, 16 November 1984, 4–6.

Blakely, Robert J. *To Serve the Public Interest: Educational Broadcasting in the United States.* Syracuse, N.Y.: Syracuse University Press, 1979.

Bozell, L. Brent III, and Brent H. Baker, eds. *And That's the Way It Isn't: A Reference Guide to Media Bias.* Alexandria, Va.: Media Research Center, 1990.

British Broadcasting Company. "About the BBC: BBC Channels." BBC Web site. http://www.bbc.co.uk/info/channels.

Brown, Les. *Keeping Your Eye on Television.* New York: Pilgrim Press, 1979.

Brown, Les. *Television: The Business Behind the Box.* New York: Harcourt Brace Jovanovich, 1971.

Burke, John E. *An Historical-Analytical Study of the Legislative and Political Origins of the Public Broadcasting Act of 1967.* New York: Arno Press, 1979.

Buzenberg, Bill. "Seven Ideas for Becoming More Indispensable Locally (It's About Adding Value)." In "Increasing Your Community Value: Becoming Indispensable Locally," 5–13. 2001. Public Radio International Web site. http://www.pri.org/PublicSite/public/pdf/community_value.pdf.

Cahalan, Joseph M. "Congress, Mass Communications and Public Policy—the Public Broadcasting Act of 1967." Ph.D. diss., New York University, 1971.

Cannon, Carl M. "NPR." *Forbes Media Critic* (1995): 70–75.

Carnegie Commission on Educational Television. *Public Television: A Program for Action.* New York: Bantam, 1967.

Caro, Robert A. *The Years of Lyndon Johnson: Means of Ascent.* New York: Alfred A. Knopf, 1990.

"CEOs Optimistic About 2004 Outlook." *Satellite News,* 8 March 2004. Hoovers Online. http://www.hoovers.com/free, Search terms: Sirius Satellite Radio, News.

Chafe, William. *The Unfinished Journey: America Since World War II.* 2d ed. New York: Oxford University Press, 1991.

Chicago Public Radio. "About Odyssey." Chicago Public Radio Web site. http://www.chicagopublicradio.org/programs/odyssey/odyssey_about.asp.

Christopher, L. Carol. "The King of Coffee Talk." *Quill.* December, 1999.

Colker, David. "The New Competition in Non-commercial Radio." *Los Angeles Herald Examiner,* 13 September 1982.

Collins, Mary. *National Public Radio: The Cast of Characters.* Washington, D.C.: Seven Locks Press, 1993.

Colson, Charles. Memo to H. R. Haldeman, 9 July 1971. In *Richard Nixon's Secret Files,* ed. Bruce Oudes, 290. New York: Harper and Row, 1989.

Congressional Quarterly. "Charges of Liberal Bias Stall Public Broadcasting Bill." *Congressional Quarterly Weekly Report,* 22 February 1992, 400–402.

——. "Public Broadcasting: Will Political Attacks and New Technologies Force Big Changes?" *The CQ Researcher,* 18 September 1992, 809–32.

Corporation for Public Broadcasting. Annual Reports. FY 1969–FY 1976. Washington, D.C.: Corporation for Public Broadcasting.

——. "Audience 88 Newsletters." Washington, D.C.: Corporation for Public Broadcasting. Audience Research Analysis, 1988. ARAnet Publications page, http://www.aranet.com/library/pdf/doc-0019.pdf.

——. "Brief Biography of Donald Quayle." Archives of the Corporation for Public Broadcasting: Donald R. Quayle Files. National Public Broadcasting Archives Web site. http://www.lib.umd.edu/NPBA/papers/quayle.html.

——. "From Wasteland to Oasis: A Quarter Century of Sterling Programming." CPB 1991 Annual Report. Washington, D.C.: Corporation for Public Broadcasting, 1991.

——. "Public Broadcasting's Services to Minorities and Diverse Audiences: A Report to the 107th Congress and the American People Pursuant to Pub. L. 100–626." December 2002. http://www.cpb.org/pdfs/minority/2002/02_minority_rpt.pdf.

——. "Recipients of the Edward R. Murrow Award." CPB Web site. http://www.cpb.org/about/awards/murrow/murrowlist.html.

——. *A Report to the People: Twenty Years of Your National Commitment to Public Broadcasting, 1967–1987.* Washington, D.C.: Corporation for Public Broadcasting, 1987.

——. "Summary of Corporation for Public Broadcasting Authorizations and Appropriations, Fiscal Years 1969–1997." Washington, D.C.: National Public Radio, 1996. Obtained from Sarah Sloan, NPR.

Crisell, Andrew. Review of *Public Broadcasting and the Public Interest,* ed. Michael P. McCauley, Eric E. Peterson, B. Lee Artz, and DeeDee Halleck. *European Journal of Communication* 18, no. 4 (December 2003): 550.

Dart, Bob. "GOP Firm in PBS Aid Debate: Democrats Say Cuts Jeopardize Popular Shows." *Wisconsin State Journal,* 20 January 1995.

——. "Hill Story Puts Face to NPR Voice: Nina Totenberg Becomes the News." *Atlanta Journal-Constitution*, 21 October 1991.

DeParle, Jason. "I.O.U.s at NPR: All Things Considered—Except One." *New Republic*, May 1983, 17–18.

Douglas, Susan J. *Inventing American Broadcasting, 1899-1922*. Baltimore, Md.: Johns Hopkins University Press, 1987.

Duggan, Joseph P. "Some Things Considered: Does 'Public Radio'—Financed by the Taxpayers—Represent the Citizenry's Views?" *The Alternative: An American Spectator* 10, no. 6 (March 1977): 13–15.

Ely, Elissa. "Lying and Meatloaf." An *All Things Considered* commentary. January 2001. A streaming audio presentation is available at http://www.npr.org/programs/atc/commentaries.

Engelman, Ralph. *Public Radio and Television in America: A Political History*. Thousand Oaks, Calif.: Sage, 1995.

Fisher, Marc. "The Soul of a News Machine." *Washington Post Magazine*, 22 October 1989, 16–23, 37–42.

Foust, James C. *Big Voices of the Air: The Battle Over Clear Channel Radio*. Ames: Iowa State University Press, 2000.

Fox, Nicols. "Public Radio's Air Wars." *Columbia Journalism Review* (January/February 1992): 9–10.

——. "NPR Grows Up." *Washington Journalism Review* (September 1991): 30–36.

Francisco, Patricia W. "The Life and Times of MPR." *Minnesota Monthly* 21, no. 1 (January 1987): 50–57.

"From Space to Car, Satellite Radio Is Making Waves World Over." *Asia Intelligence Wire*, 30 November 2003. Hoover's Online. http://www.hoovers.com/free. Search terms: Sirius Satellite Radio, News.

Garrison-Sprenger, Nicole. "MPR to Drop PRI for Program Distribution." *The Minneapolis-St. Paul Business Journal*, 9 February 2004. Available from http://www.bizjournals.com/twincities/stories/2004/02/09/daily27.html.

Garry, Kenneth John. "The History of National Public Radio: 1974–1977." Ph.D. diss., Southern Illinois University at Carbondale, 1982.

Gelfand, Mark. "Ralph Lowell—Brief Life of a 'Grand Bostonian': 1890–1978." Harvard Magazine Web site. http://www.harvard-magazine.com/issues/mj97/vita.html. May–June 1997.

Gibson, George H. *Public Broadcasting: The Role of the Federal Government, 1912-76*. New York: Praeger, 1977.

Giovannoni, David. "The Cheap 90. Public Radio Listeners: Supporters and Non-Supporters." Washington, D.C.: Corporation for Public Broadcasting. Audience Research Analysis, 1985. Available from ARAnet Publications page, http://www.aranet.com/library/pdf/doc-0004.pdf.

——. "The Critical Distinctions Between Public and Commercial Radio." Washington, D.C.: National Public Radio, June 1980. Audience Research Analysis. ARAnet Publications Page. http://www.aranet.com.

——. "A Long View of Public Radio's National Audience Growth: Availability and Accessibility Revisited. Part 1: 1970 to 1983." Washington, D.C.: Corporation for Public Broadcasting, February 1992. Audience Research Analysis. ARAnet Publications page. http://www.aranet.com.

——. "A Long View of Public Radio's National Audience Growth: Availability and Accessibility Revisited. Part 2: 1983 to Today." Washington, D.C.: Corporation for Public Broadcasting, March 1992. Audience Research Analysis. ARAnet Publications Page. http://www.aranet.com.

——. Memo to Public Radio Stations about Program Affinity, Audience Response, and Program Economics. 16 September 1996.

——. "The Personal Importance of Public Radio." Washington, D.C.: Corporation for Public Broadcasting, 1988. Audience Research Analysis. ARAnet Publications page. http://www.aranet.com/library/pdf/doc-0010.pdf.

——. "How Public Radio Gained Two Million Listeners." Washington, D.C.: Corporation for Public Broadcasting, 1982. Audience Research Analysis. ARAnet Publications page. http://www.aranet.com/library/pdf/doc-0003.pdf.

Giovannoni, David, Thomas J. Thomas, and Theresa R. Clifford. "Public Radio Programming Strategies." Washington, D.C.: Corporation for Public Broadcasting, 1992. Audience Research Analysis. ARAnet Publications page. http://www.aranet.com/library/pdf/doc-0064.pdf.

Giovannoni, David, Thomas J. Thomas, Theresa R. Clifford, John F. Berky, and Richard H. Madden. "Programming Economics." Washington, D.C.: Corporation for Public Broadcasting, 1989. Audience Research Analysis. ARAnet Publications page. http://www.aranet.com/library/pdf/doc-0023.pdf.

Glass, Ira. "The Producer of the Future." In "PRI Envisions 2005." PRI Web site. http://www.pri.org/infosite/networknews/pri_envision.pdf. 18–20. 26 May 2000.

Haney, James Michael. "A History of the Merger of National Public Radio and the Association of Public Radio Stations." Ph.D. diss., University of Iowa, 1981.

Hart, Benjamin. "Ventriloquist Journalism at National Public Radio." *Policy Review* (Spring 1984): 75–78.

Head, Sydney W., and Christopher H. Sterling. *Broadcasting in America: A Survey of Electronic Media*. 6th ed. Boston: Houghton Mifflin, 1990.

Henry, Neil, and Lucy Howard. "Going Private in Public." *Newsweek*, 7 December 1981, 105–6.

Herman W. Land Associates. "The Hidden Medium: A Status Report on Educational Radio in the United States." Prepared for National Educational Radio. New York, 1967.

Hill, Harold E. *The National Association of Educational Broadcasters: A History*. Urbana, Ill.: National Association of Educational Broadcasters, 1954.

"The History of Car Talk." Car Talk Web site. http://cartalk.com/content/about/history.

Hockenberry, John. *Moving Violations*. New York: Hyperion, 1995.

Holt, Samuel C. O. *The Public Radio Study*. Washington, D.C.: Corporation for Public Broadcasting, 1969.

Horowitz, David, and Laurence Jarvik, eds. *Public Broadcasting and the Public Trust*. Los Angeles: Second Thoughts Books, 1995.

Hoynes, William. *Public Television For Sale: Media, the Market, and the Public Sphere*. Boulder, Colo.: Westview Press, 1994.

Husseini, Sam. "The Broken Promise of Public Radio." *The Humanist* (September/October 1994): 26–29.

"Innovations Boost Satellite Radio." *Satellite News*, 20 January 2004. Hoovers Online. http://www.hoovers.com/free. Search terms: Sirius Satellite Radio, News.

"It's an SDX Hat Trick for National Public Radio: Three Journalism Awards in One Year." *The Quill*, July 1992, 38.

Jacobs Media. "Competitive Scan." Prepared for the Corporation for Public Broadcasting. January 2001.

Jansky, C. M., Jr. "The Beginnings of Radio Broadcasting." Transcript of remarks presented at the WHA Family Dinner at the University of Wisconsin, 24 November 1958. Pamphlet Collection, State Historical Society of Wisconsin, Madison.

Kahn, Frank J., ed. *Documents of American Broadcasting.* 4th ed. Englewood Cliffs, N.J.: Prentice-Hall, 1984.

Kirkish, Joseph Brady. "A Descriptive History of America's First National Public Radio Network: National Public Radio, 1970 to 1974." Ph.D. diss., University of Michigan, 1980.

Klein, Naomi. Remarks made in the keynote address at the international conference of the Union for Democratic Communications. Ottawa, Ont., Canada. 18 May 2001.

KUT-FM. "KUT GM Named 'General Manager of the Year' at National Conference." KUT-FM Press Release. 17 July 2003. http://www.kut.org/site/PageServer?pagename=7_17_03.

Lagemann, Ellen C. *The Politics of Knowledge: The Carnegie Corporation, Philanthropy, and Public Policy.* Middletown, Conn.: Wesleyan University Press, 1989.

Lashner, Marilyn A. "The Role of Foundations in Public Broadcasting, Part I: Development and Trends." *Journal of Broadcasting* 20, no. 4 (1976): 529–47.

———. "The Role of Foundations in Public Broadcasting, Part II: The Ford Foundation." *Journal of Broadcasting* 21, no. 2 (1977): 235–54.

Lasswell, Harold D. "Educational Broadcasters as Social Scientists." *Quarterly of Film, Radio, and Television* 7 (1952): 150–62.

Livingston Associates. "Training Programs." Livingston Associates Web site. http://www.livingstonassociates.net/services/training.html.

Looker, Thomas. *The Sound and the Story: NPR and the Art of Radio.* Boston: Houghton Mifflin, 1995.

Mander, Mary S. "The Public Debate About Broadcasting in the Twenties: An Interpretive History." *Journal of Broadcasting* 28, no. 2 (1984): 167–85.

McCauley, Michael P. "From the Margins to the Mainstream: The History of National Public Radio." Ph.D. diss., University of Wisconsin-Madison, 1997.

McChesney, Robert W. "Public Broadcasting in the Age of Communication Revolution." *Monthly Review* 47, no. 7 (1995): 1–19.

———. *Telecommunications, Mass Media, and Democracy: The Battle for the Control of U.S. Broadcasting, 1928-1935.* New York: Oxford University Press, 1993.

McCourt, Tom. *Conflicting Communication Interests in America: The Case of National Public Radio.* Westport, Conn.: Praeger, 1999.

McKinsey&Company. "Public Service Broadcasters Around the World: A McKinsey Report for the BBC." January 1999.

Miami Dolphins. "Administration Profile: H. Wayne Huizenga." Miami Dolphins Web site. http://www.miamidolphins.com/contacts/administration/admin_huizenga_w.asp.

Minnesota Public Radio. "Minnesota Public Radio Organizational Structure." MPR Web site. http://access.minnesota.public.radio.org/aboutMPR/docs/structure.htm.

——. "SCPR Names Bill Davis New CEO." Minnesota Public Radio Press Release. 18 December 2000. MPR Web site. http://www.access. minnesota.public.radio.org/press_releases/releases/20001219_scprceo.html.

Montopoli, Brian. "All Things Considerate: How NPR Makes Tavis Smiley Sound Like Linda Wertheimer." *Washington Monthly* (January/February 2003).

Mullally, Donald P. "Radio: The Other Public Medium." *Journal of Communication* 30, no. 3 (1980): 189–97.

NAEB. *The Nixon Administration Public Broadcasting Papers: A Summary, 1969–1974.* Urbana, Ill.: National Association of Educational Broadcasters, 1979.

Nord, David Paul. "The FCC, Educational Broadcasting, and Political Interest Group Activity." *Journal of Broadcasting* 22, no. 3 (1978): 321–38.

NPR. "About Fresh Air." NPR Web site. http://freshair.npr.org/about_fa.jhtml.

——. "About the Show," *Day to Day* Web site. http://www.npr.org/programs/day/about.html.

——. "Cokie Roberts, Senior News Analyst." NPR Web site. http://www.npr.org/about/people/bios/croberts.html.

——. "Margaret Low Smith Named Vice President for NPR2, NPR's New Satellite Radio Unit." NPR Press Release. http://www.npr.org/about/press/001017.npr2.html. 17 October, 2000.

——. "Mark Handley: President, New Hampshire Public Radio." NPR Board of Directors Bios. http://www.npr.org/about/people/bios/mhandley.html.

——. "National Public Radio: What Is It? Who Listens? How Is It Funded?" Washington, D.C.: National Public Radio, 1993.

——. "NPR and African American Public Radio Stations Announce Agreement with Tavis Smiley to Develop New Morning Show." NPR Press Release. 31 May 2001. http://www.npr.org/about/press/010531.tavissmiley.html.

—— "NPR Announces Partnership with CPRN Music Service." NPR Press Release. 5 May 2003. http://www.npr.org/about/press/030505.cprn.html.

——. NPR Annual Reports, FY 1977–FY 2002. Washington, D.C.: National Public Radio.

——. "NPR Discussions." NPR Web page. http://www.npr.org/yourturn/index.html.

——. "NPR Establishes Major Production Center in California: NPR West Opens November 2, Expanding Network's Presence and Reach." NPR Press Release. 16 October 2002. http://www.npr.org/about/press/021016.nprwest.html.

——. "NPR Expands Westward Coverage, Presence Enhanced with New Production Center." NPR Press Release. 16 April 2002. http://www.npr.org/about/press/020416.nprwest.html.

——"The Expansion of NPR News." NPR Web site. http://www.npr.org/about/news.html.

——. "NPR Names M. J. Bear as Vice President, NPR Online." NPR Press Release. 28 January 2000. http://www.npr.org/about/press/000128.mjbear.html.

——. "NPR Now." NPR Web site. http://www.npr.org/programs/nprnow/index.html.

——. "NPR Receives $14 Million from MacArthur Foundation: $4 Million for Endowment Support, $10 Million for News/Public Affairs Programming." NPR Press Release. 13 January 2003. http://www.npr.org/about/press/030113.macarthur.html.

——. "NPR's Bob Edwards Leaving Morning Edition Host Chair to Take on New Assignments as NPR Senior Correspondent." NPR Press Release. http://www.npr.org/about/press/040323.bobedwards.html. 23 March 2004.

——. "NPR's Mideast Coverage." NPR Web site. http://www.npr.org/news/specials/mideast.

——. "NPR Stations and NPR Programming: Average Quarter Hour Listening, Monday–Sunday, 6a–12m." Based on Arbitron Spring Nationwide data. NPR Audience and Corporate Research, Spring 2003.

——. "NPR Talk," NPR Web site, http://www.npr.org/programs/nprtalk/index.html.

——. "NPR Worldwide." NPR Web site, http://www.npr.org/worldwide.

——. *Profile 2001: Demographics, Lifestyle Preferences, Consumption Patterns.* NPR Audience and Corporate Research. Compiled with data from the Mediamark Research Fall 2000 MRI Study, July 2001.

——. *Profile 2003: Demographics, Lifestyle Preferences, Consumption Patterns.* NPR Audience and Corporate Research. Compiled with data from the Mediamark Research Fall 2002/Doublebase 2002 MRI Study, July 2003.

——. *Profile 2004: Demographics, Lifestyle Preferences, Consumption Patterns.* NPR Audience and Corporate Research. Compiled with data from the Mediamark Research Doublebase 2003/Spring 2003/Fall 2003 MRI Studies, July 2004.

——. "Terry Gross Biography." NPR Web site. http://www.npr.org/about/people/bios/tgross.html.

——. "Tomorrow Radio Project Announces Stellar Test Results, Declares Victory in Multi-Channel HD Radio Research." NPR Press Release. 9 January 2004. http://www.npr.org/about/press/040109.tomorrowradio.html.

——. "Wait, Wait . . . Don't Tell Me!" Web Site. http://www.npr.org/programs/waitwait/about.html.

National Rifle Association, Institute for Legislative Action. Legislative Action Center. http://capwiz.com/nra/state/main/?state=NY&view=media.

Odenwald, Dan. "Knocking God's Party: Moyers, PBS hear from Angry Conservatives." *Current*, 2 December 2002, 18.

Pepper, Robert M. "The Formation of the Public Broadcasting Service." Ph.D. diss., University of Wisconsin–Madison, 1975.

Peters, Leslie, ed. *Audience 98: Public Service, Public Support.* Washington, D.C.: Audience Research Analysis and Corporation for Public Broadcasting, 1999. Available from the ARA Web site, http://www.aranet.com/library/pdf/doc-0100.pdf.

Peters, Leslie, and David Giovannoni. "Principled Pragmatism." A report to the Corporation for Public Broadcasting. Audience Research Analysis. June 2003.

Porter, Bruce. "Has Success Spoiled NPR? Becoming Part of the Establishment Can Have Its Drawbacks." *Columbia Journalism Review* (September/October 1990): 26–32.

Public Radio Collaboration. "Whose Democracy Is It?" http://www.whosedemocracy.org.

Public Radio International. "About Laura Walker." In "PRI Envisions 2005." PRI Web site. http://www.pri.org/infosite/networknews/pri_envision.pdf, 7. 26 May 2000.

——. "Capitol Hill Bureau From PRI." Inside PRI: PRI Programs. PRI Web site. http://www.pri.org/PublicSite/inside/index.html.

——. PRI Programs. Public Radio International Web site. http://www.pri.org/Public-Site/inside/index.html.

——. "PRI's Public Radio Channel: Connecting the World to Your Life." PRI Web site. http://www.pri.org/PublicSite/listeners/sirius_schedule.html.

Public Radio News Directors Incorporated. "Training: PRNDI NewsWorks." PRNDI Web site. http://www.prndi.org/training.php.

Public Radio Weekend. Web site. http://www.publicradioweekend.org.

Radio Diaries. "About Radio Diaries," Radio Diaries Web site. http://www.radiodiaries.org/aboutus.html.

Reeves, Michael G., and Tom W. Hoffer. "The Safe, Cheap, and Known: A Content Analysis of the First (1974) PBS Program Cooperative." *Journal of Broadcasting* 20, no. 4 (1976): 549–65.

Robertson, Lori. "Quicker *and* Deeper?" *American Journalism Review* (June/July 2004). http://www.ajr.org/Article.asp?id=3700.

Rossow, Marshel D., and Sharon Dunwoody. "Inclusion of 'Useful' Detail in Newspaper Coverage of a High-Level Nuclear Waste Siting Controversy." *Journalism Quarterly* 68, nos. 1–2 (1991): 88–94.

Ryan, Charlotte. "A Study of National Public Radio." *EXTRA!* (April/May 1993): 18–21, 26.

Salyer, Stephen. "Realizing Radio's Power to Transform Lives." July 2001. Available on the page "From PRI's President." PRI Web site. http://www.pri.org/PublicSite/public/index.html.

——. "Monopoly to Marketplace—Competition Comes to Public Radio." *Media Studies Journal* 7, no. 3 (Summer 1993): 176–83.

"Satellite and Wireless Services Gain Traction." *Satellite News*, 20 January 2004, Hoover's Online, http://www.hoovers.com/free. Search terms: Sirius Satellite Radio: News.

Schaeffler, Jimmy. "Satellite Radio Growth Beats Expectations." *Satellite News*, 15 December 2003. Hoovers Online. http://www.hoovers.com/free. Search terms: Sirius Satellite Radio, News.

Severin, Werner J. "Commercial vs. Non-Commercial Radio During Broadcasting's Early Years." *Journal of Broadcasting* 22, no. 4 (1978): 491–504.

Schudson, Michael. *The Good Citizen: A History of American Civic Life*. New York: Martin Kessler Books/Free Press, 1998.

——. *Good Citizens and Bad History: Today's Political Ideals in Historical Perspective*. Monograph reproduction of keynote address at "The Transformation of Civic Life: A Conference on Michael Schudson's *The Good Citizen*." College of Mass Communication. Middle Tennessee State University, 12 November 1999.

Shimp, Terence A. *Advertising Promotion: Supplemental Aspects of Integrated Marketing Communications*. Fort Worth, Tex.: The Dryden Press, 2000.

Tavares, Frank, and David Giovannoni. "You Get Who You Play For." In *Audience 98: Public Service, Public Support*, ed. Leslie Peters, 33–34. Washington, D.C.: Corporation for Public Broadcasting, 1999. ARAnet Publications, Audience Research Analysis, http://www.aranet.com/library/pdf/doc-0100.pdf.

Siemering, William H. "National Public Radio Purposes." National Public Broadcasting Archives, University of Maryland, College Park, Md. Elizabeth Young Papers, B1, F11, 1970.

Sky Radio. "Now Airing on Delta Airlines: Sky Business." Sky Radio Web site. http://www.skyradionet.com/delta.cfm.

Smith, Leslie F., John W. Wright II, and David H. Ostroff. *Perspectives on Radio and Television: Telecommunication in the United States.* 4th ed. Mahwah, N.J.: Lawrence Erlbaum, 1998.

Smulyan, Susan. *Selling Radio: The Commercialization of American Broadcasting, 1920-1934.* Washington, D.C.: Smithsonian Institution Press, 1994.

SRI Consulting Business Intelligence. "Innovators (formerly Actualizers)." SRI Web site. http://www.sric-bi.com/VALS/innovators.shtml.

——. "The VALS Segments." SRI Web site. http://www.sric-bi.com/VALS/types.shtml.

——. "Welcome to VALS." SRI Web site. http://www.sric-bi.com/VALS.

Starr, Jerold M. "Public Television in the Digital Age: Town Hall or Cyber Mall?" In *Public Broadcasting and the Public Interest*, ed. Michael P. McCauley, Eric E. Peterson, B. Lee Artz, and DeeDee Halleck, 238–51 Armonk, N.Y.: M. E. Sharpe, 2003.

Station Resource Group. "Listener Support and Underwriting: Revenue, Costs, and Net Return to Operations." May 2004. http://www.srg.org/funding/o2revenueupdate.pdf.

——. "Public Radio Income 80–98." A spreadsheet based on data from the Corporation for Public Broadcasting. Provided to author by Tom Thomas.

Stavitsky, Alan G. "The Changing Conception of Localism in U.S. Public Radio." *Journal of Broadcasting and Electronic Media* 38, no. 1 (Winter 1994): 19–33.

——. "Guys in Suits with Charts: Audience Research in U.S. Public Radio." *Journal of Broadcasting and Electronic Media* 39, no. 2 (Spring 1995): 177–89.

——. "Listening for Listeners: Educational Radio and Audience Research." *Journalism History* 19, no. 1 (Spring 1993): 11–18.

Sterling, Christopher H., and John M. Kittross. *Stay Tuned: A Concise History of American Broadcasting.* 2nd ed. Belmont, Calif.: Wadsworth, 1990.

Stimson, Leslie. "Commercial HD Radios Debut at CES." RW Online. 2 January 2004. http://www.rwonline.com/reference-room/iboc/o2_rw_ces_preview.shtml.

Stone, David M. *Nixon and the Politics of Public Television.* New York: Garland, 1985.

StoryCorps. "About StoryCorps," StoryCorps Web site. http://www.storycorps.net/about.

"The News Turns Worse at National Public Radio." *BusinessWeek*, 4 July 1983, 41–42.

Thomas, Thomas J., and Theresa R. Clifford. "Audience 88: Issues and Implications." Washington, D.C.: Corporation for Public Broadcasting, 1988. Audience Research Analysis. ARAnet Publications page, http://www.aranet.com/library/pdf/doc-0017.pdf.

——. "Audience 88: Making Choices: Strategies and Targets." Audience 88 Newsletter, no. 5. Washington, D.C.: Corporation for Public Broadcasting, 1988. Audience Research Analysis, ARAnet Publications page. http://www.aranet.com/library/pdf/doc-0019.pdf.

Thomas, Thomas J., Theresa R. Clifford and David Giovannoni. "Programming and Audience Trends." Washington, D.C.: Corporation for Public Broadcasting, 1993. Audience Research Analysis, ARAnet Publications page. http://www.aranet.com/library/pdf/doc-0094.pdf.

To The Point. Web site. http://www.moretothepoint.com.

Transom.org. "J.J.Sutherland's Topic." http://talk.transom.org/WebX?128@142.HueUau6ojMC.o@.eeaf812.

Tucker, William. "Public Radio Comes to Market." *Fortune*, 18 October 1982, 205, 208, 210.

"Two Decades at a Glance." *Minnesota Monthly* 21, no. 1 (January 1987): 58.

University of Wisconsin Extension, "The University of Wisconsin Extension Telecommunications Center." Promotional pamphlet, 1972.

U.S. Congress. *The Radio Act of 1912*. Public Law 264. 62nd Congress. 13 August 1912. Available in Frank J. Kahn, ed., *Documents of American Broadcasting*, 4th ed. pp. 14–22. Englewood Cliffs, NJ: Prentice-Hall, 1984.

——. *The Radio Act of 1927*. Public Law 632. 69th U.S. Congress. 2nd session. 23 February 1927. Available in Frank J. Kahn, ed., *Documents of American Broadcasting*. 4th ed. Englewood Cliffs, N.J.: Prentice-Hall, 1984.

U.S. Congress, House. *Congressional Record*. 90th Cong., 1st sess., 1967. Public Broadcasting Act of 1967. S. 21.

——. 90th Cong. 1st sess. *House of Representatives Report on the Public Broadcasting Act of 1967*. 21 August 1967. H. Rept. 572. Washington, D.C.: United States Government Printing Office.

——. *Conference Report on the Public Broadcasting Act of 1967*. 90th Cong. 1st sess. 18 October 1967. H. Rept. 794. Washington: Government Printing Office, 1967.

——. Committee on Interstate and Foreign Commerce. 1st session 90th Congress. Hearings, Public Television Act of 1967. 90-09.

U.S. Congress, Senate. *Congressional Record*. 90th Cong., 1st sess., 1967. Public Broadcasting Act of 1967.

——. *Report on the Public Broadcasting Act of 1967*. 90th Cong. 1st sess. 11 May 1967. S. Rept. 222. Washington, D.C.: Government Printing Office.

——. Committee on Commerce, Subcommittee on Communications. 90th Cong. 1st sess. *The Public Television Act of 1967: Hearings Before the Subcommittee on Communications of the Committee on Commerce*. Washington, D.C.: Government Printing Office, 1967.

U.S. Department of State. "Ambassador Delano E. Lewis." Web site of U.S. Embassies and Consulates. http://usembassy.state.gov/pretoria/wwwham5.html.

U.S. Federal Radio Commission. "FRC Interpretation of the Public Interest: Statement Made by the Commission on 23 August 1928, Relative to Public Interest, Convenience, or Necessity." In Frank J. Kahn, ed., *Documents of American Broadcasting*, 4th ed., 57–62. Englewood Cliffs, N.J.: Prentice-Hall, 1984.

Walker, Laura. "The Sound of 2005." In "PRI Envisions 2005." PRI Web site. http://www.pri.org/infosite/networknews/pri_envision.pdf. 8–11. 26 May 2000.

Warnock, Tom. "An Early Look at *All Things Considered*." *Educational Broadcasting Review* 5, no. 3 (June 1971): 61–62.

Wasserman, Carol. "Coyotes Roar." An *All Things Considered* commentary. March 2001. Streaming audio presentation available at http://www.npr.org/programs/atc/commentaries.

WBUR.org. "About the Show." *The Connection* Web site. http://www.theconnection.org/about.

WEAA-FM. "Who Is WEAA." WEAA-FM Web site. http://www.weaa.org/about/who_is_weaa.php.

Wesleyan University. "Douglas J. Bennet biography." Wesleyan University Web site. http://www.wesleyan.edu/home/DJB_Bio.htm.

WGBH-Boston. "Says You" Web sites. http://www.wgbh.org/schedules/program-info?program_id=30608; http://www.wgbh.org/radio/saysyou.

Wilkinson, Lawrence. "The Audience(s) of the Future." In "PRI Envisions 2005." PRI Web site. http://www.pri.org/infosite/networknews/pri_envision.pdf. 14–16. 26 May 2000.

Witherspoon, John, and Roselle Kovitz. *A History of Public Broadcasting*, with an update by Robert K. Avery and Alan G. Stavitsky. 1987; Washington, D.C.: Current, 2000.

Zorn, Eric. "At Its Peak, NPR Falls Through the Bottom Line." *Chicago Tribune*, 1 August 1983. Personal files of James L. Baughman.

Zuckerman, Laurence. "Has Success Spoiled NPR?" *Mother Jones* (June/July 1987): 32–39, 44–45.

Frequently Consulted Newspapers, Magazines, and Other Periodicals

Broadcasting (now *Broadcasting and Cable*)
Chicago Tribune
Current
Educational Broadcasting Review
In These Times
Los Angeles Times
NAB Highlights
NAEB Letter
NAEB Newsletter
NATRB Reporter
Newsweek
New York Times
Public Telecommunications Letter
Public Telecommunications Review
Time
Variety
Washington Post

Oral History Interview Transcripts

Michael P. McCauley NPR Oral History Collection at the National Public Broadcasting Archives, Hornbake Library, University of Maryland, College Park, Md. (NPR OHC).
Douglas Bennet, 31 July 1995.
Ronald Bornstein, 3 July 1995.
William Buzenberg, 28 May 1998.
Ted Clark, 23 August 1995.
Barbara Cochran, 15 August 1995.
Neal Conan, 15 August 1995.

Jeffrey Dvorkin, 9 June 2000.

Edward Elson, 2 November 1995.

Deborah Emanation, 13 October 1995.

Richard Estell, 5 July 1995.

Lee Frischknecht, 4 August 1995.

David Giovannoni, 30 August 1995, 10 July 2003.

Robert Goldfarb, 12 September 1995.

Joseph Gwathmey, 3 August 1995.

Susan Harmon, 20 September 1995.

Samuel C. O. Holt, 23 August 1995.

Al Hulsen, 2 August 1995.

Laurence Jarvik, 11 August 1995.

Jay Kernis, 8 September 2003.

Thomas Kigin, 28 May 1998.

William Kling, 26 July 1995.

Kevin Klose, 7 June 2000, 10 September 2003.

Richard Kolm, 31 August 1995.

Herman Land, 3 November 1995.

Delano Lewis, 15 August 1995.

Frank Mankiewicz, 14 August 1995.

Cleve Mathews, 30 June 1995.

Steve Meuche, 31 July 1995.

George Miles, 25 August 1995.

Jack Mitchell, 28 April 1995, 19 September 1995, 25 September 1995, 26 May 1998.

Donald Mullally, 12 July 1995.

Adam Clayton Powell III, 1 August 1995, 20 August 2003.

Donald Quayle, 14 August 1995.

Steve Rathe, 3 August 1995.

Jeff Rosenberg, 14 August 1995.

Jim Russell, 3 August 1995.

Karl Schmidt, 11 July 1995.

Robert Siegel, 21 August 1995.

William Siemering, 8 August 1995.

Scott Simon, 23 August 1995.

Norman Solomon, 21 September 1995.

Susan Stamberg, 16 August 1995.

Steve Symonds, 24 September 1995.

Tom Thomas, 23 September 2003.

Sanford Ungar, 16 August 1995.

Joe Welling, 10 July 1995.

Linda Wertheimer, 18 August 1995.

John Witherspoon, 1 August 1995.

Elizabeth Young, 22 September 1995.

Nicholas Zapple, 3 December 1996.

Bob Zelnick, 11 August 1995.

Burt Harrison Papers. Public Radio Oral History Project. National Public Broadcasting Archives. College Park, Md.
    Lee C. Frischknecht, 2 November 1978.
    Robert Mott, 24 July 1978.
    Donald Quayle, 23 October 1978.
    Jerrold Sandler, 24 October 1978.
    John Witherspoon, 31 October 1978.
    Elizabeth Young, 10 October 1978.

MANUSCRIPT COLLECTIONS AND ARCHIVES

Carnegie Commission on Educational Television Papers, 1963–1967. State Historical Society of Wisconsin, Madison, Wis. Cited as CC MSS.
Carnegie Commission on the Future of Public Broadcasting Papers. State Historical Society of Wisconsin, Madison, Wis. Cited as CC2 MSS.
Jimmy Carter Library. National Archives and Records Administration, Atlanta, Ga. Cited as Carter MSS.
    Margaret A. McKenna Files.
    Hamilton Jordan Files.
    Office of Hispanic Affairs.
    Domestic Policy Staff files (Stuart Eizenstat, Richard Neustadt).

Gerald R. Ford Library. National Archives and Records Administration, Ann Arbor, Mich. Cited as Ford MSS.
    Philip W. Buchen Files.
    Dean Burch Files.
    Gerald R. Ford Congressional Papers.
    Gerald R. Ford Vice Presidential Papers.
    Max L. Friedersdorf Files.
    Robert A. Goldwin Papers.
    Robert Hartmann Papers.
    William T. Kendall Files.
    Bobbie Greene Kilberg Files.
    Kenneth A. Lazarus Files.
    Charles H. McCall Files.
    Frederick Lynn May Files.
    Ron Nessen Papers.
    Richard Parsons Files.
    William Timmons Files.
    White House Central Files.

Lyndon Baines Johnson Library. National Archives and Records Administration. Austin, Tex. Cited as LBJ MSS.
    Task Force Reports.
    White House Confidential File.

National Association of Broadcasters Records, 1938–1982. State Historical Society of Wisconsin. Madison, Wis. Cited as NAB MSS.
National Association of Educational Broadcasters Records, 1925–1977. State Historical Society of Wisconsin. Madison, Wis. Cited as NAEB MSS.
National Public Broadcasting Archives. University of Maryland. College Park, Md. Cited as NPBA MSS.
  Lee C. Frischknecht Papers.
  Joseph Gwathmey Files.
  Samuel C. O. Holt Papers.
  Frank Mankiewicz Papers.
  NPR Board of Directors Files.
  NPR Oversight and Investigation Files.
  Tom Warnock Files.
  Elizabeth L. Young Papers.

Nixon Presidential Materials. National Archives and Records Administration. College Park, Md. Cited as Nixon MSS.
  Patrick J. Buchanan Papers.
  Leonard Garment Materials.
  Nixon Annotated News Summaries.
  Nixon Handwriting Files.
  White House Central Files.
  White House Special Files.

Ronald Reagan Library. National Archives and Records Administration. Simi Valley, Calif. Cited as Reagan MSS.
  White House Alphabetical Files (CPB, NPR, PBS).
  White House Subject Files.

WHA Radio and Television Papers. University of Wisconsin. Madison, Wis. Cited as WHA MSS.

INDEX